British rural landscapes on film

MANCHESTER
1824

Manchester University Press

British rural landscapes on film

Edited by
PAUL NEWLAND

Manchester University Press

Published by Manchester University Press
Altrincham Street, Manchester M1 7JA
www.manchesteruniversitypress.co.uk

British Library Cataloguing-in-Publication Data
A catalogue record for this book is available from the British Library

Library of Congress Cataloging-in-Publication Data applied for

ISBN 978 0 7190 9157 5 hardback

First published 2016

Typeset by Out of House Publishing
Printed in Great Britain
by TJ International Ltd, Padstow

Contents

Figures

Contributors

Mark Broughton is a senior lecturer in cultural studies at the University of Hertfordshire. He has published on the use of landscape gardens and sculpture in cinema. He is the author of a forthcoming BFI TV Classic on *Brideshead Revisited* and is working on publications about Nigel Kneale (for Manchester University Press) and psychedelic film.

Andrew Higson is Greg Dyke Professor of Film and Television and head of the Department of Theatre, Film and Television at the University of York. He has written widely on British cinema, from the silent period to the present day, and on questions of national cinema. His books include *Waving the Flag: Constructing a National Cinema in Britain* (1995), *English Heritage, English Cinema: The Costume Drama Since 1980* (2003) and *Film England: Culturally English Filmmaking since the 1990s* (2011). He is also editor of *'Film Europe' and 'Film America': Cinema, Commerce and Cultural Exchange, 1920–1939* (with Richard Maltby, 1999), *British Cinema, Past and Present* (with Justine Ashby, 2000) and *Young and Innocent? The Cinema in Britain, 1896–1930* (2002).

Stella Hockenhull is a senior lecturer in film studies at the University of Wolverhampton and is particularly interested in landscape and British cinema. She is the author of *Aesthetics and Neo-Romanticism in Film: Landscapes in Contemporary British Cinema* (2013).

Keith M. Johnston is a senior lecturer in film and television studies at the University of East Anglia. He is the author of *Coming Soon: Film Trailers and the Selling of Hollywood Technology* (2009) and *Science Fiction Film: A Critical Introduction* (2011), was one of the co-editors of *Ealing Revisited* (2012) and published 'The Great Ealing Film Challenge' (95 articles covering each of the Ealing films produced between 1938 and 1959) in the *Huffington Post* (2012–13). Fuelled by the discovery of 1950s 3D trailers, his current research into the history of British stereoscopic 3D media has been published in the *Historical Journal of Film, Radio and Television, Film History, Convergence: The International Journal of Research into New Media Technologies* and the *Journal of Popular Film and Television.*

Patrick Keiller studied architecture at University College London, becoming an architect in 1976, and fine art at the Royal College of Art. His earliest audio-visual works were exhibited at the Tate Gallery in 1982. During the 1980s, he made a series of short films in which images of landscape were accompanied by fictional narration, a method employed in the feature-length *London* (1994) and *Robinson in Space* (1997), the latter an exploration of England's material economy, extended as a book in 1999. In 2000, he completed *The Dilapidated Dwelling*, a study of the UK's housing predicament. He has taught in schools of architecture and fine art since 1974, and between 2002 and 2011 was a research fellow at the Royal College of Art, where he developed *The City of the Future*, a project with early film that led to a series of installations, the exhibition *Londres, Bombay* (Le Fresnoy, Tourcoing, 2006) and the film *Robinson in Ruins* (2010). A related exhibition *The Robinson Institute* (Tate Britain), with an accompanying book *The Possibility of Life's Survival on the Planet*, followed in 2012. His essay collection *The View from the Train: Cities and Other Landscapes* was published in 2013.

Gideon Koppel originally trained as a sound recording engineer at Utopia Studios London, receiving credits on numerous music projects with bands such as Duran Duran, Queen, and Donovan. He then returned to full-time education, first at the London College of Printing and then as a postgraduate at the Slade School of Fine Art. Koppel's work as a filmmaker and artist has been broadcast worldwide and exhibited in galleries from the Tate Modern in London to MoMA in New York. After his film installation for the Japanese fashion label Comme des Garçons was shown at the Florence Biennale, Koppel made film and television commercials. His feature film *sleep furiously* with a soundtrack by Aphex Twin was one of the most critically acclaimed British films of the year – nominated for numerous awards including the Golden Leopard at the Locarno International Film Festival and winning the 2010 Guardian First Feature Film Award. Koppel is an associate fellow of Green Templeton College, University of Oxford.

Paul Moody has research interests that cover early British cinema, national identity, the horror film and contemporary international film policy. He is currently working on a history of EMI Films and is the director of the annual Calling the Tune Film Festival.

Paul Newland is a reader in film studies at Aberystwyth University. He was previously a post-doctoral research associate at the University of Exeter, where he worked on the film producer Gavrik Losey's archive in the Bill Douglas Cinema Museum. He is the author of *The Cultural Construction of London's East End* (2008) and *British Films of the 1970s* (2013), and editor of *Don't Look Now: British Cinema in the 1970s* (2010). He has published widely on constructions of space and place in film, for example in the articles 'Global Markets and a Market Place: Reading BBC Television's *EastEnders* as the Anti-Docklands' (*The Journal of British Cinema and Television*, 2008), 'Folksploitation: Charting the Horrors of the British Folk Music Tradition in *The Wicker Man* (Robin Hardy, 1973)' (*British Cinema in the 1970s*, ed. Robert Shail, 2008), and 'To the West There Is Nothing … Except America: The Spatial Politics of *Local Hero*' (*Visual Culture in Britain*, 2011).

Duncan Petrie is professor of film and television at the University of York. He has a long-standing research interest in Scottish cinema that has produced two monographs: *Screening Scotland* (2000) and *Contemporary Scottish Fictions: Film, Television and the Novel* (2004); a co-edited collection, *Bill Douglas: A Lanternist's Account* (1993); and various journal articles and book chapters. His other books include several monographs co-written with Rod Stoneman: *Creativity and Constraint in the British Film Industry* (1991), *The British Cinematographer* (1996), *Shot in New Zealand: The Art and Craft of the Kiwi Cinematographer* (2007), *A Coming of Age: 30 Years of New Zealand Cinema* (2008) and *Educating Film-Makers: Part, Present and Future* (2014). He has also co-edited a number of collections, including *New Questions of British Cinema* (1992) and *The Cinema of Small Nations* (2007) with Mette Hjort. Duncan is co-principal editor of the *Journal of British Cinema and Television*. At the University of Exeter he established and directed the Bill Douglas Centre for the History of Cinema and Popular Culture and has also served on various industry bodies including the board of South West Screen and the Scottish Screen Lottery Panel.

Tom Ryall is emeritus professor of film history at Sheffield Hallam University. His books include *Alfred Hitchcock and the British Cinema* (1986), *Britain and the American Cinema* (2001) and *Anthony Asquith* (2005). He has contributed various articles on British and American cinema to collections such as *The Oxford Guide to Film Studies* (1998), *The Cinema of Britain and Ireland* (2005), *The British Cinema Book* (2009) and *A Companion to Alfred Hitchcock* (2011).

Suzanne Speidel is a senior lecturer in film studies at Sheffield Hallam University. Her publications include chapters in *Introduction to Film Studies* (ed. Jill Nelmes, 2007), *The X-Files and Literature* (ed. Sharon Yang, 2007) and *Joseph Conrad and the Performing Arts* (2009). She is currently completing a monograph, *Adapting*

Forster, for Palgrave Macmillan. She received a BA in English Literature and a PhD from the University of Sheffield.

Kate Woodward is a lecturer in film studies at Aberystwyth University. The main focus of her research is both Welsh and English language film from Wales. Her monograph on the Welsh Film Board was published in 2012. She has also published papers in the journals *Critical Studies in Television* and *Cyfrwng: Media Wales Journal*.

Acknowledgements

The editor would firstly like to thank all of the contributors to this book for their hard work, generosity and enthusiasm for the project. He would particularly like to thank Gideon Koppel and Patrick Keiller for agreeing to be interviewed.

Many thanks to the staff at Manchester University Press, who were supportive of this book from the beginning.

Thanks to Przemyslaw Sobkowicz for his help with the images.

PN, Aberystwyth, October 2015

Introduction: approaching British rural landscapes on film

Paul Newland

It is obvious that landscape as such is not a *genre* in the dominant cinema, as it is still in visual media; the institution of cinema prefers generic categories that revolve around narrative.

Sergei Eisenstein[1]

In *A Canterbury Tale* (Michael Powell and Emeric Pressburger, 1944), three pilgrims arrive in Chillingbourne, a fictional Kent village near Canterbury. The Second World War is raging elsewhere, but here, a land girl, Alison (Sheila Smith); a British soldier, Sergeant Peter Gibbs (Dennis Price); and an American GI, Bob Johnson (John Sweet), find some respite. Their status as outsiders in this rural landscape is central to the narrative, which sees them gradually getting to know the Kentish community that lives here, and coming to enjoy its way of life. As Andrew Moor puts it, they 'begin to commune with the spirit of the place.'[2] *A Canterbury Tale* was shot by cinematographer Erwin Hillier in and around the villages of Chilham, Fordwich, Selling, Shottenden, Wickhambreaux and Wingham.[3] This archetypally rural southern English landscape – all lush, tree-covered hills, rolling, sun-baked fields and dusty tracks – is celebrated in the film as something to savour, and, importantly, as something to defend and protect during a period of war.

The film begins with an unseen narrator speaking lines from the *General Prologue* to Chaucer's *The Canterbury Tales*. We see shots of the landscape with a horseback procession of medieval pilgrims, and then a famously daring match cut suddenly takes us from a hawk flying high in the summer sky in the Middle Ages to a Second World War fighter aircraft coming in low across the fields. Over these images the narrator makes a memorable speech

1 *A Canterbury Tale*

that reflects on the potential relationship between Chaucer's characters and contemporary Kent:

> Six hundred years have passed. What would they see, Dan Chaucer and his goodly company today? The hills and valleys are the same. Gone are the forests since the enclosures came. Hedgerows have sprung. The land is under plough. And orchards bloom with blossom on the bough. Sussex and Kent are like a garden fair. But sheep still graze upon the ridges there. The pilgrims' walk still winds above the weald, through wood and brake and many a fertile land. But though so little has changed since Chaucer's day, another kind of pilgrim walks the way.

A Canterbury Tale is a film that is primarily engaged with notions of 'belonging' in a rural landscape within the contexts of a modern, mechanised, global war. But one of the key themes of the film is the potentially transformative nature of this rural landscape. The film is engaged with the threat of change to the countryside, and, especially, the potentially destructive nature of modernity.

Later in the film, the mysterious gentleman farmer and local magistrate, Thomas Colpeper (Eric Portman), gives a lecture and magic lantern show in which he too evokes a sense of deep past in this specific rural location. Colpeper speaks of how one might today feel the presence of past pilgrims seeking blessings:

Well, there are more ways than one of getting close to your ancestors. Follow the old road, and as you walk, think of them and of the old England. They climbed Chillingbourne Hill just as you do. They sweated and paused for breath just as you did today. But when you see the bluebells in the spring and the wild thyme and the broom and heather, you are only seeing what their eyes saw. You ford the same rivers. The same birds are singing. When you lie flat on your back and rest, watch the clouds sailing, as I often do, you are so close to those other people that you can hear the road, and their laughter and talk, and the music of the instruments they carried. And when I turn the bend of the road, where they too saw the towers of Canterbury, I feel I've only to turn my head and see them on the road behind me.

Through the figure of Colpeper and other villagers, the Kent countryside in *A Canterbury Tale* comes to stand for a vision of what might be at stake if Britain (or in this case specifically, England) cannot be saved.[4] As Tom Ryall notes in Chapter 3 – in which he considers the representation of the rural landscape in Second World War films – *A Canterbury Tale* has its roots in a mythical vision of the rural English past. Indeed, Ian Christie has written elsewhere of the film as an expression of 'Neo-Romanticism'.[5] But too often there has been slippage between notions of the 'British' and the 'English' countryside. The ubiquitous nature of these images of the southern English landscape in particular (as evidenced in *A Canterbury Tale*) that come to stand for a wider idea of Britain needs to be engaged with and critiqued. Several contributors to this book do this, including Kate Woodward (in her work on Wales) and Duncan Petrie (in his work on Scotland).

In his influential book *The Making of the English Landscape* (1954), W. G. Hoskins appeared to share the primary concerns of Powell and Pressburger's film. Hoskins wrote: 'Especially since the year 1914, every single change in the English landscape has either uglified it, or destroyed its meaning, or both.'[6] Interestingly, Hoskins also noticed the profound temporality of the countryside: 'everything in the landscape is older than we think'.[7] Like *A Canterbury Tale*, Hoskins's still widely read book demonstrates a sense of melancholy for a lost rural idyll.

Such rural nostalgia had previously been evidenced by the creation of the National Trust in 1895 and the Council for the Preservation of Rural England in 1926. The appearance of these organisations can be understood within the contexts of the rapid urbanisation and industrialisation of Britain during the nineteenth century – between 1801 and 1911 the proportion of the population living in cities rose from 20 to 80 per cent.[8] In many ways the idea that the countryside should be somehow an unchanging (and thus protected) refuge from industrial (and now post-industrial) urban modernity has endured into the twenty-first century. But, as we will see, this idea is ideologically charged, and is bound up with issues of conservatism, nostalgia and bourgeois taste.

One point *A Canterbury Tale* appears to be making is that we should not forget how the legends of Albion, Mercia, Elmet, Sir Gawain, John Barleycorn,

Robin Hood, Rob Roy, Math (*Mabinogion*) and 'Arcadian plenitude' continue to inform ideas of Britain and its constituent nations.[9] These myths have played key roles in the development of an imagined countryside for many years. As the art historian Christiana Payne puts it, 'An element of myth pervaded nineteenth-century attitudes to the countryside, and our own attitudes are undoubtedly affected by similar myths.'[10] Indeed, according to Payne, pervasive myths about the countryside have had a profound influence on western European culture since classical times. These myths tend to perpetuate the idea that people are happier in the countryside, and that country people were more content and more virtuous in the past than they are now.[11] *A Canterbury Tale* certainly evokes the enduring power of these ideas through its depiction of the Kent rural landscape as a magical, mythical, mysterious world.

But the film also features the famous cathedral city of Canterbury as the final destination of the pilgrims, and London too (as a socio-cultural, political and economic nexus) always feels *present* in the film – it is the home of a number of the characters and is mentioned explicitly several times by others. It is important to recognise, then, as the geographer David Matless argues, that the 'rural' needs always to be understood in terms of its relationship to the city and the suburb, 'and approached as a heterogeneous field.'[12] In other words, as John Rennie Short demonstrates, 'the countryside has always been a counterpoint. Its usage first appeared in English in the sixteenth century with the growth of London.'[13]

The countryside and the city – and the dense and complex relationship between the two – have played key roles in the development (and maintenance) of a spatialised British imagination (or, indeed, set of 'imaginations').[14] As Michael Bunce argues – invoking the influential ideas of Ferdinand Tönnies – the modern shift from *Gemeinschaft* (pre-industrial, communal society) to *Gesellschaft* (the associational, goal-oriented living typical of agrarian and industrial societies) might have fostered 'some nostalgia for countrysides left behind'.[15] *A Canterbury Tale* certainly offers an examination of what *Gesellschaft* living might look like and mean – and how and why it operates as something to be 'returned to' and cherished – in a period of modern warfare. A number of contributors to this book deal with tensions that develop between notions of rural and urban life. In his chapter on rural landscapes in the British silent era, for example, Andrew Higson notes that films such as *The Lure of Crooning Water* (Arthur Rooke, 1920), *Fox Farm* (Guy Newall, 1922) and *Mist in the Valley* (Cecil Hepworth, 1923) explore contrasts between bifurcated rural and urban socio-cultural milieus.

Just as it informs how we imagine the 'urban', the British countryside plays a key role in the construction and maintenance of ideas of the 'national'. As Tim Edensor notices, the 'national' remains 'the pre-eminent spatial construct'.[16] We know that national identities are informed by landscapes and their stories, traditions, myths and legends.[17] Edensor advocates that landscapes are 'apt to act upon our sense of belonging so that to dwell within them, even if for a short time, can be to achieve a kind of national self-realisation, to return to 'our' roots where the self, freed from its inauthentic – usually urban – existence, is re-authenticated.'[18]

But what are the key aspects of this seemingly authentic life that rural landscapes speak of? David Lowenthal writes of the 'insularity' of English countryside; its 'imagined stability'.[19] England's iconic, privileged landscapes, more than any other British landscapes, are consistently circulated and recirculated through popular culture.[20] Anybody familiar with cultural representations of the English countryside no doubt thinks of (as Edensor aptly puts it) 'parish churches, lychgates, haystacks, thatched or half-timbered cottages, rose-leaden gardens, village greens, games of cricket, country pubs, rural customs, hedgerows, golden fields of grain, plough and horses, hunting scenes, and a host of characters including vicars, squires, farmers, gamekeepers, … part of a series of interlinked cues which are widely shared at home and abroad.'[21] Images such as these – as indeed portrayed in *A Canterbury Tale* – retain what Edensor terms 'an affective and cognitive power that serves exclusive variants of nationalism'.[22]

Cinema has offered one of the primary means of circulating such images over the past century. But British poetry has often engaged with the experience of rural landscape. One cannot imagine the verse of Blake, Wordsworth, Coleridge or Clare, for example, without powerful evocations of rural scenes, and in recent years just one example of the wide-ranging contemporary landscape poetry can be found in Alice Oswald's *Dart*, which charts the Devon river. Furthermore, there have been numerous depictions of the rural landscape in canonical British novels. One need only think of the work of Jane Austen, Thomas Hardy's Wessex (as depicted in novels such as *Far from the Madding Crowd*) and the work of Charles Dickens and Emily Brontë in particular. In contemporary fiction, novels such as Graham Swift's *Waterland* (1983) vividly evoke specific rural landscapes and use them to facilitate narrative and characterisation. It is unsurprising, then, that British literature that so vividly brings landscape to life should be adapted into films, such as *Waterland* (Stephen Gyllenhaal, 1992), which was shot on location in East Anglia.

The aims of this book

In recent years there has been a significant rise in scholarly interest in the spatiality of cinema across the social sciences and humanities, but especially within the disciplines of film studies and cultural geography. Scholars have used films to think about how spaces and places form within the popular imagination, and in doing so have noticed how far specific films can facilitate our understanding of how territories are imaginatively constructed. Most of this critical inquiry has tended to focus on issues related to city and urban locations, and how complex issues of modernity are worked though in built spaces.[23] *British Rural Landscapes on Film* offers new insights into how rural areas in Britain have historically been represented on film, from the silent era through both world wars and on into the twenty-first century. The contributors to this book demonstrate that the country-side has provided Britain (and its constituent nations and regions) with a dense range of spaces in which contested cultural identities have been (and continue to be) worked through. Films show us, then, that key aspects of Britishness appear to be bound up with the iconography and topography of rural areas. *British Rural Landscapes on Film* demonstrates that British cinema provides numerous examples of how national identity and the identity of the countryside have partly been constructed through filmic representation, and how British rural films can allow us to further understand the relationship between the cultural identities of specific areas of Britain and the ontology of the landscapes they inhabit. The diverse and varied essays in this book draw on a range of popular and alternative films and genres in order to demonstrate how far film texts come to prefigure expectations of rural social space, and how these representations come to shape – and be shaped by – the material and embodied circumstances of what we might think of as 'lived' rural experience. Contributors to this collection are particularly interested in issues surrounding the British 'cinematic countryside', and how far concepts of the rural – as displayed in British films – feed into wider questions of modernity versus tradition, self versus other, and issues of nationhood, the global and the local.

What is landscape?

Before thinking about the ways in which British rural landscapes operate in film in more detail, we need to engage with the question of what precisely a landscape *is*, or might be considered to be. The English noun 'landscape' remains fairly new to the language. Its origins can be found in the Dutch word *landschap* – meaning 'region' or 'province'. It entered the English language (as 'landskip') in the seventeenth century as 'a piece of fashionable artistic jargon'.[24] But 'landscape' remains a contested term in the fields of geography and art history. For some, such as Simon Schama, a landscape can be best understood as an imaginative projection.[25] Indeed, for Stephen Daniels and Denis Cosgrove, 'A landscape is a cultural image, a pictorial way of representing, structuring or symbolising surroundings.'[26] This evidences the development and continuing relevance of the Marxist notion of landscape as representation. Similarly, landscapes can also be understood as 'narratives' or, at least, as key elements of storytelling.[27]

Landscapes can also be considered to be spaces that are experienced, worked and lived, as opposed to just things to be framed and 'looked at'. For example, the geographer J. B. Jackson developed an interest in everyday landscapes and 'vernacular' experience, focusing on dwelling and embodied practice.[28] And Carl O. Sauer championed a branch of cultural landscape studies in which knowledge is gained by observation and fieldwork.

So, the notion of 'landscape' is still being debated. But landscapes serve to reveal key aspects of human life – everyday, real human existence and survival on the one hand and the imagined relationship between humans and the natural environment on the other. As the art historian Richard Mabey points out, 'Landscapes have always been looked on to bridge the gap between two opposed sets of human needs: for some haven of continuity on one hand, and the vitality of nature on the "other" for familiar environment, fashioned by human hands, and then again something that transcends the man-made and the artificial.'[29] But in addition to this we have to engage with other important considerations. For example, the working countryside is often not seen to be a 'landscape' (especially by those that work it). Furthermore, British landscapes cannot be properly understood without consideration of their complicated histories of ownership and use.

In his book *Landscape* (2007), the geographer John Wylie works through a series of tensions that become apparent when thinking about landscape. Wylie considers issues of proximity/distance; issues of observation/inhabitation; the tension between the eye of the observer and the land observed; and tensions between concepts of culture and nature.[30] Teasing out these problems, Wylie usefully points out that 'landscape is both the phenomenon itself *and* our perception of it'.[31] Furthermore, he advocates that 'landscape is not only something we see, it is also a way of seeing things, a particular way of looking at and picturing the world around us'.[32] This idea is developed in a slightly different way by David Matless, who puts it that, 'if landscape carries an unseemly spatiality, it also shuttles through temporal processes of history and memory'.[33] As *British Rural Landscapes on Film* shows, cinema in Britain continues to facilitate this process in a wide variety of ways.

Rural landscapes are often viewed as idyllic. But this vision of course effectively hides poverty and homelessness in the countryside, and, as Paul Cloke puts it, 'establishes a political and cultural expectation of orthodoxy which actively seeks to purify rural space from transgressive presences and practices'.[34] So, one should recognise different visions and realities of such landscapes, and acknowledge the presence of marginalised rural 'Others'. To understand the countryside, as Cloke notices, one needs to engage with and understand 'the embodied practices of people in relation to the potentially transformative agency of animals, plants, weather and technology'.[35] It is worth pointing out here that in British cinema there has been a tradition of representation of rural 'Others' as backward, lawless, violent, and criminal – witness, for example, the notorious depiction of ribald Cornishmen in *Straw Dogs* (Sam Peckinpah, 1971). These representations can sometimes work against popular conceptions of the British rural landscape, which are often bound up, as we have seen, with bourgeois nations of value and taste.

Raymond Williams has remarked that 'a working country is hardly ever a landscape. The very idea of landscape implies separation and observation.'[36] In other words, landscapes can play ideological roles in the development of social life. They can support a set of ideas, values and assumptions about the way a society is organised. There is a long history of such ideologically informed ideas of the countryside. As Denis Cosgrove points out, the idea of landscape 'emerged as a dimension of European elite consciousness at an identifiable period in the evolution of European societies: it was refined and elaborated over a long period during which it expressed and supported a range of political, social and moral assumptions and became a significant aspect of taste'.[37] This concept – which was developing during the fifteenth and sixteenth centuries – encapsulated idealised visions of landscape that effectively concealed the real material conditions of rural life. In other words, landscape has often been rendered the property of the detached observer.[38] In this way, landscapes can operate as 'visual ideology'.[39]

The idea of landscape in Britain has often been closely identified with landscape art.[40] One key aspect of the development of landscape art is the notion of perspective. Wylie points out that 'perspective enabled a commanding, objective and controlled grasp of space and spatial relations'.[41] Indeed, as Cosgrove puts it, 'linear perspective provides both the certainty of our reproductions of nature in art and underlies the power and authority, the divine creativity of the artist'.[42] Cosgrove focuses on the socio-historical implications of perspective, and deals with the issue of landscape as a 'way of seeing' the world.[43] The majority of landscape painters working in England in the late seventeenth century produced idealised or classical landscapes, and these very often tended to be imaginary.[44] Most of these painters worked in the tradition of Claude Lorrain, developing balanced compositional frames with recessive depth.[45] Wylie argues that this tradition of painting landscape has tended to be seen as a particular 'visual mode of observing and knowing'.[46] British landscape paintings of the classical tradition were effectively products of the Restoration.[47] Post-Restoration, noblemen employed decorative painters to embellish the interiors of their mansions, and portraitists to depict themselves and their families.[48] This means that many images of nineteenth-century English agricultural landscapes show them to be at odds with the harsh social, political and economic realities of agricultural labourers.[49]

Other key movements in British landscape art are worth considering here, as these movements have often influenced the ways in which the rural has been depicted in British cinema. For example, the idea of the 'picturesque' developed during the late eighteenth century. This effectively encapsulated a new way of viewing and experiencing nature.[50] The originator of this idea, William Gilpin, argued in his *Essays on Prints* (1768) that the picturesque was the kind of beauty agreeable in a picture. Gilpin was drawn to places of varied topography, such as the Wye Valley, the Lake District and the Scottish highlands. He admired views that were rough, harsh and broken. In these places, nature was experienced as a 'picture'.[51] His books, such as *Observations on the River Wye* (1770), catered for an expansion in the British taste for landscape after 1760. The picturesque essentially sets up a picture frame between the observer and the landscape. Viewers of picturesque landscapes are not embedded in these landscapes, then. They stand apart, as observers.[52]

Another tradition of British landscape art that has fed into developments in British rural cinema is the 'pastoral' (which means 'pertaining to shepherds'). Pastoral paintings present an often idyllic celebration of simple country life. John Rennie Short points out that 'an agricultural life, it is argued, is more wholesome, more spiritually nourishing, more natural'.[53] It is significant that the pastoral was usually a view of the countryside from the town.[54] Certainly a great many British rural landscape films can be said to demonstrate an awareness of pastoral concerns. This is especially true of morale-boosting war-time documentary films such as *Britain at Bay* (Harry Watt, 1940), *Listen to Britain* (Humphrey Jennings and Stewart McAllister, 1942) and *Summer on the Farm* (Ralph Keene, 1943). As Sue Harper has pointed out, the Ministry of Information 'favoured documentaries about the *transformation* of landscape by war, and the ways in which it could be made more productive'.[55] *Britain at Bay*, for example, features shots of fields and farmsteads that Powell and Pressburger's *A Canterbury Tale* would later echo, and a memorable J. B. Priestley narration declaring this to be 'one of the most beautiful countrysides in the world'. *Summer on the Farm* has shots of a range of individuals happily picking crops in the fields together. Furthermore, *Listen to Britain* similarly shows farm workers happily toiling under light, fluffy cumulus clouds on hot, sunny days. But this poetic film – which had a big impact overseas – features images of fighter aircraft flying overhead, and tanks pressing forcefully through the landscape in shots that would be echoed in *A Canterbury Tale*. Having said this, as Andrew Moor notes, *A Canterbury Tale* 'blatantly subverts the stylistic properties of documentary realism'.[56]

One other way of seeing the rural landscape in Britain – a way that has influenced a number of British filmmakers – is the 'sublime'. In *A Philosophical Enquiry into the Sublime and the Beautiful* (1757), Edmund Burke wrote of the passion caused by great and sublime in nature – 'astonishment'. While pastoral beauty was thought to bring about pleasant feelings, the sublime encapsulated a response of astonishment and awe. The sublime, then, encapsulates wild nature. These landscapes are vast and powerful.

In his introduction to the edited collection *Landscape and Film* (2006), Martin Lefebvre develops a number of ideas about the relationship between cinema and landscape. He points out that 'every unit of meaning in a film – whether an action, a view of an object, etc. – implies a setting (or settings)'.[57] Therefore, implicit in any film is the presence of, creation of, and requirement of landscapes. Lefebvre further argues that 'the form of landscape is thus first of all the form of a view, of a particular gaze that requires a frame'.[58] This clearly chimes with the ideas of the geographers Denis Cosgrove and Stephen Daniels, among others.

To a degree it has been demonstrated that cinema more broadly developed out of the desire to represent landscapes. As Tom Gunning has shown, for example, during the nineteenth century the fascination with landscapes gave rise to new technologies of motion pictures and mobile viewpoints.[59] These included panoramas, magic lanterns and dioramas. Gunning notices the central importance of the representation of landscape in the development of cinema: as a way of seeing, but also as an industry.[60] Here we might think of the 'panoramic view' landscape films of Thomas Edison and Biograph. Gunning argues that 'the films realise the centuries-old fantasy of penetration that had remained literally impossible in landscape painting'.[61] The new technologies that saw the representation of landscape move from panoramas to motion pictures 'endeavoured to increase the sensation of immersion into a represented space' and pursued 'an almost obsessive goal of total spectator involvement'.[62] As Andrew Higson demonstrates in Chapter 1, promotional material for phantom rides seems to suggest that the scenery provided as much of an appeal to spectators as the experience of speed afforded by these films shot from the front of moving trains. But, interestingly, despite the technological and aesthetic advancements of cinema after innovations such as phantom rides, Gunning advocates that the fixed image of landscape and its contemplation 'still provided the privileged mode of landscape viewing'.[63]

British rural landscape and film genre

Sue Harper once argued that 'there is a relative paucity of landscape in British cinema; images of the countryside tend to be unevenly marked after the coming of sound, and their appearance is spasmodic'.[64] As Tom Ryall notes in Chapter 3, this is a provocative statement which he nevertheless concedes is borne out by the evidence provided by war-time British cinema. But *British Rural Landscapes on Film* demonstrates that the countryside has actually played a very important role (or, indeed, a variety of roles) in the construction of British national cinema and, through this, modern British national identity. For example, in his chapter on British pre-war film publicity, Paul Moody notices that rural landscapes were employed by publicists 'as a metaphor for a national commonality'. But it is fair to say that different genres have placed different emphases on the function of rural landscape.

Sue Harper has written very usefully about the function of the landscape in film melodramas from the 1930s to the 1950s such as *The Water Gypsies* (Maurice Elvey, 1931), *The Constant Nymph* (Basil Dean, 1933) and *The Mill on the Floss* (Tim Whelan, 1937).[65] Harper argues that the function of landscape in these films 'was to be an index of sexual and social conservatism'.[66] In *Lorna Doone* (Basil Dean, 1934), for example, Dean 'gave prolonged attention to the Devon hills and clefts, which were treated as objects of more complexity and power than the protagonists'.[67] Sequences in this film were shot on location on Exmoor in

Somerset. But, interestingly, most of the film was shot at ATP Studios in Ealing. This leads Harper to make an interesting series of points about what she deems to be a relative lack of depictions of landscapes through the means of location shooting in many of these films. Indeed, she even goes as far as to argue that, during the 1950s, 'none of the popular films evoke pastoral imagery or celebrate the landscape'.[68] Furthermore, 'the bigger studios like Denham or Pinewood had back lots, where landscape could be represented, but they were controlled by management'.[69] But, while it is important to recognise that many of the rural landscapes we see in films from the 1930s to the late 1950s were indeed constructed on studio back lots, we should not downplay the complex (and often seemingly contradictory) roles that rural landscapes shot on location have played throughout the history of British cinema.

During the period before and after the Second World War, as we have seen, films such as *A Canterbury Tale* represented the English rural landscape as an idyllic but also strange, mysterious space. Other films of the 1940s perhaps even more unequivocally mark the landscape as a thing of beauty to be cherished and fought for, as Tom Ryall notes in his chapter on rural imagery in Second World War British cinema. Ryall demonstrates here how pastoral imagery was employed as propaganda not only in the films of the period such as *This England* (David MacDonald, 1941) and *Tawny Pipit* (Bernard Miles and Charles Saunders, 1944) but also in paratextual material such as posters and film magazines. He also notes the ways in which Stanley Baldwin (the British prime minister for much of the inter-war period) often invoked England's rural heritage (thus effectively again 'Othering' the cultures of the Celtic nations in the process).

But other films of the war period more obviously invite a range of contradictory readings. For example, *Went the Day Well?* (Alberto Cavalcanti, 1942) is a complicated film at the level of its depiction of rural landscape. Sue Harper argues that in this film 'there is a powerful desire to validate the village life and landscape'.[70] In Chapter 3, Tom Ryall also notices a 'darker' sense of the rural in this film. The famous Gainsborough melodrama *The Wicked Lady* (Leslie Arliss, 1945), set on a rural estate and shot partly on location at Blickling Hall, Norfolk, uses this rural location to speak of the elemental passions stirring in the characters on the 'highway'. But its overall aesthetic perhaps owes more to the efficacies of studio shooting noticed by Sue Harper. *Great Day* (Lance Comfort, 1945), shot on location in Denham, Buckinghamshire (where much of *A Canterbury Tale* was shot), is a film with 'pastoral overtones' that tells the story of a visit by Eleanor Roosevelt to a small, fictional English village, Denley.[71] But, according to Brian McFarlane, this is a film 'which does not set out to celebrate village life but to subject it to scrutiny, not to idealise it but to dramatise a network of feelings, some positive, some not'.[72]

One of the key ideas that *British Rural Landscapes on Film* engages with – and indeed critiques – is the notion of 'heritage' in Britain, and its relationship to space and place. In the so-called British heritage film, rural landscapes are often initially presented through impressive long shots.[73] These landscapes, as Sarah Cardwell has demonstrated, are shown to be 'controlled, peaceful, unthreatening'.[74] The archetypal heritage films – Ismail Merchant and James Ivory's *Howards End* (1992) and *The Remains of the Day* (1993), for example – depict a vision of a primarily English (again) rural landscape that encapsulates a nostalgic, rose-tinted view of the British countryside.[75] As Andrew Higson puts it in his path-finding work on British heritage cinema, in films such as these the past is displayed as 'visually spectacular pastiche' inviting a 'nostalgic gaze' that 'resists the ironies and social critiques so often suggested narratively'.[76] The heritage vision of rural landscape has become the representational paradigm in British cinema against which all others have since tended to be judged. But there is other, non-bourgeois rural heritage evident in British cinema too. In this book, Mark Broughton's chapter on *The Go-Between* (Joseph Losey, 1971) – shot in Norfolk – uncovers how far the American director and his collaborators (including the British dramatist and screenwriter Harold Pinter) deployed a rural location 'rhetorically' in order to allow it to comment on the history of landed power in England. Broughton shows how a variety of landscapes circulating around one impressive rural locale are used in this film to evidence and articulate tense power relations and 'different ways of understanding the estate's socio-cultural structure'. Stella Hockenhull also pays attention to debates on heritage (and indeed develops them) in her chapter on the 'dirty' uncivilised topographies of recent costume dramas and literary adaptations *Jane Eyre* (Cary Fukunaga, 2011) and *Wuthering Heights* (Andrea Arnold, 2011). Hockenhull argues that these films offer a rather 'pessimistic' *mise-en-scène* in which the idyllic country houses of the 1980s and 1990s heritage films are replaced by 'vast, cavernous castles, filthy peasant dwellings and wild, remote rural landscapes'.

In an attempt to shift debates about film representations of the British countryside away from traditional notions of 'heritage', Catherine Fowler and Gillian Helfield have reflected upon the nature of the 'rural' and what they call 'rural cinema'. One of their key arguments in their edited collection *Representing the Rural: Space, Place, and Identity in Films about the Land* (2006) is that, while the rural milieu is frequently cast as a site of heritage and bourgeois cultural tradition, this is not always the case. Indeed, for Fowler and Helfield, rural cinema can be distinguished from heritage cinema. As they point out, 'the heritage film may demonstrate a harmonious relationship between man and nature and between peasant and fellow members of the rural community. ... Within rural cinema, however, the mood is not always nostalgic.'[77] Furthermore, rural cinema is primarily concerned with the relationship between the land and its inhabitants, and how this relationship develops in terms of a merging of physical and social landscapes.[78] This is not usually a concern of what we might think of now as classic heritage films, which instead depict the countryside as spectacle.

In terms of how they represent landscape, British rural films are often characterised by tensions that develop between notions of heritage, realism, the pictorial, spectacle and the generic requirements of narrative and characterisation. In
her *The History of the British Film, 1906–1914* (1945), Rachael Low suggests that
there were two distinct lines of early development in British filmmaking: 'narrative' and 'pictorial'. Films with an interest in the beauty of pictorial composition can be traced through the work of filmmakers such as Cecil Hepworth and
Maurice Elvey. But, as Andrew Higson argues in his chapter in this book, there
are in fact four distinct but overlapping ways in which rural settings are used
in British silent films. Firstly, there is the basic function of providing a 'relatively neutral narrative space' in which the story can unfold. Secondly, there is
their function as spectacular aesthetic display. Thirdly, there is their function of
offering an appeal to the tourist gaze. And fourthly, rural settings in these films
can perform ideological functions that offer a 'particular reading of the nation'.
Higson further argues that what we can see here is the emergence of a respectable, middlebrow national art cinema. He employs films such as *Tansy* (Cecil
Hepworth, 1921) and *Comin' Thro' the Rye* (Cecil Hepworth, 1923) to demonstrate how rich pictorial imagery and picturesque settings effectively produced
cinematic attractions.

In his chapter on 3D stereoscopic films, Keith Johnston notes that the
terms 'realism' and 'spectacle' loom large in discussions of landscape in British
cinema and can be used in discussions of the work of the 1930s British documentary movement and British 'New Wave' of the 1960s. Johnston argues
that 1950s 3D films offered a spectacle that could 'bring the landscape to
the audience or ... draw the eye into that landscape'. Intriguingly, these films
might thus be placed 'within a continued cultural geography tradition of tension between landscape as something to be subjectively immersed within or
objectively distanced from'.

In his still-influential mid-1980s discussion of British 'New Wave' films – *A
Kind of Loving* (John Schlesinger, 1962) in particular, but also *Room at the Top*
(Jack Clayton, 1958) and *This Sporting Life* (Lindsay Anderson, 1963) – Andrew
Higson similarly engaged with the tensions between 'realism' and 'spectacle' in
landscape shots:

> Landscape and townscape shots – that is, expansive shots of rural or urban scen-
> ery – must at one level construct a *narrative space* in which the protagonists of
> the drama can perform the various actions of the plot. Narratives require space in
> which they can unfold. But because the British New Wave films were promoted
> as realist, landscape and townscape shots must always be much more than neutral
> narrative spaces. Each of these location shots demands also to be read as a real his-
> torical *place* which can authenticate the fiction. There remains a tension between
> the demands of narrative and the demands of realism, however, with the narrative
> compulsion of the film working continually to transform place once more back
> into space. This tension can be transcended when landscape and townscape shots

are incorporated into and as the movements of the narration itself. In these cases, place becomes a signifier of character, a metaphor for the state of mind of the protagonists in the well-worn conventions of the naturalist tradition.[79]

Writing about what he calls 'That Long Shot of Our Town from That Hill', Higson remarks, 'Although these images are coded as spectacular, they can still be clawed back into the narrative system of the films according to the logic of point-of-view shots and establishing shots.'[80] Drawing on Stephen Heath's argument that 'narrative never exhausts the image … Narrative can never contain the whole film which permanently exceeds its fictions', Higson's point here is that these British 'kitchen sink' films, usually discussed in terms of their 'gritty realism', are actually often poetic in nature, especially when their landscape shots transcend the ordinary and make it 'strange, beautiful'.[81] But, engaging with and problematising Higson's argument here, B. F. Taylor asks 'when I watch these opening images, do I really consider them as "spectacle"? Does my desire to see what happens next become suspended by my wanting to gaze at these particular images?'[82] Taylor does not believe that such landscape images 'create problems for the narrative as a result of their "visibility"'.[83] These arguments serve to highlight the highly complex, fluid relationship between narrative and pictorial aspects of British landscapes on film.

A number of examples of the ways in which rural landscapes can develop a wide range of potential meanings can be found in the British horror genre. Peter Hutchings employs the term 'dark heritage' in order to encapsulate menacing cityscapes and landscapes 'in their own way just as picturesque and marketable as their more conventionally pretty counterparts'.[84] What is interesting here is the way in which Hutchings notices how in some films tensions are generated by the conventional pictorial beauty of rural landscapes on the one hand and the generic concerns of narrative and characterisation on the other. In horror films, indeed, the beauty of the countryside can sometimes operate as a fillip to horrific goings-on in the narrative. A key example of this can be found in the seventeenth-century-set *Witchfinder General* (Michael Reeves, 1968), which presents the lush green beauty of the East Anglian landscape as a space in which unspeakable horrors are being perpetrated by Vincent Price's character (Matthew Hopkins) and his acolytes. This film was shot in Norfolk and Suffolk, in and around beauty spots such as Kentwell Hall, Lavenham and Orford Castle. Similarly, other location-shot horror films such as *The Wicker Man* (Robin Hardy, 1973), *Blood on Satan's Claw* (Piers Haggard, 1971) and *Killer's Moon* (Alan Birkinshaw, 1978) employ rural landscapes that might otherwise often be termed conventionally beautiful as the uncanny, troubling locations of horrific activity.

So, even seemingly beautiful locations can have a potentially wide range of cultural meanings. Indeed, John Rennie Short points out that 'European folklore is populated with demons and dangers who dwell in the forest'.[85] Furthermore, Tanya Krzywinska writes that 'the sacred landscapes of ancient Britain have become entrenched in the popular imagination under the seductive sign of "transgression"'.[86] Bearing this in mind, films such as *Blood on Satan's Claw* and *The Wicker Man*, which place pagan sacrifice 'centrally as the source of horror'[87] – as well as the 1970s curio *Psychomania* (Don Sharp, 1972) – might be read as articulations of a counter-cultural moment that saw – through the activities of the hippy movement – the embrace of non-urban, anti-modern, transgressive lifestyles. In other words, beautiful, picturesque landscapes are often linked in British films to peripheral and 'Other' cultural traditions, old and new.

Interestingly, traditions in the representation of rural landscapes in British horror films can be understood within the contexts of much older ways in which places have been imagined. For example, Rosenthal points out that 'until around 1760 the general reaction to uncultivated landscape was distaste. It was preferred cultivated, because farming rendered it ordered and intelligible, made it into patterns of fields and tracks intimately connected with the village and the great house for the benefit of which the ground was farmed.'[88] In other words, wild landscapes have often been imagined as uncontrolled and uncontrollable. As Rosenthal further puts it, 'the look of a landscape reveals the society which inhabits it. A cultivated one denotes civilization, but because a wild one indicates a more savage population, the onus is always to maintain the development of agriculture.'[89] So, it is no surprise to see untamed landscapes being used in a range of films in sequences in which a sense of threat is fuelling the narrative.

But this is not just the case in horror films. Another famous example can be found in the opening of David Lean's *Great Expectations* (1946), which provides a memorable cinematic evocation of the famous scene in Dickens's novel where Pip meets Magwitch. David Lean shot this eerie sequence in the wild, mysterious St Mary's marshes in northern Kent. A similar landscape can be seen facilitating the dark atmosphere of *The Long Memory* (Robert Hamer, 1953), a grimy noir-esque crime thriller that features sequences shot in the gloomy marshland around Gravesend. *The Hide* (Marek Losey, 2009), a film about violent goings-on in a remote wooden ornithologist's shelter, was also shot on marshland, in this case on the Isle of Sheppey.

Other rural landscapes in British films often seem to have darker and more troubling atmospheres in their own right. Hutchings writes of an uncanny landscape 'suffused with a sense of profound and sometimes apocalyptic anxiety'.[90] This landscape 'can signify Britishness as much as, if not more than, the critically privileged heritage dramas'.[91] One example Hutchings uses is the chilling, largely deserted coastal locations used in *The Damned* (Joseph Losey, 1963), which seem fitting for a film about a government secretly preparing for life after nuclear war.[92]

But, in a range of British films, the rural landscape operates as a welcome temporary refuge from city life and the quotidian problems associated with it. For example, we might think of the use of the countryside in the 1940s melodramas *Love on the Dole* (John Baxter, 1941), *Millions Like Us* (Sidney Gilliat and Frank

2 *Brief Encounter*

Launder, 1943) and *It Always Rains on Sunday* (Robert Hamer, 1947). We might also think of the suburban love story *Brief Encounter* (David Lean, 1945), which features a trip taken by car out to the countryside by the adulterous middle-class lovers Laura (Celia Johnson) and Alec (Trevor Howard) – a key rural tryst sequence was shot at Middle Fell Bridge, which crosses Langdale Beck, in the Lake District (Cumbria).

These types of journeys are not just the preserve of melodrama. The Lake District also memorably features in *Withnail & I* (Bruce Robinson, 1987), which has two inebriated, out-of-work actors (played by Richard E. Grant and Paul McGann) briefly escaping the cold, damp misery of their late 1960s life in a Camden flat by driving in a battered old Jaguar up to a remote, run-down rural cottage. This theme of a journey out of the city to the country has endured in a wide range of British films. For example, the drive out of urban East London into the Essex countryside undertaken by a teenager, Mia (Katie Jarvis), her mother (Kierston Wareing) and her mother's boyfriend (Michael Fassbender) in Andrea Arnold's *Fish Tank* (2009) is in many ways reminiscent of journeys taken out of industrial towns into the country in a number of British social realist 'kitchen sink' films (including those mentioned by Higson in his dissection of shots of towns from hills mentioned earlier). In *Fish Tank*, as in a number of Ken Loach films including *Kes* (1969), tensions are set up between the prison-like urban lives of the young protagonists (and the socio-cultural and economic pressures governing these lives) and the apparent freedoms (albeit temporary) of the countryside. As Higson demonstrated, shots of industrial towns from grassy hills are a recurring theme of British New Wave films in particular, such as *Saturday Night and Sunday Morning* (Karel Reisz, 1960). It seems that even a temporary escape to grassy slopes above their home towns can lead downtrodden and troubled characters to experience a different, slower rhythm to the rapidly mechanised rhythms that govern their everyday urban (and suburban) lives.

Almost every corner of rural Britain has been captured and presented memorably on film. Northern England plays a key role in films as diverse as *Whistle Down the Wind* (Bryan Forbes, 1961) and *Raining Stones* (Ken Loach, 1993). *Four Lions* (Chris Morris, 2010) and *Yasmin* (Kenneth Glenaan, 2004) see Asian British characters engaging with the rural landscape of the north in very different ways. The landscapes of rural south-west England have performed a range of roles in British films, too. One might think of *A Cottage on Dartmoor* (Anthony Asquith, 1929) and *Love Story* (Leslie Arliss, 1944) – the latter a film that sees, as Sue Harper puts it, the composer heroine 'artistically inspired by the Cornish landscape, whose wildness she emulates in her emotional life'.[93] *The Titfield Thunderbolt* (Charles Crichton, 1953) draws much of its bucolic atmosphere from the rolling hills of Somerset and Oxfordshire. *The French Lieutenant's Woman* (Karel Reisz, 1981) makes memorable use of the woods high above Lyme Regis on the Dorset coast. *Land Girls* (David Leland, 1998) depicts the goings-on on a Somerset farm during the Second World War. *Hot Fuzz* (Edgar Wright, 2007) – shot around Wells – pokes fun at the Ealing-esque backwardness and apparent strangeness of contemporary small-town rural life. As we have seen, *A Matter of Life and Death* (Michael Powell and Emeric Pressburger, 1946) features memorable beach sequences shot at Saunton Sands, Devon, but the same dune system was employed very differently, and to horrific effect, in *The Shout* (Jerzy Skolimowski, 1978). The rural south-east features in a range of genre films. For example, Mark Broughton shows in his chapter how Norfolk functions to great effect in *The Go-Between* (Joseph Losey, 1971). Another key representation of East Anglia – in addition to *Witchfinder General*, as mentioned earlier – can be found in *The Tomb of Ligeia* (Roger Corman, 1964), an adaptation of Edgar Allan Poe starring Vincent Price and Elizabeth Shepherd and shot at Castle Acre priory, Swaffham, in Norfolk.

Duncan Petrie's work on Scottish cinema has demonstrated the ways in which the landscapes of Scotland have often been represented as wild and untamed. As he shows in his chapter in this book, this 'rural periphery' is often marked as geographically distant from the rules and conventions of metropolitan society. Petrie uses *I Know Where I'm Going!* (Michael Powell and Emeric Pressburger, 1945) to demonstrate how far characters in Scottish cinema are often connected to (or indeed are manifestations of, or embodiments of) wild landscapes, an example being the figure of Torquil McNeil (Roger Livesey), the Laird of Kiloran. He also shows how the figure of the urban outsider in a rural Scottish landscape fuels the drama in films such as *Whisky Galore!* (Alexander Mackendrick, 1949), *The Wicker Man* (Robin Hardy, 1973) and *Local Hero* (Bill Forsyth, 1983).[94] But, in addition to this, Petrie's chapter notices a more recent strain of Scottish films such as *Another Time, Another Place* (Michael Radford, 1983) and *The Winter Guest* (Alan Rickman, 1997), which instead choose to depict liminal coastal landscapes that connect modern Scotland to Scandinavia perhaps more than they do neighbouring England. In her chapter, too, Kate Woodward explores the ways in which *On the Black Hill* (Andrew Grieve, 1987) explores another liminal space that straddles the border between England and rural Wales.

Rural landscapes have been employed to stage historical dramas. Examples include English Civil War films of varying aesthetic approaches, such as *Cromwell* (Ken Hughes, 1970) and *Winstanley* (Kevin Brownlow and Andrew Mollo, 1975). The psychedelic curio *A Field in England* (Ben Wheatley, 2013), which recalls these earlier films in some ways, was shot in the landscape around Guildford, Surrey.

The rural landscapes of Britain have also played a hugely important role in a very broad range of experimental film work. Between 3 and 21 March 1975, for example, avant-garde British landscape films were screened at the Tate Gallery in London, including William Raban's *Boardwalk*, Renny Croft's *Stream Walk* and David Pearce's *Heath Light*.[95] Other important British landscape films of the 1970s include *River Yar* (William Raban and Chris Welsby, 1972), *Seven Days* (Chris Welsby, 1974), *Akenfield* (Peter Hall, 1974) and *Requiem for a Village* (David Gladwell, 1975). Moving into the 1980s, one might consider the work of Peter Greenaway (*The Coastline*, 1983) and Margaret Tait's films of Orkney (for example, the study of an Orkney croft, *Landmakar*, 1981) as key landscape work. Patrick Keiller's *ouevre* – especially *Robinson in Ruins* (2010) as well as Andrew Kötting's *Gallivant* (1996) and Gideon Koppel's *sleep furiously* (2008) have more recently engaged with tensions between stasis and change in depictions of rural landscapes of Britain. Keiller and Koppel are interviewed by Paul Newland in this book about their engagement with British rural landscapes in their work.

Rural landscapes have also played important roles in children's films, often (but by no means always) signifying places of warm, vivid memories. Indeed, Owain Jones has written about how childhood and rurality are combined in a range of British films such as *Chitty Chitty Bang Bang* (Ken Hughes, 1968), *The Railway Children* (Lionel Jeffries, 1970), *Tales of Beatrix Potter* (Reginald Mills, 1971) and *The Secret Garden* (Agnieszka Holland, 1993).[96] In her chapter on children's cinema in this book, Suzanne Speidel shows how contemporary films such as the Harry Potter series and the Nanny McPhee films depict the rural landscape 'through an array of visual allusions'. She notices the ways in which these films present landscapes as a kind of bricolage of 'pastoral extremity' and 'garish artificiality', mixing a range of iconography to produce 'unfeasibly picturesque' qualities that often verge on pastiche.

Lastly, several films have performed the roles of curious British takes on the 'road movie'. These include *The Magical Mystery Tour* (1967), a television film that documents the Beatles taking a surreal trip from London to Cornwall. Made a few years later, the epic *O Lucky Man!* (Lindsay Anderson, 1973) encompasses much of England and Scotland and depicts the countryside as rural idyll on the one hand but also as strange, secretive and even dangerous on the other. *Radio On* (Chris Petit, 1979) follows a lone male character on a strange road trip along the M4/A4 corridor west from London to Bristol and beyond. More recently, *Sightseers* (Ben Wheatley, 2012) evidently echoes the classic television film *Nuts in May* (Mike Leigh, 1976) in its depiction of a troubled, eccentric young English couple who travel around rural northern England in a Volvo, camping and killing as they go. Britain might not provide the sense of unlimited space seen in US road movies or indeed films shot across mainland Europe, but it has a significant range of rural landscapes that have informed (and continue to inform) many key British films at the level of the representation of national and regional identities, the identities of communities and individuals.

The functions of rural landscapes in British films are wide-ranging and often contradictory. While landscapes in narrative films are often memorable as pictorial images in their own right, they are never purely 'to be looked at' and admired as spectacle, because they always exist within other contexts, not least the contexts of editing schemas that facilitate (or indeed sometimes problematise) narrative progression. So, when it comes to film, the potentially pictorial nature of rural landscape always has to be considered alongside other formal and aesthetic properties. That is to say, rural landscapes in British films can play highly complex roles that perform many seemingly opposing functions, often at the same time. We might think that cameras out on location in rural Britain are capturing 'real' landscapes or indeed developing or constructing 'imagined' landscapes, but there is always a discernable slippage between 'real' and 'imagined' within these contexts that needs to be more fully and carefully engaged with. As we have seen from the debates in geography and art history mentioned earlier, landscapes are spatial constructs that can never have one simple set of semiotic connotations. Just as spaces and places exist in a state of flux, landscapes in films can also shift and change, depending on the ways in which they are framed from shot to shot, the shifts in behaviour and performance of figures placed in them and alongside them (and indeed seen viewing them), industrial contexts, exhibition contexts, and audiences' emotional and intellectual engagement with them (which might or might not be based on personal memories of locations or a personal level of engagement with representations of these locations that can only be understood within other textual and paratextual contexts). It is hoped that this book goes some way to engaging with these issues, while pointing the way towards further research.

Notes

1 Sergei Eisenstein, quoted in Martin Lefebvre, 'Introduction', in Martin Lefebvre (ed.), *Landscape and Film* (New York and Oxford: Routledge, 2006), pp. xi–xxxi; p. xi.
 2 Andrew Moor, *Powell & Pressburger: A Cinema of Magic Spaces* (London and New York: I.B. Tauris, 2005), p. 88.
 3 Michael Powell's fascination with landscape is also visible especially in *Edge of the World* (1937), *I Know Where I'm Going!* (1945), *Black Narcissus* (1947) and *Gone to Earth* (1950). *A Matter of Life and Death* (1946) also makes landscape a central feature. The surgeon views the landscape through a camera obscura, and Peter (David Niven) 'lands' in England on a wide sand beach (this sequence was shot at Saunton Sands in Devon).
 4 Moor, *Powell & Pressburger*, p. 88.
 5 Ian Christie, *Arrows of Desire: The Films of Michael Powell and Emeric Pressburger* (London: Faber and Faber, 2005), p. 75.
 6 W. G. Hoskins, *The Making of the English Landscape* (Harmondsworth: Penguin, 1985), p. 298. See also John Wylie, *Landscape* (London and New York: Routledge, 2007), p. 30.
 7 Hoskins, *The Making of the English Landscape*, p. 12.
 8 Moor, *Powell & Pressburger*, p. 90.
 9 Blake Morrison, 'Dream country', *The Guardian Review* (5 May 2012), p. 2.
10 Christiana Payne, *Toil and Plenty: Images of the Agricultural Landscape in England, 1780–1890* (New Haven and London: Yale University Press, 1993), pp. 1–2.
11 Payne, *Toil and Plenty*, p. 24.
12 David Matless, *Landscape and Englishness* (London: Reaktion Books, 1998), p. 17.
13 John Rennie Short, *Imagined Country* (London: Routledge, 1991), p. 31.
14 See Raymond Williams, *The Country and the City* (London: Chatto and Windus, 1973).
15 Michael Bunce, 'Reproducing rural idylls', in Paul Cloke (ed.), *Country Visions* (Harlow: Pearson/Prentice Hall, 2003), pp. 16–30; p. 16.
16 Tim Edensor, *National Identity, Popular Culture and Everyday Life* (Oxford and New York: Berg, 2002), p. 37.
17 Stephen Daniels, *Fields of Vision: Landscape Imagery and National Identity in England and the United States* (Cambridge: Polity Press, 1993), p. 5.
18 Edensor, *National Identity, Popular Culture and Everyday Life*, p. 40.
19 David Lowenthal cited in Edensor, *National Identity, Popular Culture and Everyday Life*, p. 1.
20 Edensor, *National Identity, Popular Culture and Everyday Life*, p. 40.
21 Edensor, *National Identity, Popular Culture and Everyday Life*, p. 41.
22 Edensor, *National Identity, Popular Culture and Everyday Life*, p. 43.
23 See, for example, Stephen Barber, *Projected Cities: Cinema and Urban Space* (London: Reaktion Books, 2002); Charlotte Brunsdon, *London in Film: The Cinematic City since 1945* (London: British Film Institute, 2007); David Clarke (ed.), *The Cinematic City* (London: Routledge, 1997); Francois Penz, *Urban Cinematics: Understanding Urban Phenomena through the Moving Image* (Bristol: Intellect, 2012); Mark Shiel and Tony Fitzmaurice (eds), *Screening the City* (London: Verso, 2003).
24 Richard Mabey, 'Landscape: terra firma?', in Nicholas Alfrey, Paul Barker, Margaret Drabble, Norbert Lynton, Richard Mabey, David Matthews, Kathleen Raine,

William Vaughan, *Towards a New Landscape* (London: Bernard Jacobson, 1993) pp. 62–8; p. 65.

25 Simon Schama, *Landscape and Memory* (New York: Vintage, 1996), p. 61.

26 Stephen Daniels and Denis Cosgrove, 'Introduction: iconography and landscape', in Denis Cosgrove and Stephen Daniels (eds), *The Iconography of Landscape: Essays on the Symbolic Representation, Design and Use of Past Environments* (Cambridge: Cambridge University Press, 1988), pp. 1–10; p. 1.

27 Andrew Horton, 'Reel landscapes: cinematic environments documented and created', in Iain Robertson and Penny Richards (eds), *Studying Cultural Landscapes* (London: Arnold, 2003), pp. 71–92; p. 71.

28 See Tim Cresswell, *Place: A Short Introduction* (Oxford: Blackwell, 2004); Wylie, *Landscape*, p. 18.

29 Mabey, 'Landscape: terra firma?', pp. 63–4.

30 Wylie, *Landscape*, pp. 1–11.

31 Wylie, *Landscape*, p. 7 (emphasis in original).

32 Wylie, *Landscape*, p. 7.

33 Matless, *Landscape and Englishness*, p. 13.

34 Paul Cloke, 'Knowing ruralities?', in Paul Cloke (ed.), *Country Visions* (Harlow: Pearson/ Prentice Hall, 2003), pp. 1–13; p. 3.

35 Cloke, 'Knowing ruralities?', p. 5.

36 Raymond Williams cited in Wylie, *Landscape*, p. 68.

37 Denis Cosgrove, *Social Formation and Symbolic Landscape* (Madison, Wisconsin: University of Wisconsin Press, 1984), p. 8.

38 Cosgrove, *Social Formation and Symbolic Landscape*, p. 49.

39 Cosgrove, *Social Formation and Symbolic Landscape*, p. 47.

40 Wylie, *Landscape*, p. 55.

41 Wylie, *Landscape*, p. 58.

42 Cosgrove, *Social Formation and Symbolic Landscape*, p. 52.

43 Cosgrove, *Social Formation and Symbolic Landscape*, p. 58.

44 Luke Herrmann, *British Landscape Painting of the Eighteenth Century* (London: Faber and Faber, 1973), p. 12.

45 Tom Gunning, 'Landscape and the fantasy of moving pictures: early cinema's phantom rides', in Graeme Harper and Jonathan Rayner (eds), *Cinema and Landscape: Film, Nation, and Cultural, Geography* (Bristol: Intellect, 2010), pp. 31–70; p. 34.

46 Wylie, *Landscape*, p. 5.

47 Michael Rosenthal, *British Landscape Painting* (London: Phaidon, 1982), p. 10.

48 Rosenthal, *British Landscape Painting*, p. 21.

49 Payne, *Toil and Plenty*, p. 23.

50 Gunning, 'Landscape and the fantasy of moving pictures', p. 34.

51 Gunning, 'Landscape and the fantasy of moving pictures', p. 35.

52 For more on aesthetic approaches to British landscape films see Stella Hockenhull, *Aesthetics and Neo-Romanticism in Film: Landscapes in Contemporary British Cinema* (London and New York: I. B. Tauris, 2014).

53 Short, *Imagined Country*, p. 30.

54 Short, *Imagined Country*, p. 28.

55 Sue Harper, 'The ownership of woods and water: landscapes in British cinema 1930–1960', in Graeme Harper and Jonathan Rayner (eds), *Cinema and Landscape: Film,*

Nation, and Cultural Geography (Bristol: Intellect, 2010), pp. 147–60; p. 153 (emphasis in original).

56 Moor, *Powell & Pressburger*, p. 114.

57 Martin Lefebvre, 'Between setting and landscape in the cinema', in Martin Lefebvre (ed.), *Landscape and Film* (New York and Oxford: Routledge, 2006), pp. 19–60; p. 21.

58 Martin Lefebvre, 'Introduction', p. xv.

59 Gunning, 'Landscape and the fantasy of moving pictures', p. 41.

60 Gunning, 'Landscape and the fantasy of moving pictures', p. 52.

61 Gunning, 'Landscape and the fantasy of moving pictures', p. 55.

62 Gunning, 'Landscape and the fantasy of moving pictures', p. 64.

63 Gunning, 'Landscape and the fantasy of moving pictures', p. 41.

64 Harper, 'The ownership of woods and water', p. 149.

65 Harper, 'The ownership of woods and water', p. 151.

66 Harper, 'The ownership of woods and water', p. 151.

67 Harper, 'The ownership of woods and water', p. 151.

68 Harper, 'The ownership of woods and water', p. 150.

69 Harper, 'The ownership of woods and water', p. 150.

70 Harper, 'The ownership of woods and water', p. 154.

71 Brian McFarlane, *Lance Comfort* (Manchester: Manchester University Press, 1999), p. 71.

72 McFarlane, *Lance Comfort*, p. 74.

73 Sarah Cardwell, 'Working the land: representations of rural England in adaptations of Thomas Hardy's novels', in Catherine Fowler and Gillian Helfield (eds), *Representing the Rural: Space, Place, and Identity in Films about the Land* (Detroit: Wayne State University Press, 2006), pp. 19–34; p. 25.

74 Cardwell, 'Working the land', p. 26.

75 See Jefferson Hunter, *English Filming, English Writing* (Bloomington: Indiana University Press, 2010); John Pym, *Merchant Ivory's English Landscape: Rooms, Views and Anglo-Saxon Attitudes* (New York: Harry N. Abrams, 1995).

76 Andrew Higson, 'Re-presenting the national past: nostalgia and pastiche in the heritage film', in Lester Friedman (ed.), *British Cinema and Thatcherism: Fires Were Started* (London: Wallflower, 2nd edition, 2006), pp. 91–109; p. 91.

77 Catherine Fowler and Gillian Helfield, 'Introduction', in Catherine Fowler and Gillian Helfield (eds), *Representing the Rural: Space, Place, and Identity in Films about the Land* (Detroit: Wayne State University Press, 2006), pp. 1–14; pp. 5–6.

78 Fowler and Helfield, 'Introduction', p. 6.

79 Andrew Higson, 'Space, place, spectacle: landscape and townscape in the kitchen sink film', in Andrew Higson (ed.), *Dissolving Views: Key Writings on British Cinema* (London: Cassell, 1996), pp. 133–56; p. 134.

80 Higson, 'Space, place, spectacle', p. 138.

81 Higson, 'Space, place, spectacle', p. 137.

82 B. F. Taylor, *The British New Wave: A Certain Tendency?* (Manchester: Manchester University Press, 2006), p. 111.

83 Taylor, *The British New Wave*, p. 111.

84 Peter Hutchings, 'Uncanny landscapes in British film and television', *Visual Culture in Britain*, 5: 2 (2004), pp. 27–40. See also David Bell, 'Anti-idyll: rural horror', in Paul

Cloke and Jo Little (eds), *Contested Countryside Cultures* (London: Routledge, 1997), pp. 94–108.

85 Short, *Imagined Country*, p. 8.

86 Tanya Krzywinska, 'Lurking beneath the skin: British pagan landscapes in popular cinema', in Robert Fish (ed.), *Cinematic Countrysides* (Manchester: Manchester University Press, 2007), pp. 75–90; p. 84.

87 Krzywinska, 'Lurking beneath the skin', p. 78.

88 Rosenthal, *British Landscape Painting*, p. 9.

89 Rosenthal, *British Landscape Painting*, p. 16.

90 Hutchings, 'Uncanny landscapes in British film and television', p. 29.

91 Hutchings, 'Uncanny landscapes in British film and television', p. 28.

92 Hutchings, 'Uncanny landscapes in British film and television', p. 33.

93 Harper, 'The ownership of woods and water', p. 154.

94 See Paul Newland, 'Folksploitation: charting the horrors of the British folk music tradition in *The Wicker Man* (Robin Hardy, 1973)', in Robert Shail (ed.), *British Cinema in the 1970s* (London: British Film Institute, 2008), pp. 119–28. See also Paul Newland 'To the west there is nothing … except America: the spatial politics of *Local Hero*', in *Visual Culture in Britain*, 12: 2 (2011), pp. 171–83.

95 See Lucy Reynolds, 'Avant-garde British Landscape films at the Tate Gallery', www.luxonline.org.uk/histories/1970-1979/landscape_tate.html (accessed 12 June 2013).

96 Owain Jones, 'Idylls and otherness: childhood and rurality in film', in Robert Fish (ed.), *Cinematic Countrysides* (Manchester: Manchester University Press, 2007), pp. 177–94; pp. 181–2.

1

Silent landscapes: rural settings, national identity and British silent cinema

Andrew Higson

Landscape and national cinema

Since the beginnings of cinema in the 1890s, landscape has played a crucial role in the development of British national cinema. A sense of national specificity in British films has been asserted in part through the representation of particular types of place, and through presenting such places in particular ways. From short scenic films in the late 1890s and early 1900s to the heritage films of the late twentieth and early twenty-first centuries, the representation of a particular version of traditional, rural England and the display of particular types of rural landscapes has been central to the articulation of national identity in British films. And of course it is a particular version of *England* and *Englishness* that has held sway in some of the most prominent understandings of *British* cinema.[1]

In this chapter, I offer some reflections on the use of rural landscapes in British films of the silent period, and the ways in which those films and their landscapes were promoted and taken up in contemporary critical debate.[2] These reflections will touch on the role of landscape in articulating national identity and on the centrality of the concept of the picturesque in the film culture of the period. It will also become clear that, in contemporary critical debate, picturesque Englishness is very often seen as synonymous with high-quality photography. It is also worth remarking that 1895 saw not only the first public performances of films but also the foundation of that key British institution, the National Trust, known at the time as the National Trust for Places of Historic Interest or Natural Beauty. To put it another way, the debates about and the development of British cinema in this period were by no means taking place in a vacuum.

In what follows, I will draw on examples from the late 1890s to the late 1920s, and from fiction and non-fiction films alike. Cecil Hepworth, one of the leading British filmmakers of the silent period, will inevitably figure large in my account, since his work was central to the critical debate of the period about landscape, British cinema and national identity.[3] Thus, in 1912, Frederick Talbot noted of the Hepworth Company that it produced 'some of the best films prepared especially to suit British and Colonial tastes'.[4] What contemporary commentators particularly appreciated was the company's 'unsurpassed skill in the representation of typically English scenes' and the 'delicacy of touch and the beauty of [the] countryside settings' of so many of its films.[5] Of the 1916 version of *Comin' Thro' the Rye*, for instance, the *Bioscope* remarked that it had 'never seen a film which embodied more thoroughly the true inner spirit, as well as the outward appearance, of the English countryside'.[6] Of the 1919 film *Broken Threads*, *The Cinema* commented: 'It makes one proud that a British producer can record for the screen such typical homeland scenery, that shown at home will make many a heart thrill with pride, whilst shown abroad will give the foreigner a true conception of our country's beauty.'[7] Indeed, as Hepworth himself remarked in his autobiography, 'it was always in my mind from the very beginning that I was to make English pictures, with all the English countryside for background and with English atmosphere and English idiom throughout'.[8]

These are typical of the terms in which landscape in British films was discussed at the time: an un-self-conscious sense of what was typically *English* (rather than British), a sense that the English countryside was at its best naturally beautiful (although the concept of the picturesque, rather than the formally beautiful, is probably more appropriate here), and a sense that, for many commentators, the best British films were able to present such countryside scenes in an aesthetically pleasing manner that could be described as 'delicate'. All of this was bound up in a concept of national identity in which tradition played a central role.

The early development of British cinema: storytelling versus pictorialism

In a discussion of aesthetic developments more generally in British films of the early 1910s, the renowned historian of British cinema Rachael Low suggests that there were in fact two distinct lines of development, each with their own more or less well-formulated theories and advocates. On the one hand, there was the line that stressed the role of the scenario writer and which therefore concentrated on the construction of the narrative, continuity, efficiency and cohesiveness – and, above all, comprehensibility. This we might call the classic narrative tendency. On the other hand there was the line that stressed the importance of pictorial composition, less in terms of relevance to the story than in terms of realism and beauty, and more or less static concepts of image construction such as 'grouping'.[9] This we might call the pictorialist tendency. We might see the former as an attempt to decisively move on from the stage of the cinema of attractions, while the latter recognises the continuing visual appeal of those attractions and is more overt about the processes of integrating the pleasures of the scenic and the travelogue, the theatrical tableau and the lantern image, with the pleasures of the extended dramatic narrative.

Low suggests that the distinction between the different tendencies can be illustrated by Barker and Haldane's *East Lynne* (1913), which she sees benefiting from a well-constructed scenario, and the Hepworth/Bentley production of *David Copperfield* (1913), which is full of beautiful pictorial compositions. The distinction is not hard and fast, of course, and indeed both films were discussed at the time in terms of the discourses of realism and authenticity, Englishness and landscape.

Both films were made in 1913 and contributed to a sense that there had been a turnaround in the quality of British films that year. In response, one of the two leading British trade papers of the period, *Kinematograph and Lantern Weekly*, proclaimed that 'the All-British film is rapidly coming into its own'. *East Lynne* was a key film in this development: 'the staging, photography and acting of the film … are all perfect, and on every hand the film is being spoken of as the best yet turned out by an English firm'.[10] Similar accolades were heaped on three Hepworth productions of 1913: *Drake's Love Story* ('this very fine production'[11]), *David Copperfield* ('the finest cinematograph film ever made by a British producer'[12]) and *Hamlet* ('no finer film has ever been screened'[13]). All in all, it could be claimed that:

> There is a marked increase in the respect with which English film productions are regarded in these days. Since *East Lynne*, *Waterloo*, and now *Ivanhoe*, we have heard remarkably little of the impossibility of getting good photographic results with the English climate. Still more remarkable is the absence of the once almost universal state of mind which led to condemnation of an English film because it was English – sometimes without even the form of inspection.[14]

As will be evident, several of these notable films were adaptations of canonical literary texts, bio-pics of national heroes or re-enactments of key moments in the national past. Such subject matter was not insignificant to those making claims for a turnaround in the fortunes of British cinema:

> The charge against British manufacturers that they have allowed their national history and literature to be adapted for the cinematograph by foreign producers in other lands has often been heard, and has, up to the present, been partially justified. Latterly, however, our own manufacturers, in spite of overpowering odds where their number is concerned, have been making magnificent efforts to build up a library of national film masterpieces, produced and acted by British artists on British soil. And in this movement the Hepworth Manufacturing Company … have been leaders.[15]

So began the review of *David Copperfield* in the other leading British trade paper of the period, *The Bioscope*. Central to the film's critical success was what was deemed an authentic reproduction of Dickens's novel. Even *The Dickensian* was impressed:

> The film not only includes all the most prominent characters and all the necessary incidents of the book to make the story intelligible to the lay reader, but they have been enacted in the actual places in which the novelist laid them. With the

narrative so well maintained, the scenery accurate and the acting so life-like and natural, the film should be a popular success wherever it is shown and no Dickens lover should miss the opportunity of seeing it.[16]

But, in trying to be so faithful to the narrative and its setting, the film ends up parading a series of relatively discrete attractions in a highly episodic narrative, with much of the work of narration having to be provided by the spectator from outside the bounds of the film text. As Low puts it, whereas *East Lynne* is much more assured as a piece of continuous storytelling, *David Copperfield* 'is perfected piece by piece, its quality in the individual shots rather than in the manner of the combination'.[17]

Without some foreknowledge of the story of *David Copperfield*, it is often difficult to determine who characters are and why they act in the way that they do. The pictorialist images, charming though they are, often seem superfluous to narrative development. But there is no doubt that they are beautifully photographed and make the most of some delightful scenery, especially characterful old buildings, gardens, country lanes and coastal settings. The camera stands well back from the characters and is thus able to make the most of the scenery, with skyline, background and foreground frequently visible in classically balanced pictorial compositions. And frequently these compositions seem staged for the camera rather than having a genuinely useful function as narrative space: this is pictorialist cinema rather than classic narrative cinema.

As advertisements in the trade press indicated, there were many attractions on offer in this production, among them the use of landscape and other exterior locations:

Barker's All-British Masterpiece, *East Lynne*, Adapted from Mrs Henry Wood's Famous Novel. Perfect Staging! Perfect Photography! Perfect Acting![18]

The scenery is all that could be desired to produce a photoplay of the very highest standard of excellence.[19]

According to the *Bioscope*, 'all else is subordinated to pictorial effect, which perhaps is at it should be in a picture play. Particularly beautiful are the scenes at Boulogne ... being excellent examples of photography and of great intrinsic beauty.'[20]

Meanwhile, American publicity for this 'Fragrant Memory of the Dear Old Past' announced that it was 'staged in the beautiful and historic Severn valley'.[21] If we take such proclamations into account, it is clear that, while *East Lynne* may have had a relatively strong, coherent narrative, and a greater sense of continuity than some other British films of the period, it was still a bundle of attractions in which a pictorialist representation of landscape and local detail played its part.

This is particularly true of some lovingly photographed picturesque scenery: the grand country house and its gardens, quaint old cottages, country lanes, the cliffs and beach, some old walls and archways, a pond with swans, and so on.

Reviewers praised this 'really delightful and dainty piece of work' with 'one of the most charming settings that the story has ever received'. This applied to the

> picturesque costumes ... the beautiful mounting and scenic effects ... [even] the *atmosphere* of the period ... In many of the scenes – especially in the beautiful gardens of East Lynne – you can almost detect the scent of lavender coming towards you from the old-fashioned pleasaunce, completing the illusion that you are assisting at a real living representation instead of a mimic production.[22]

The same reviewer commented that:

> there are a number of pretty scenes that I can imagine audiences going into ecstasies over. The village wedding ... is a specially picturesque and charming scene ... [but] there are many other scenes that are certain to be appreciated for their beauty, quaintness and distinct charm in every detail.[23]

It is interesting to find this conjunction of terms – 'a picturesqueness and an attention to detail'[24] – in the critical discourse around the film, since it suggests that this picturesque construction of old England is not nostalgic but authentic. Ideology thus masquerades as realism. It is also worth noting that *East Lynne*, for all the narrative continuity that Low notes, is still shot primarily in wide, tableau-style long takes, without a great deal of analytical editing, which enables the cinematographer to make the most of the picturesque charms of the locations.

Hepworth, Newall and Elvey: the emergence of a middlebrow art cinema

As the distinction between classic narrative filmmaking and pictorialist film-making developed, it was certainly the Hepworth Company that became the prime exponent of the pictorialist style of filmmaking in Britain. Reviews of the 1913 film *Drake's Love Story* underline this view of Cecil Hepworth's films, and the general tenets of the pictorialist tradition. For the *Bioscope*, 'As an example of the arts of photography and scenic arrangement it is ... almost perfect.'[25] The *Kine Weekly* reviewer agreed:

> The outstanding feature of the production and one which calls for unstinted praise, is the tasteful and picturesque stage settings of the play. Set among old world gardens and beautiful buildings of the period – no cheap stage imitations these, but the real thing – the figures move in a setting in exquisite keeping with the story. The art of the producer has emphasised all that is lovely in these scenic backgrounds, whilst the art of the photographer has preserved them for all time.[26]

But if,

> pictorially, the film could scarcely be improved upon, as a drama, perhaps, it is not quite so good. Sometimes the Hepworth Company seem inclined to neglect the play for the picture, and in the present instance we carry away with us a memory of exquisite *tableaux*, wonderfully arranged and perfectly reproduced, rather than of

a stirring and charming romance. Admittedly, it is difficult to fashion an historical happening into a play if one is to remain faithful to the original, but one fancies that the action might have been 'speeded up' a trifle without in any way lessening its value as a true tale.[27]

This tension between the picturesque image and halting narrative development is typical of the pictorialist strand of British filmmaking. *Kine Weekly* thought it was still there in Hepworth's film *Mist in the Valley* (1923), made ten years later: there is no doubt in their reviewer's mind that 'the scenery is very charming' and that any attempt to exploit the film should 'stress the picturesque qualities of the picture'. But, if 'there is a great deal of picturesque scenery … none of the characters have much appeal, as they are put into such entirely unconvincing situations … It is a pity that the producer has seen fit to take such a very illogical and unconvincing story on which to expend such a lot of excellent camera work.'[28] Lionel Collier, the *Kine Weekly*'s review editor, added, 'there remains little to hold the interest or entertain except the settings which, though pleasing in themselves, cannot be regarded as a substitute for story value'.[29] The tension between the image and the narrative was noted too in Henry Edwards's *Owd Bob* (1924). Filmed around Lake Windermere in the Lake District ('the artistic values of which are very good'), reviewers noted that 'the settings are very beautiful' but 'the story is apt to become a little wearisome'.[30]

The work of another acclaimed English filmmaker of the early 1920s, Guy Newall, in films such as *The Lure of Crooning Water* (1920) and *Fox Farm* (Arthur Rooke, 1922), seems more inclined towards the classic narrative tendency. Yes, the English landscape remains vital to these films – and it was Newall's professed aim to make 'very, very English' films[31] – but the use of landscapes tends to be less heavily foregrounded in publicity and reviews. This is perhaps because those landscapes are more thoroughly integrated as narrative settings, by comparison with the overt pleasures of the picturesque setting as an attraction in its own right in Hepworth films from the same period, such as *Tansy* (1921) and *Comin' Thro' the Rye* (1923).

Even so, the pictorial qualities of the landscape remain important in the production and critical reception of Newall's films. Thus, in a review of *Fox Farm*, *Kine Weekly* described Newall as 'a producer with an eye to dramatic and picturesque effect'.[32] And, in an otherwise somewhat critical review of *Boy Woodburn* (1922) – 'it bears traces of hasty production and incomplete editing, and its story is rambling and neither new nor very convincing' – the *Kine Weekly* reviewer noted that 'there is plenty of charm in some of the details of characterisation and setting … [and] pictorially, it is excellent, with many good landscape effects'.[33] Thus, while 'it is not a bad film by any means', the reviewer wrote, 'it gets perilously near to being a boring one, despite its pictorial merits and the sentimental-humorous appeal of its many charming studies of animals'.[34] Newall had even bought his own farm for *Boy Woodburn*: 'Having used the farm I specially acquired for *Boy Woodburn* ... I naturally can't use it for [my] next production [*Fox Farm*]. But there is a particularly picturesque farm within a couple of miles of my own, and I have already arranged for it to figure on the screen as the farm of Warwick Deeping's novel.'[35] While these settings and pictorial values undoubtedly add to the claims for realism made for Newall's films, just as important is the naturalistic acting style of Newall and Duke – what a fan magazine described as 'their artistic and sincere rendering of their respective roles' in *The Lure of Crooning Water*.[36]

Fox Farm is typical of Newall's work in that there is much more scene dissection, cross-cutting, analytical editing and parallelism than in Hepworth's films. It remains narratively languorous and episodic in construction, however, rambling slowly through the lives of its characters. The film, like its hero Jesse Falconer, demonstrates a love of the countryside and it displays its wares in almost documentary style, offering us a dissection of contemporary English rural life. As Christine Gledhill remarks, Newall employs 'a descriptive camera which captures rather than enacts the situations and exchanges of the characters'. It might also be remarked that the countryside is almost a character in its own right, 'imbued with metaphysical force of a kind found in Thomas Hardy and Mary Webb', as Gledhill suggests. Particularly remarkable is a lovely, picturesque scene in a bluebell wood with a river running by; equally charming is the Falconers' house, dripping with honeysuckle and ivy. Newall pushes for a relatively intense psychological realism, with a restrained, undemonstrative acting style that dwells subtly on small details and with characters defined in terms of ambiguity and complexity rather than stereotypicality.[37]

As Linda Wood has demonstrated, Maurice Elvey was another filmmaker noted in the late 1910s and early 1920s for his efforts to celebrate a pastoral vision of Englishness and the English countryside.[38] Like Hepworth and Newall, his work too was characterised by a tension between pictorialist splendour and narrative drive. Of a 1917 film, the *Bioscope* wrote, '*Mary Girl* enables us to enjoy a story breathing English sentiment showing an English countryside and introducing English rural types'.[39] A year later, *Kine Weekly* remarked of his adaptation of *Adam Bede* (1918) that 'the settings are a procession of English beauties' which bring 'to our eyes corners of the loveliest county in England'.[40] In a letter published in defence of this film in a fan magazine of the period, the writer asked whether there was 'any necessity for this continual running down of English productions ... I think it is about time a protest was made against a certain section of people who seem blind to the beautiful scenery and natural unaffected acting of English productions.'[41] Evidently not everyone shared these sentiments. Another letter published a few weeks later in the same fan magazine commented:

> I notice there's been a great deal of discussion of late in your paper about the superiority of British and American films ... Every picturegoer, however patriotic, who

wishes to be just, will own that British pictures will have to be improved before they come anywhere near the American standard, not just in scenery and buildings.[42]

What is clear from the critical debates of the period is that the promotion of a specifically British cinema in the 1910s and early 1920s was intimately bound up with the filmic presentation of certain types of scenery and properties. Such attractions, as we've seen, were frequently provided as backdrops to adaptations of 'national' literature, or re-workings of 'national' history. This is true of another Elvey film from 1918, his bio-pic *Nelson*, produced as propaganda at the tail end of the Great War.

While much of the film deals with Nelson's exploits at sea, these are counterbalanced by scenes of his home life, introduced in one intertitle with the telling phrase 'England, home and beauty'. The scenes of Nelson's homeland construct a familiar scene of a picturesque and peaceful rural England, a space of great trees, of ivy-covered houses, of leafy glades and rose-covered walks, and of a quaint bridge over a charming pond. The *Kine Weekly* reviewer concluded that 'Mr Elvey has spared no pains to find settings that for sheer beauty could surely not be equalled throughout the rest of England.' The way such settings were filmed 'prove that Mr Elvey is an artist … at last we have a British success that is at the same time an artistic success'.[43] What, perhaps surprisingly, goes unremarked is that these pastoral attractions are housed in an extremely episodic story, lacking the fluid narrative continuity of the contemporary American film. This remains an insistently attractionist cinema, wherein a pictorialist representation of rural England is one of the key attractions.[44]

Hepworth's, Elvey's and Newall's films shared a delight in a certain version of the English countryside. In their emphasis on beautiful scenery, and, especially in Newall's films, on fine character acting, they also represented the development of what we might now identify as a middlebrow-quality cinema, a middle-class art cinema. Thus *Kine Weekly* cautioned that

> *Fox Farm* is an artistic production which should not be exploited by means of stunts or teasers. … Mention Guy Newall and Ivy Duke, drawing particular attention to the clever acting of the film, for the acting will attract the type of audience with which this film will be popular. The beautiful scenery of the English countryside and the artistic nature of the production are other features of the film which it would be well to exploit. If you have any system of classifying your patrons, *Fox Farm* is the sort of film which it would pay to advertise amongst the more educated and artistic members.[45]

Such statements are indicative of a growing recognition and exploitation in the late 1910s and early 1920s of that audience we would now call the art-house crowd. Thus an article published in *Kine Weekly* in 1924 noted that 'there is an artistic public; and although it is not large, it is mightily influential'. Pictorial values are important to such audiences – although 'it is as well to remember also that beautiful pictures are not wasted even upon the eightpenny seats'.[46]

Projecting a national landscape: 'a typically British school of film-making'

Landscape, national identity, patriotism and national cinema were constantly bundled together in the debate about British cinema in the 1910s and 1920s. Thus *Drake's Love Story* had 'the outstanding merit of being genuinely English'.[47] 'First and last it is an English play in an English setting, and as such it will undoubtedly have a multitude of admirers when shown in picture theatres throughout the country.'[48] *East Lynne*, 'a bold bid for British supremacy', was deemed so important and so successful that 'it is the duty of every English exhibitor to see this production'.[49] A decade on and the Hepworth Company was celebrated by the *Bioscope* as a 'typically British school of film-making', while the fan magazine the *Picturegoer* described its films as 'representative of English thought, ideals, and character, without any imitation of other countries whatsoever'.[50] The picturesque landscapes and gardens that populated Hepworth productions enabled those films to represent 'English art in its cleanest, grandest form'.[51]

Pictures and the Picturegoer described Arthur Rooke's *The Lure of Crooning Water* as 'without question one of the finest pictures ever made in this country'.[52] *Kine Weekly* agreed: '*The Lure of Crooning Water* is as near perfection as anything which has yet emanated from a British studio.'[53] *Kine Weekly* was equally positive about Newall's later film, *Fox Farm*: 'Pictures of this excellence show what strides the British Industry is making.'[54] A couple of years later, *Owd Bob* too could be described as 'a typically British production', not least because 'the scenery in the Lake District is extremely beautiful'.[55] *Kine Weekly* reported that 'Samuelson's patriotic film' *A Couple of Down and Outs* (1923) was being prepared for 'the All British Film Week' of 1924,[56] while the *Daily Telegraph* predicted that 'if the continuous applause which punctuated the exhibition of [the film to an invited audience] be any criterion, *A Couple of Down and Outs* will be one of the most popular items in the programme of the All-British Film Weeks next year'.[57]

The British Film Weeks of 1924 were an attempt to promote a specifically British national cinema – by creating a protected market in British picture houses.[58] The focus on the domestic, at the level of both production and exhibition, did not always sit easily with the efforts made by some British filmmakers to target the American market. In an interview around the time of the release of his film *Owd Bob*, Henry Edwards pointed out the difficulties of making specifically national films and assuming that they might be suitable for export to the US: 'It is no good ... going out to make films for the American market if we are to produce typically British pictures. I do not know that British pictures appeal at all to the Americans if they are really English in sentiment.' This was not to say that such films shouldn't be made, however,

> provided that the stories are carefully chosen, and the money is spent judiciously, good British films can still make money in this country if the public will give our best the encouragement they deserve. The English public have so long been served with the recherché dishes which are served out by American companies, that just plain roast beef is dull in comparison, *although there are people who prefer it.*[59]

What we can see emerging in this critical discourse, and in the films that this discourse valorises, is a model for a national cinema. Certain standards for British filmmaking were being defined – what the films should look like, what sorts of stories they should tell, the moral tone they should adopt, the nation they should envision. This was much more than an assertion that British audiences should be able to watch British films: the debate concerned the differences between not only British and American films but also the quality film and the mere commercial pot-boiler. What we can see here, in effect, is the emergence of a respectable national art cinema. The formal terms of this cinema – the rich pictorial imagery, the tableau-style shots composed in depth with minimal scene dissection, and the languorous, episodic narratives – were both characteristic of other European (art) cinemas of the 1910s and distinct from the rapid-cutting and shallow space of the American film.[60]

But might American audiences also appreciate such films? If, to use Henry Edwards's splendid phrase, some British audiences preferred plain roast beef to Hollywood's recherché servings, there were certainly others who argued that American audiences *did* in fact enjoy British scenes and British sentiments, and that British filmmakers should make every effort to respond to these desires. It was frequently asserted that it was vital that British filmmakers, and not foreign filmmakers, should make films about British subjects. One of the great advantages of such films, it was often argued, was that British filmmakers could use genuine British settings, and that those settings allowed a flavour that only British filmmakers could achieve. Publicity for *East Lynne* proclaimed that the film had been 'produced by Britishers, who know their Country and its Customs. We have not made the glaring errors which are so common in Photo-Play Productions ... of British Books or Historical Subjects, filmed under another flag than the Union Jack.'[61] Compare too the *Bioscope* review of *Drake's Love Story*:

> One's first sensation in seeing this very fine production by the Hepworth Company is a feeling of gratification that the splendid chapter of English history which it represents has been immortalised in pictures not by a foreign firm but by a company essentially and entirely British. For too long we have been forced to endure the ignominy of having our first literary masterpieces and our noblest historical passages flung back in our faces, as it were, by people of another land, and, apart from other considerations, we must all be ready appreciatively to recognise the laudable

efforts of Messrs. Hepworth to remove this ancient reproach and to establish the art of manufacture on quite as high and as national a basis in our own as it is in other countries. It is quite certain that no foreign producer could have caught the spirit of Elizabethan England, so far as scenery is concerned, with the success possible to a British company, and from this point of view the film is a triumph.[62]

Compare too Martin Lane, writing in 1923: 'What I want to plead ... is that if English history is to be screened it should be done by Englishmen.' Too many films about the British national past had been made by American companies, he felt. And they generally did so

not with the happiest results so far as English susceptibilities are concerned. They have not been true to British tradition and they have lacked the necessary atmosphere. But they have proved one thing – that the Americans love things British and that they believe in their right to annex the historical past for their own purposes. ... They rave about the beauties of our countryside, with its lordly castles, its historic homes, its quaint manor houses, its picturesque cottages, its hill and dale, its moor and fen, our time-worn institutions, our antiquities and curiosities, and our legends and stories. They would like to convey them wholesale across the herring-pond, and in many cases they have. ... From these facts, it may be forcefully argued, I think, that Americans generally would like to witness on the screen the episodes which have had these places for a backdrop in days gone by, and that this is sufficient reason for contending that there is money in the exploitation of our national beauties and inheritances.[63]

Lane goes on to add that, 'besides the Americans there is the Colonial market to consider, and I believe the Colonies would simply lap up such pictures', concluding with the statement that 'it is the Englishman's duty to deal with the stories of his own country and to try to capture the foreign markets with them'.[64]

The cameraman Charles Rosher, returning to Britain in 1929 after nearly 20 years in Hollywood, expressed the similar view that 'there is in America a big demand for films based on big figures in British history. Over there they love pomp and ceremony, the costumes and pageantry associated with everything of the old English periods, and if properly treated, I believe such subjects would go big over there.' However, as the *Bioscope* went on to say, Rosher 'was inclined to agree with a suggestion that British directors were apt, in filming such subjects, to sacrifice pictorial entertainment to unerring fidelity to tradition and historical fact and he felt that in that respect American film producers had appeared to enjoy a distinct advantage'.[65]

The functions of landscape in British silent cinema

Whether films were made for the American market or not, rural landscape was, as we've seen, frequently noted as a means of promoting a film as British, especially when it could be rolled up with historical subject matter. Landscape in this sense is thus a key marker of national identity. What this suggests, and what I think is emerging from my analysis more generally, is that rural settings performed a variety of different sorts of functions in British films of the silent period. I want to suggest that there are in fact four distinct but overlapping ways in which rural settings were used, four key reasons for displaying rural Britain, and especially selected parts of rural England, on screen.

Firstly, there is the most basic function of providing a relatively neutral narrative space in which the story can unfold, or, more broadly, a diegetic setting within which non-fictional events can take place. But secondly, as will have become clear from many of the reviews I have quoted from, that relatively neutral diegetic space also functions as an appealing aesthetic display: rural settings, in other words, are presented, and/or received, as spectacular. Thirdly, and closely related to the second point, is the idea of rural settings as appealing to what has been called the tourist gaze, whether the gaze of the English urban-dweller or of the virtual visitor from America or the empire. Fourthly, and finally, rural settings are often called upon to perform an ideological function, to offer a particular reading of the nation, a particular embodiment of national identity. Clearly these functions may overlap in any particular film, particularly insofar as they are to a great extent a product of the reception process. Promotional material or critical responses will thus take up films in different ways to those intended by the producer, for instance, while different readers will construct different interpretations of the films from each other, and so on.

It is worth unpacking the details of the functions I have ascribed to use of rural settings in British films. Firstly, when rural settings are used simply as diegetic or narrative space – as the space demanded by the events of the film – they appear as relatively neutral spaces, the details of which are simply about filling out the diegesis, enabling a realistic effect. Of course, no space can really be neutral, or meaningless, and will always be invested with some sort of significance beyond its narrative or diegetic use. But, at the level of analysis, we might, momentarily at least, focus on this idea of space as neutral, stripped of meaning, simply offering room for the story to develop. Cecil Hepworth's *Tansy* is about a shepherdess, so it makes sense that much of the film is shot on the sort of rolling downland where sheep typically graze. On a more modest scale, but staying with Hepworth, one might note the parkland setting for the procession of the pack of cards in *Alice in Wonderland* (1903), the fields through which the Tilly girls and their sailor suitors briefly cycle in *Tilly's Party* (1911) or the wild seashore setting for *A Fisherman's Love Story* (1912). *East Lynne* is a costume drama organised around the comings and goings at a country house, so needs to portray an England in keeping with the period and the setting depicted. The very title of *Fox Farm* dictates certain sorts of narrative spaces, while Elvey's 1922 Sherlock Holmes adaptation *The Hound of the Baskervilles* offers several shots of pastoral landscapes in keeping with the opening title, 'Midst the desolate silence of the Devonshire Moorland'.

In many filmed dramas, however, the countryside is not simply a neutral narrative space but provides a spectacular backdrop to the action – and thus very often functions as an attraction in its own right, as we have seen in so many of the reviews quoted above. Rural settings are thus carefully aestheticised, presented as spectacle, according to the formal conventions of the vista or the panorama. The high vantage point occasionally afforded the spectator in *Tansy*, for instance, displays vast stretches of rolling countryside. The sheer pictorial composition of several of Hepworth's and Newall's films means that they draw attention to themselves as more than mere *mise-en-scène*. Thus the cliffs, seascapes and rocky shore of Lulworth Cove, and the gardens and grounds of various country houses, provided a spectacular backdrop to the theatrical performances of Sir Johnston Forbes-Robertson and the rest of the Drury Lane theatre company in Hepworth's 1913 production of *Hamlet*. The 1912 British & Colonial Kinematograph Company film *The Mountaineer's Romance* provides some spectacular rural settings in the Derbyshire Peak District as the backdrop to its drama. It is never simply spectacle, however, since the more troubling the narrative becomes, the more rugged is the setting. Generally in picturesque, when proper Englishness is under threat, the landscape can become more sublime, more terrible, as in *The Mountaineer's Romance* or in the scene beneath the towering cliffs at Boulogne in *East Lynne*, when Lady Isabel, convalescing far from the security and stability of her home and family, once more and fatefully meets the villainous Levinson. But, when landscape is required to function as spectacle, the landscape space is consciously selected, or framed, the image designed or composed to stress the awe-inspiring nature of the setting. As such, this representation of space will benefit from an attractionist, shot-based aesthetic, one that is more akin to the self-contained tableau than the shallow space and fast cutting of the American cinema of the 1910s and 1920s.

But the pleasures of rural England could also form the background to a much more classically narrated film such as Hitchcock's *The Farmer's Wife* (1928). This light romantic comedy is at the same time a visual celebration of English rural life and landscape, populated with beautiful thatched farmhouses and grand vistas and shot on location in Devon and Surrey.[66] For all their picturesque spectacle, however, they remain narrative settings (captured in establishing shots) or mere backdrop to the interplay of the characters, in a film remarkable for its American-style visual narration rather than any pictorialist aesthetic. Even so, the trade press recommended to exhibitors that promotional material should exploit 'the English atmosphere and scenery', commenting that 'some of the Devonshire shots are outstandingly beautiful, and merited the applause they obtained at the Trade show'.[67]

Another Hitchcock film made the same year and with a similarly picturesque semi-rural setting was *The Manxman* (1929). This too is remarkable for its fluid visual narration, especially its ability to construct a drama by cutting between the looks exchanged by its central characters. But it too is equally remarkable for its beautiful location photography, its pastoral rural imagery and its shots of the coastline, the sea and the traditional labour of the fisherman, underlining what is often remarked of Hitchcock's British films: his eye for documentary detail, what the *Bioscope* called the 'unflinching realism' of *The Manxman*.[68] Settings, photography and atmosphere were identified by *Kine Weekly* as having 'a strong appeal. There are a number of delicate seascapes and landscapes which have rare pictorial beauty.'[69]

Such rural settings often seem designed to function not simply as spectacle but as an appeal to the tourist gaze. They beckon city-dwellers to the countryside, they beckon Britons living elsewhere in the empire back to the old country and they invite American tourists to explore the English atmosphere. Early scenics – short observational documentaries – like Hepworth's *Thames River Scenery* series of around 1899 seem designed to work in this way. In the Hepworth Company catalogue, it was suggested that the 'photographic panorama of the scenery' in *Thames Panorama – Under Chertsey Bridge* would appeal to 'all lovers of the "Royal Thames" – and their name is legion'.[70] The surviving prints of these films present England as a charming, semi-rural space and were clearly composed for pictorial beauty. The 1903 catalogue draws attention to the pastoral imagery in *Thames River Scenery – Magna Charta Island and Panorama of House Boats*: 'the beautifully wooded island' with its 'very picturesque little cottage' and its strong historical connections, and 'the effect of the sunlight on the rippling water [which] is very beautifully rendered'.[71] *Thames River Scenery – Wargrave* offers 'a very beautiful panorama of one of the prettiest portions of the Upper Thames' and 'a great deal of varied and beautiful scenery'.[72]

Phantom rides, filmed by a camera strapped to the front of a train or other moving vehicle, also provided scope for the display of rural landscapes, and literally played out the gaze of the traveller passing through the countryside. Judging from the promotional material, the scenery was as much of an appeal as the sheer experience of speed afforded by these films. Thus the Hepworth catalogue underlined the fact that *View from an Engine Front – Shilla Mill Tunnel* offers 'a panoramic representation of some of the most beautiful of the Devonshire scenery'.[73] *View from an Engine Front – Devonshire Scenery* 'is one of the most varied "Phantom Ride" pictures ever taken, for during its run the audience is carried through all varieties of beautiful scenery' including 'some beautiful glimpses of hill and valley, river and wood'.[74]

The travelogue, developing out of these precursors and others such as the lantern slide travel lecture, was also very much designed to appeal to the tourist gaze. One strand of the travelogue – what we might call the heritage travelogue – delights in presenting historical sites identified with key figures from the national past, or, as in films like the 1914 *Old London*, simply provides evidence of the antiquity of England. One of the trade papers noted in 1918 'the growing demand for reproductions in pictures, of famous British scenery'.[75] In the films that offered such reproductions, the discourses of tourism are repeatedly bound up with the discourses of historical authenticity. Numerous travelogues feed off the Shakespeare industry, such as *Shakespeare Land* (Kineto, 1910) and *Shakespeare's Country*.[76] Both films are replete with picturesque scenes from around Stratford upon Avon, featuring heritage properties (especially Tudor buildings), traditional street scenes, rural idylls (including the River Avon) – and of course the obligatory shot of Anne Hathaway's Cottage. A typical image would be the stunning view of Guy's Cliff Mill in Warwick, from *Shakespeare Land*, displaying an extraordinary old country house seen across water and a meadow, framed with all the artfulness of the classic late nineteenth-century pictorialist photograph.

Sometimes such imagery would be narrativised, as in the Hepworth production of Dickens's *David Copperfield*, one of the promotional taglines for which claimed that its numerous scenes were 'taken on the actual spots that have been made so famous by the author in his novel'.[77] In the same vein was the British & Colonial Kinematograph Company bio-pic of 1914 *The Life of William Shakespeare*, many of whose scenes were shot on location in and around Stratford. This was indicative of efforts made to authenticate the fiction – 'to ensure accuracy in every particular'[78] – by, for instance, drawing on the services of Shakespearean experts and using furniture from Anne Hathaway's Cottage.[79] American reviewers also stressed the perceived authenticity of the production: 'the greatest pains have been taken to reproduce in costumes, properties and settings the actual atmosphere of the old Elizabethan life'.[80] Back in Britain, the *Kine Weekly* reviewer praised the film for both its scenario, which 'so cleverly chose and interwove the interesting points in the life of the Bard', and 'the scenery and interior views, which, to my mind, are some of the most beautiful and typically English scenes we have yet filmed'.[81] Stills reproduced in the same trade paper certainly suggest that this was another very picturesque film, with several charming rural landscapes and period buildings as well as the obligatory sheep and pond.[82]

Sometimes the very practice of tourism would be narrativised too, as in *The Mountaineer's Romance*. The opening title of the film reads: 'This photoplay was enacted in the beautiful Peak District around Derbyshire.' With the setting established as a real geographical space, the drama can begin to unfold – and the drama in this particular film involves some locals taking a group of American tourists on a trip through the Peak District.

The landscape of invented tradition

As the extracts from contemporary reviews demonstrate, rural space is rarely treated as a neutral narrative space, or even gazed upon simply as a spectacular space. On the contrary, that space is often read metaphorically. In the discussion above, we have repeatedly seen commentators focusing on landscapes and other rural settings in terms of their assumed mythic, symbolic or ideological significance. The particular types of rural space on display present a very specific vision of the nation, usually reducing Britain to England, and England very often to the south country. It is the England of invented tradition, a construction of Englishness in terms of a rural, pre-industrial myth, traditional, conservative and nostalgic. It is a pastoral vision of the nation – and, as Terry Morden notes, 'in Britain, the pastoral has a particular resonance. It lies deep within the national consciousness providing the dominant and enduring image of the British land'.[83]

Alun Howkins demonstrates that this took a very specific form in the late Victorian period as the ideal representation of the nation:

> a strain emerged within English politics and ideas in the 1880s which linked the rural to a general crisis in urban society. This in turn produced a cultural response in the 1890s and 1900s which, by 1914, had spread far across English art and letters, music and architecture, producing a ruralist version of a specifically English culture.[84]

This rural England remains picturesque; crucially, it is populated and cultivated, rather than wild or sublime. As Martin J. Wiener points out, it is an England imbued with the 'ideals of stability, tranquillity, closeness to the past … this countryside of the mind was everything industrial society was not – ancient, slow-moving, stable, cosy and "spiritual"'.[85] One can see this vision of England in the work of writers such as Thomas Hardy, composers such as Ralph Vaughan Williams, garden designers such as Gertrude Jekyll and artists such as Helen Allingham – but one can see it also in many of the films to which I have already referred.

Such a vision of the countryside in British films is invariably layered over other uses of rural space, as outlined above. Thus the real historical spaces displayed in so many travelogues are selectively chosen and framed to foreground this vision. It is important to note the extent to which this rural myth of old England is presented as normative, as unquestionable, as essentialist. Thus it was said of Hepworth's 1916 version of *Comin' Thro' the Rye* that, 'in his search for backgrounds, Mr Hepworth seems to have ransacked the country for open-air beauty of the most perfectly and essentially English type'.[86]

Most of the films I have discussed here, and the critical discourse that surrounded them, engaged with this rural myth, this England of invented tradition, this rose-tinted vision of the nation. Sometimes the sense of an escape from modernity, technology and the city is writ large in the films or in the discourse around them, especially during the Great War and in the years that followed. *Tubby's Rest Cure*, for instance, an episode of Hepworth's 1916 twelve-part comic series about the exploits of Tubby, appeared at the height of the war, and showed Tubby leaving the city for a bucolic version of the country on his doctor's advice. This was not the only film to link the pastoral vision of the countryside to the idea of the rest cure as a means of relieving the stresses of modern urban life. *Kine Weekly*'s synopsis of *The Lure of Crooning Water*, for instance, describes Ivy Duke's character as going 'for a kind of rest-cure to a country farm'.[87] During the production of *Boy Woodburn*, the same paper reported that 'Ivy Duke, who hates London, is delighted to get back to the rolling moorland' where the film was being shot.[88]

The contrast between country and city, and the different values they represented, was often played out narratively in the films. In *Fox Farm*, for instance, the ideal couple played by Newall and Duke are associated with the countryside and rural solitude, while the adulterous couple are associated with the urban, with the crowd, with motorised vehicles and with the mechanised entertainment of a fairground. In *The Lure of Crooning Water*, Duke's character taints the farming community she visits by bringing with her the moral dangers of the city-dweller's lifestyle.

Most of Hepworth's surviving films from the early 1920s play on this same country/city, tradition/modernity bifurcation. *Mist in the Valley* contrasts the city, which drives one of the central characters to suicide, with the stabilities and pleasantries of the countryside, the village and traditional village life. In *Tansy*, the one villainous character, Clem, is associated with modern technology. In *Comin' Thro' the Rye*, Sylvia, introduced in an intertitle as 'the Most Heartless Little Flirt in the Whole Country', is associated with suburban space, while Paul Vasher falls into her wayward clutches when he leaves the English countryside and visits the city of Rome. In each case, the traditional English countryside is set against modernity and against the loose morals of those associated with the city or with technology. This is a theme that can be traced right back to the beginning of Hepworth's career and the 1900 film *How It Feels to Be Run Over*. Here, the calm of a country road is destroyed by a motor car careering wildly towards the camera, eventually running over the camera operator.

Some conclusions

Landscapes are a means of shaping how we see rural geographical space, a means of capturing and presenting such space visually. As Martin Lefebvre puts it, 'the form of landscape is ... first of all the form of a view, of a particular gaze that requires a frame. With that frame, nature turns into culture, land into land-scape.'[89] Landscape – the framing of a view of rural space – thus always already has a mythic dimension, and works at a symbolic or ideological level. The pictur-esque landscape is doubly mythic, since the picturesque too is about making the world into a picture.

Each of the films I have discussed provides a very specific projection of national identity, a projection that is closely linked to how images of the land, of rural space, are captured and presented, how they are embellished, but also how they themselves embellish our vision of the nation. Throughout the 1910s and

1920s, one can find commentators struggling to promote particular images of the nation and to encourage filmmakers to consolidate those images – often, as noted above, to combat images provided from abroad, and especially America. At the close of the period on which I have concentrated, Sir Stephen Tallents, a senior civil servant, wrote a pamphlet arguing that what he called 'the art of national projection' deserved far more attention.[90] This is less about articulating a vision of national identity for domestic consumption and more about projecting an image of the nation abroad.

> If a nation would be truly known and understood in the world, it must set itself actively to master and employ the new, difficult and swiftly developing modes which science has provided for the projection of national personality. … No civilized country can to-day afford either to neglect the projection of its national personality or to resign its projection to others.[91]

Tallents saw cinema as unquestionably 'the greatest agent of international communication at the moment', and therefore a key institution in this process.[92] He was of course particularly interested in the developing non-theatrical market with which he and John Grierson were so involved, noting that the American film industry dominated commercial film exhibition worldwide, having 'turned every cinema in the world into the equivalent of an American consulate'.[93] He also argued that Britain should be projected both as a traditional rural island with a grand history and as a modern, industrialised, forward-looking nation. Generally, as in the work of Hepworth, these two images are mutually exclusive, but Tallents argued for them to be brought together, by seeing rural tradition as a key image for the tourist industry and by noting the importance of agricultural science.

Hepworth's cinema is profoundly paradoxical, since it uses one of the technologies of globalised modernity to project a sense of traditional English nationhood. This underlines once again the extent to which images of the nation, and the space of the nation, are ideological constructions, designed to elicit a particular form of reception and consumption. His cinema is in part about a traditional iconography of English landscapes, but it is also about a particular formal approach, an aesthetic. It is not just that it presents a certain type of landscape but that it presents those landscapes in a way that cannot be fully absorbed or contained by the narrative drive of the films. This can be understood as a particular English film aesthetic, one that bucks against the narrative-led Hollywood aesthetic and insists instead on a pictorialist extension of the cinema of attractions, one that delights in the presentation of picturesque rural landscape. Of course, storytelling is important in this national cinema aesthetic, but it is not overwhelming.[94]

As David Clarke and Marcus Doel argue, this early English cinema aesthetic owes a great deal to pre-cinematic landscape traditions that are closely wedded to a traditional, conservative ideology of English national identity.[95] But, if this provides a powerful model for a national cinema, it is important to remember that, in British picture houses of the period, there were a great many Hollywood films, at least from the early 1910s onwards, and a lesser but still significant number of British films that focused on images and themes of modernity, industry, the city, mechanisation and so on, and that presented such images as positive. Some of these films were actualities and documentaries, from the many films of cinema's first decade that showed moving traffic in the city centre, to *Day in the Life of a Coalminer* (1910), to John Grierson's *Drifters* (1929). But some of them were fiction films – and, in the 1920s, some of these films could be very popular, as with the *Squibs* films (1921–1923), starring Betty Balfour, or Elvey's 1929 version of *Hindle Wakes* (1927), set in a Lancashire mill town. A less well-known film, *When Greek Meets Greek*, a 1923 Walter West production promoted as part of 'the British National Program', was also about 'life in the Industrial Districts'. The 'outstanding feature' of this story was 'the inclusion of a number of very striking scenes illustrating the activities and variety of processes employed in the making of steel'. Shot on location in a factory, 'they are certain to add immensely to the popularity of the picture throughout the country, and particularly in the industrial areas where great factories of a similar kind are to be found. While these scenes in no way interfere with the progress of the story, they impart to it a sense of realism, which makes it immeasurably more effective.'[96]

Such films had to contend both with the pervasiveness of Hollywood and with a deeply entrenched ideology of Englishness that saw modern England as rooted in a countryside that represented tradition, stability and tranquillity, a refuge from modernity.[97] Films set in the past, with their narratives unfolding in the countryside and their landscapes presented in a picturesque and pictorialist manner, therefore had a particularly strong claim on the 'national cinema' label. Given the mythic vision of the countryside as the 'true England', however, and as such films as *The Lure of Crooning Water* show, it was not necessary for narratives to be set in the past in order to maintain a sense of continuity with the past or to proclaim a deep sense of national identity. Simply to represent rural England was enough, or at least that particular version of rural England that had taken hold of the imagination of intellectuals and the people alike since the late nineteenth century.

Notes

1 I discuss these issues at more length in *Waving the Flag: Constructing a National Cinema in Britain* (Oxford: Oxford University Press, 1995); *English Heritage, English Cinema: The Costume Drama in the 1980s and 1990s* (Oxford: Oxford University Press, 2003); 'A green and pleasant land: rural spaces and British cinema', in Catherine Fowler and Gillian Helfield (eds), *Representing the Rural: Space, Place and Identity in Films about the Land* (Detroit: Wayne State University Press, 2006); 'Re-presenting the national past: nostalgia and pastiche in the heritage film', in Barry K. Grant (ed.), *Film Genre Reader IV* (Austin: University of Texas Press, 2012), pp. 602–27 (a revised version of an essay first published in 1993).

2 This chapter would not have been possible without the presence of the wonderful British Silent Film Festival, which ran annually between 1998 and 2012; this chapter was first presented at the sixth edition of the *festival:* 'Location! Location! Location!', held at the Broadway Media Centre, Nottingham, in April 2003. Most of the papers presented at that event are included in Laraine Porter and Bryony Dixon (eds), *Picture Perfect: Landscape, Place and Travel in British Cinema before 1930* (Exeter: University of Exeter Press, 2007). I'm also grateful to Miranda Bayer and Clare Watson for their research assistance.

3 I have written at length elsewhere about the work of Cecil Hepworth. See, for instance, 'Figures in a landscape: the performance of Englishness in Hepworth's Tansy', in Alan Burton and Laraine Porter (eds), *The Showman, the Spectacle and the Two-Minute Silence: Performing British Cinema before 1930* (Flicks Books, 2001), pp. 53–62 and 'The heritage film, British cinema, and the national past: *Comin' Thro' the Rye*', in Andrew Higson, *Waving the Flag: Constructing a National Cinema in Britain* (Oxford: Oxford University Press, 1995).

4 Frederick A. Talbot, *Moving Pictures: How They Are Made and Worked* (William Heinemann, 1912), p. 151.

5 'The royal command picture play', *The Bioscope* (5 October 1916), p. 109; Lionel Collier, 'British pictures and the public', *Kinematograph Weekly* (1 February 1924), p. 40.

6 'The royal command picture play', p. 109.

7 *The Cinema*, quoted in an advertisement in *Kinematograph and Lantern Weekly* (13 December 1917), p. 3. (See also the full-page illustration of Hepworth property in *Pictures and the Picturegoer* (13 December 1919), p. 689).

8 Cecil M. Hepworth, *Came the Dawn: Memories of a Film Pioneer* (Phoenix House, 1951), p. 144.

9 Rachael Low, *The History of the British Film, 1906–1914* (London: George Allen and Unwin, 1949), chs. 7 and 8, esp. pp. 247–8.

10 'Weekly notes', *Kinematograph and Lantern Weekly* (15 May 1913), front page.

11 Review of *Drake's Love Story*, *The Bioscope* (27 February 1913), p. 673.

12 'A British masterpiece', *The Bioscope* (21 August 1913), p. 607.

13 'Editorial notes', from *Our News*, a Gaumont promotional supplement to *Kinematograph and Lantern Weekly* (10 July 1913), p. xxv.

14 'Weekly notes', *Kinematograph and Lantern Weekly* (31 July 1913), p. 1442.

15 'A British masterpiece', *The Bioscope* (21 August 1913), p. 607.

16 'David Copperfield on the cinematograph', *The Dickensian*, 9 (October 1913), p. 267.

17 Low, *The History of the British Film, 1906–1914*, p. 247.

18 Advertisement in supplement to *Kinematograph and Lantern Weekly* (29 May 1913), p. lxviii.

19 Advertisement in *Kinematograph and Lantern Weekly* (24 July 1913), p. 1414.

20 'East Lynne', *The Bioscope* (29 May 1913), p. 677.

21 Unidentified playbill, held at the British Film Institute Library.

22 'East Lynne: reminiscent and appreciative', *Kinematograph and Lantern Weekly* (29 May 1913), p. 545.

23 'East Lynne', p. 549.

24 *Morning Advertiser* (23 May 1913), quoted in an advertisement in *Kinematograph Monthly Film Record* (June 1913), p. 97.

25 Review of *Drake's Love Story*, *The Bioscope*, p. 673.

26 Review of *Drake's Love Story*, *Kinematograph Monthly Film Record* (April 1913), p. 111.

27 Review of *Drake's Love Story*, *The Bioscope*, p. 673.

28 Review of *Mist in the Valley*, *Kinematograph Weekly* (8 March 1923), p. 64.

29 Lionel Collier, 'Trade shows reviewed', *Kinematograph Weekly* (8 March 1923), p. 61.

30 'Henry Edwards' picture *Owd Bob*', *Kinematograph Weekly* (30 October 1924), p. 67; review of *Owd Bob*, *Kinematograph Weekly* (6 November 1924), p. 55.

31 Unidentified source, quoted in Rachael Low, *The History of the British Film, 1918–1929* (London: George Allen and Unwin, 1971), p. 146.

32 Review of *Fox Farm*, *Kinematograph Weekly* (3 August 1922), p. 44.

33 Review of *Boy Woodburn*, *Kinematograph Weekly* (11 May 1922), p. 65.

34 Review of *Boy Woodburn*, *Kinematograph Weekly* (11 May 1922), p. 60.

35 Guy Newall quoted in 'British studios', *Kinematograph Weekly* (4 May 1922), p. 54.

36 'A magnificent British film', *Pictures and the Picturegoer* (14 February 1920), p. 156.

37 Christine Gledhill, *Melodrama and Realism in Twenties British Cinema* (British Film Institute Education Pamphlet, December 1991).

38 See Linda Wood, *The Commercial Imperative in the British Industry: Maurice Elvey, a Case Study* (London: British Film Institute, 1987), esp. pp. 11–12, 35.

39 *The Bioscope* (16 December 1917), quoted in Wood, The Commercial Imperative in the British Industry, p. 35.

40 Review of *Adam Bede*, *Kinematograph and Lantern Weekly* (18 November 1918), p. 81.

41 'Concerning *Adam Bede*' (letter), *Pictures and the Picturegoer* (9 September 1918), p. 476.

42 'Do British films improve?' (letter), *Pictures and the Picturegoer* (16 November 1918), p. 498.

43 Review of *Nelson*, *Kinematograph and Lantern Weekly* (26 December 1918), p. 54.

44 I discuss this film at more length in 'The victorious re-cycling of national history: Nelson', in Karel Dibbets and Bert Hogenkamp (eds), *Film and the First World War* (Amsterdam: Amsterdam University Press, 1995), pp. 108–15.

45 Kine Technicalities supplement, *Kinematograph Weekly* (10 August 1922), p. vi.

46 C. F. Tilney, 'Artistic effect in production', Film and Theatre supplement, *Kinematograph Weekly* (11 December 1924), p. 79.

47 Review of *Drake's Love Story*, *The Bioscope*, p. 673.

48 Review of *Drake's Love Story*, *Kinematograph Monthly Film Record*, p. 111.

49 'A bold bid for British supremacy', *Kinematograph and Lantern Weekly* (29 May 1913), p. 551.

50 Review of *Comin' Thro the Rye*, *The Bioscope* (31 January 1924), p. 52; 'JL', 'Romance of the old studios no.1 – The Hepworth Studios', *The Picturegoer* (February 1924), p. 15.

51 Gertrude M. Allen, 'The master mind of the House of Hepworth', *Pictures and the Picturegoer* (20 September 1919), p. 356.

52 'A magnificent British film', p. 156.

53 Review of *The Lure of Crooning Water*, *Kinematograph Weekly* (29 January 1920), p. 104.

54 Review of *Fox Farm*, p. 44.

55 Review of *Owd Bob*, p. 55.

56 'Samuelson's patriotic film', *Kinematograph Weekly* (1 November 1923), p. 64.

57 Quoted in an advertisement for the film in *Kinematograph Weekly* (22 November 1923), p. 34.

58 See Higson, *Waving the Flag*, pp. 32–3.

59 Henry Edwards quoted in 'British studio news and gossip', *Kinematograph Weekly* (2 October 1924), p. 104 (my emphasis).

60 See Ben Brewster, 'Deep staging in French films, 1900–1914', in Thomas Elsaesser with Adam Barker (eds), *Early Cinema: Space, Frame, Narrative* (London: British Film Institute Publishing, 1990), pp. 49–50.

61 Advertisement in supplement to *Kinematograph and Lantern Weekly* (15 May 1913), pp. xx–xxi.

62 Review of *Drake's Love Story*, *The Bioscope*, p. 673. See also the review of *Drake's Love Story* in *Kinematograph Monthly Film Record*: 'Beautiful as are so many of the settings in the photoplays which come to us from abroad, none of them assuredly can compare in simple beauty with the scenes which the Hepworth Company have provided for *Drake's Love Story.*' *Kinematograph Monthly Film Record* (April 1913), p. 111.

63 Martin Lane, 'English history on the screen', *Kinematograph Weekly* (1 March 1923), p. 58.

64 Lane, 'English history on the screen', p. 58.

65 'British epic films wanted', *The Bioscope* (27 February 1929), p. 22.

66 Donald Spoto, *The Life of Alfred Hitchcock: The Dark Side of Genius* (Da Capo, 1999), p. 102.

67 Review of *The Farmer's Wife*, *Kinematograph Weekly* (8 March 1928), p. 81.

68 *The Bioscope* (23 January 1929), p. 38, quoted in Tom Ryall, *Alfred Hitchcock and the British Cinema* (London: Croom Helm), 1986, p. 94.

69 Review of *The Manxman*, *Kinematograph Weekly* (24 January 1929), p. 65.

70 Hepworth Manufacturing Company, *A Selected Catalogue of the Best and Most Interesting 'Hepwix' Films* (1906), entry 9, p. 2.

71 Hepworth Manufacturing Company, *A Selected Catalogue of the Best and Most Interesting 'Hepwix' Films* (1903), entry 79, p. 19.

72 Hepworth Manufacturing Company, *A Selected Catalogue of the Best and Most Interesting 'Hepwix' Films* (1906), entry 36, p. 7.

73 Hepworth Manufacturing Company, *A Selected Catalogue of the Best and Most Interesting 'Hepwix' Films* (1906), entry 50, p. 8.

74 Hepworth Manufacturing Company, *A Selected Catalogue of the Best and Most Interesting 'Hepwix' Films*, (1906), entry 51, p. 9; see also entry 779, p. 104 and Tom Gunning, 'Landscape and the Fantasy of Moving Pictures: Early Cinema's Phantom Rides', in Graeme Harper and Jonathan R. Rayner (eds), *Cinema and Landscape* (Bristol: Intellect), 2010, pp. 31–70.

75 'The demand for British scenery in films', *Kinematograph and Lantern Weekly* (20 June 1918), p. 67.

76 See Roberta E. Pearson, 'Shakespeare's country: the national poet, English identity and British silent cinema', in Andrew Higson (ed.), *Young and Innocent? The Cinema in Britain, 1896–1930* (Exeter: University of Exeter Press, 2002), pp. 176–90.

77 Advertisement in *The Bioscope* (21 August 1913), p. 577; a title at the start of the film states that the film is 'arranged by Thomas Bentley … on the actual scenes immortalised by Charles Dickens'.

78 'Trade notes', *Kinematograph and Lantern Weekly* (5 February 1913), p. 67.

79 See 'Gossip', *The Picturegoer* (14 February 1914), pp. 602–3; 'Shakespeare comes to life', *The Picturegoer* (21 February 1914), p. 21; H. G., 'The life of Shakespeare', *Kinematograph and Lantern Weekly* (25 December 1913), p. 51; Robert Hamilton Ball, *Shakespeare on Silent Film: A Strange Eventful History* (London: Allen & Unwin, 1968), pp. 203–5.

80 *Motion Picture World* (24 October 1914), quoted in Ball, *Shakespeare on Silent Film*, p. 205.
81 Stroller, 'Another winner from B&C', *Kinematograph and Lantern Weekly* (12 February 1914), p. 47.
82 See stills reproduced in *Kinematograph and Lantern Weekly* (5 February 1914), p. 76.
83 Terry Morden, 'The pastoral and the pictorial', *Ten*, 8: 12 (1983), p. 19.
84 Alun Howkins, 'The discovery of rural England', in Robert Colls and Philip Dodd (eds), *Englishness: Politics and Culture 1880–1920* (London: Croom Helm, 1986), pp. 62–88; p. 63.
85 Martin J. Wiener, *English Culture and the Decline of the Industrial Spirit, 1850–1980* (Cambridge: Cambridge University Press, 1981), pp. 5–6.
86 'The royal command picture play', p. 109.
87 Review of *The Lure of Crooning Water*, *Kinematograph Weekly* (29 January 1920), p. 104.
88 Guy Newall quoted in 'British studios', p. 54.
89 Martin Lefebvre, 'Introduction', in Martin Lefebvre (ed.), *Landscape and Film* (London and New York: Routledge, 2006), pp. xi–xxxi; p. xv.
90 Sir Stephen Tallents, *The Projection of England* (London: Faber and Faber, 1932), p. 13.
91 Tallents, *The Projection of England*, pp. 11–12.
92 Tallents, *The Projection of England*, p. 29.
93 Tallents, *The Projection of England*, p. 30.
94 Compare Martin Lefebvre's discussion in his 'Between setting and landscape in the cinema', in Martin Lefebvre (ed.), *Landscape and Film* (London and New York: Routledge, 2006), pp. 19–60.
95 David B. Clarke and Marcus A. Doel, 'From flatland to vernacular relativity: the genesis of early English screenscapes', in Martin Lefebvre (ed.), *Landscape and Film* (London and New York: Routledge, 2006), pp. 213–44; see also Christine Gledhill, *Reframing British Cinema 1918–1928: Between Restraint and Passion* (London: British Film Institute, 2003).
96 'First British National program picture', *Kinematograph Weekly* (29 June 1922), p. 3, reprinted from *Film Renter* (17 June 1922).
97 See Alun Howkins, 'The discovery of rural England', in Robert Colls and Philip Dodd (eds), *Englishness: Politics and Culture, 1880–1920* (London: Croom Helm, 1986), pp. 62–88; Martin J. Wiener, *English Culture and the Decline of the Industrial Spirit, 1850–1980* (Cambridge: Cambridge University Press, 1981); Raymond Williams, *The Country and the City* (London: Hogarth Press, 1985); Patrick Wright, *On Living in an Old Country: The National Past in Contemporary Britain* (London: Verso, 1985).

2

British landscapes in pre-Second World War film publicity

Paul Moody

A romanticised concept of pastoral life was widely established in British culture by the start of the twentieth century, having been popularised by, among others, the pre-Raphaelites as an 'idealised medieval vision'[1] since the late 1800s, and used as shorthand for the essence of the British national character, the pedigree of which was located in the 'green and pleasant fields' of the (mainly English) countryside. This conflation of land and identity circulated through popular, commercial forms and contexts for mass consumption – and there was no medium as potent or ubiquitous as the cinema. Film was able to transport its audience to actual, authentic locations, not mere pictorial or literary representations, and its bucolic depictions of the countryside ensured that it would be indelibly associated with the British landscape in the public consciousness.

As early as 1903, the *British Journal of Photography* would extol the benefits that the relatively new medium could offer to the portrayal of rural life, declaring:

> [What] would not the rural councils in our now almost depopulated agricultural districts give, if they could show in the neighbouring overcrowded towns animated photographs of English rural life and industries! Actual scenes from farm life would do more to reawaken the love of country life than the most eloquent and impassioned speeches.[2]

But it was the rapid increase in cinema building in the wake of the 1909 Cinematograph Act, which helped to cultivate the development of film publicity and its appeals to national identity, as distributors had to convince a far larger audience than before of the connection they shared with the characters on screen, and ensure that this message would transfer seamlessly to a variety of venues across the country. Thus, the landscape was often referred to, with its rural complexion presented as possessing almost mythic qualities that were common to every person raised within the British Isles.

By the 1910s, regular features about film productions had begun to appear in publications other than the film trade press, initially in magazines directed at the theatregoing public. *Playgoer and Society Illustrated* began its regular series 'The Picture Playgoer', and these articles helped to disseminate similar ideas to those seen in pressbooks from the decade, whether independently or directly as a result of the content of the film company's publicity materials. The review of the artist Sir Hubert Herkomer's forays into filmmaking (he produced and directed *The Old Wood Carver* (1913) at Bushey) highlighted the scenery of his home, where his films were set, which provided 'some perfect rural pictures', and *Playgoer's* approach to most British product followed a similar format.[3] For example, the adaptation of Oliver Goldsmith's *The Vicar of Wakefield* (Frank Wilson, 1913), as rendered by the Hepworth Manufacturing Company, was described as 'essentially English' and praised for its 'high-class style of photography … combined with the beautiful scenery of Surrey and Kent'.[4] Likewise, *Playgoer* greeted the release of the London Film Company's adaptation of Arthur Conan Doyle's *The House of Temperley* (Harold Shaw, 1913) with great praise, declaring it to be 'perfect as possible in every detail' and effusively praising its 'national' qualities: 'The story of "The House of Temperley," as is well-known, is British from every point of view, and as it was enacted amid English surroundings, with every national characteristic, its realism was complete.'[5] As filmmakers and critics were still striving to establish cinema as a respectable form of entertainment, there were many reviews of this nature that highlighted what was perceived to be the defining quality of film – the realism or authenticity of the images portrayed on screen. Pressbooks would often refer to location filming as if it were an indicator of merit, with the implication that the more 'realistic' the setting, the more authentically British it was.

This approach was adopted even for films that did not fall within the complementary confines of historical or literary adaptation, such as George Pearson's *Ultus, the Man from the Dead* (1915), which in its pressbook had its rural surroundings presented as emblematic of its 'Britishness' and integral to its commercial appeal. A section describing the film's locations argued that '"British" is stamped all over it. One part of the country has provided the desert scenes; another the wonderful scenery among the hills.'[6] This theme was maintained in the publicity for the film's sequel, *Ultus and the Grey Lady* (George Pearson, 1917), which highlighted 'Delightful settings on the tranquil upper reaches of the Thames and on drowsy Cornish hills and dales, [which] furnish agreeable backgrounds to many of the incidents.'[7] The ideology present in publicity like this clearly permeated the trade press, with, for example, *The Cinema* describing *The Gay Lord Quex* (Maurice Elvey, 1917) as 'notable for some quite exceptional outdoor scenes', arguing that its 'glorious old English gardens, and some fine river scenes, will still more heighten its thoroughly English atmosphere.'[8]

While many of these examples were merely subtly suggestive allusions to the importance of the countryside to the British character, others, such as the press-book for *The Manxman* (George Loane Tucker, 1916), sought to make this connection explicit. Set on the Isle of Man, the film's marketing began with the familiar notion of a simple, quaint rural idyll, describing how 'the people of the island live very simply, and there is surprisingly little difference in the manner of living between the upper and lower classes'.[9] But this theme was developed further, conflating the initial location search into an evocation of the British race:

> For nearly a year little actual production was done. The time being spent in study-ing not only the different parts of England, Scotland and Ireland, but in becoming steeped in the atmosphere, environment and psychology of the different races, that warring in the past have united their blood, and whose descendants are the prod-uct of invasion and conquest of the Briton, by Angle, Saxon, Dane and Norman French. The modern Briton in different parts of the United Kingdom clings extraordinarily to racial characteristics of the original stock.[10]

It is interesting that an island with a complex relationship with British national identity was portrayed in this way, yet, for a film that was potentially a problem-atic commercial proposition for the distributor, this attempt to draw parallels between the heritage of the island and the wider UK was one method of attract-ing an audience throughout Britain. It said to the public that the characters and stories they were seeing on the screen had relevance to their own lives, and, as the British landscape was a universal feature of this audience's daily experience, it was regularly employed by publicists as a metaphor for a national commonality.

On occasion, 'Britishness' would be supplanted by individual British national identities, such as in the pressbook for *A Welsh Singer* (Henry Edwards, 1915), which described the film's main protagonist, Mifanwy, as possessing 'the wonder-ful voice that seems nature's gift to so many of the daughters of Wales, and while tending to her sheep on the wind-swept slopes it was her delight to sing – unheard though she might be save for the distant hills, the mists, majestic Snowdon'.[11] However, the format followed – that of the presentation of the ethereal, timeless qualities of the environment – was identical to the portrayals of other landscapes identified as 'British' and was reinforced in reviews of the film, with *The Bioscope* arguing that:

> The various camera studies, so beautifully arranged and reproduced, which are a leading feature of the film throughout, are never introduced for their own sake alone, but serve a legitimate purpose by intensifying the emotional force of the situation in which the players and scenario writer have equal shares.[12]

A Welsh Singer was also indicative of the trend throughout the teens to attempt to situate the characteristics of this enduring 'stock' in an individual female char-acter, who would embody the inherent qualities of the rural landscape she inhab-ited. And, as these promotional techniques developed, magazines such as *Nash's* and *Pall Mall* would run feature articles that sought to impose the same qualities associated with the British landscape onto the actresses themselves, not just the characters they portrayed. These articles quoted stage actresses who had begun to work in film and explored the perceived heightening of reality that filming on location was said to produce. Mary Manners, in a piece titled 'The Drama of Reality', was quoted as saying

> [The] photo-drama is nearer to nature than any spoken play, placed in ever so real a setting. The reality of the scenes in which the cinema players move and have their being, the enormous variety of places in which the action can be worked, and the knowledge on the part of the spectator that he is looking upon actualities, all contribute to the cinema's fascination.[13]

Even Sarah Bernhardt, describing her new role in a film version of *Jeanne Doré*, said:

> I like it better even than the stage ... In the first place I have always had a great aversion to shams – on the stage, as elsewhere. I have always wanted things to bear close inspection. I prefer always the real. Tinsel or any tawdry glitter always offended my taste. In moving picture work it is possible to employ real scenery. It is superb. In all moving picture art the scenery can be actual.[14]

While this link between authenticity and the 'new style' of film acting was not unique to Britain – a similar process took place in Germany during the 1910s with its film critics and actors – what was different about the British experience was how this was linked so often to the landscape.[15] And, once this notion was established, any female character that did not conform could be presented as representing the dangers of the city and the superficial pleasures that it entailed. Thus, *The Lure of Crooning Water* (Arthur Rooke, 1920) would present these threats as embodied by Georgette Verlaine (Ivy Duke), an actress from London who is sent by her doctor to Crooning Water Farm to convalesce, only to tempt the farm owner, Horace Dornblazer, into an affair. A special supplement to Stoll's *Editorial News*, dedicated to *Crooning Water*, described Georgette's first arrival at the estate in glowing terms, in contrast to her own diffidence:

> The station for Crooning Water was a little wayside halting place, down where the flowers grew and the sweet breath of the countryside laved all with health and brightness. But the pampered darling sitting by a pile of trunks on the platform had no eyes for beauty, no sense of smell for the redolent air.[16]

However, over time Georgette learns to value what the farm has to offer, but the potential she has to usurp the simple lifestyle of Horace and his family is ever present:

> Gradually, the girl began to appreciate the country and its quiet life. The busy life of the farm brought unwonted interests and the morning at Crooning Water was morning not noon. Georgette was wise enough to realise that she was benefitting

and she remembered, too, that she was a woman, that this taciturn man gave her no thought. That was a challenge to her witchery.[17]

Horace leaves his wife and follows Georgette to London, only to be rebuffed after witnessing her at a supper in which 'the lady did not comport herself as he expected Georgette to do'.[18] Georgette is revealed, like the landscape she originates from, as *uncultivated*, and Horace returns to Crooning Water to be reconciled with his wife and the honest, unpretentious rural lifestyle the film's marketing portrayed.

Of course, there were already several notable examples of female characters in British art and literature who had been explicitly associated with the rural environment, from Cathy in Emily Brontë's *Wuthering Heights* (1847), via Millais's *Ophelia* (1852), through to Hardy's *Tess of the d'Urbervilles* (1891). Yet, in the main, these women embodied the unpredictable and destructive forces of nature, in contrast to the tranquil and reassuring qualities that were projected in early film promotion. There were several factors that contributed to the latter portrayal, not least the reorganisation of traditional gender roles that took place during the inter-war period, which was accompanied by an increasing sense of 'male unease' about the status of women in society.[19] That women could be presented as passive, inextricably linked to a countryside that was pliable and suggestive of centuries of submission to male will, was one way of asserting the continuation of existing patriarchal systems. And, as the majority of the cinema audience and readership of fan magazines was female, this was also a message to women, promising that an understated, homely private life would bring them happiness. By locating this domestic idyll in a rural environment that was largely unfamiliar to cinema's predominantly urban audience, filmmakers and their publicity departments could employ the aspirational appeal of living in the countryside to affirm the importance of maintaining the status quo. In other words, in a world in which men were rapidly losing dominance, the old archetype of the wild, female free spirit ready to be tamed, which had dominated British culture for centuries, was no longer sufficient. Instead, the authoritative male was removed from the equation and female audiences were encouraged, via a variety of wish-fulfilment narratives, to be the agents of their own capitulation.

Yet this was an approach doomed to failure, for, as many contemporary British publications would lament, what most young British cinemagoers aspired to was to be found in American movies, which cast in a much more positive light the urban, material pleasures most British films sought to disparage. While much of Britain's cinematic output followed suit and shifted towards more urban productions by the 1920s, there remained a small number of filmmakers, roughly bracketed together as part of a 'pictorialist' movement, who continued to produce films in a rural setting that espoused traditional 'British' values. Cecil Hepworth was the leading figure of this approach, having developed his style since the early days of British cinema into a distinctive poetic approach. With his *Alf's Button* (1920), *Tansy* (1921), *The Pipes of Pan* (1923) and, most importantly, *Comin' Thro' the Rye* (1923), he forged a place for this style in the British cinematic consciousness. *Comin' Thro' the Rye*'s pressbook declared that Hepworth had 'captured the true spirit of the story, and depicted the romantic story in authentic costumes of the period in settings that are beautiful beyond words'.[20] The front cover was adorned with a striking still of Alma Taylor as Helen Adair, surrounded by a vast field of rye and once more making explicit the connection between the natural landscape and femininity. The rapturous reviews were also eager to emphasise the film's rural authenticity, with the American fan magazine *Photoplay* explaining to its readers that 'for this production six acres of rye were especially grown'.[21] For *The Cinema*, the 'charm of the settings' was an integral part of a 'perfect whole',[22] and *Pictures and the Picturegoer* went even further, exploring the possibility that Hepworth's approach might herald a fresh wave of films focusing on outdoor settings: 'Producers are all beginning to wake up to the fact that natural backgrounds are more beautiful than anything the property man can devise. A fact that Cecil Hepworth has been demonstrating all his movie life.'[23]

Picturegoer's prediction proved to be false, with the financial collapse of Hepworth's company before the release of *Comin' Thro' the Rye* heralding the dominance of urban locations throughout British cinema in the latter half of the 1920s. Nonetheless, by the end of the decade, the main tropes of the representation of the rural landscape in British film publicity had been established, and would cast a long shadow over future portrayals of pastoral environments in the nation's cinema. Thus, even in the late 1920s, *A Cottage on Dartmoor* (Anthony Asquith, 1928) was presented as a film that was 'deliberately set in ordinary surroundings', although this appeal to authenticity extended to the film's metropolitan locales as well.[24] But the apparent verisimilitude offered by the British landscape would even encompass reproductions of foreign locations, as seen in the small boom in First World War dramas instigated by *The Battles of the Coronel and Falkland Islands* (Walter Summers, 1927) and *The Somme* (M. A. Wetherell, 1927). The pressbook for the latter highlighted the importance of terrain to the production's authenticity, describing it starkly as about 'mud, guns, men' and noting that the mud featured in the film had to be specially manufactured.[25] But the significance of the landscape to the film's realism was identified on the pressbook's final page: 'Many of the very big scenes were filmed on the actual ground where the incidents happened, whilst where this was found to be impossible … exact replicas of the country were sought and found in England.'[26]

Towards the end of the decade, the 1927 Cinematograph Films Act would help to foster not only an indigenous industry but also an influx of foreign capital and personnel who were keen to establish the 'Britishness' of their productions in the face of intense pressure from critics and unions, concerned about the erosion of national identity and the number of jobs available to British-born workers.

Importantly, by emphasising those aspects of 'Britishness' that had the greatest cultural capital and international commercial appeal, these filmmakers often turned towards stories that lent themselves to exploitation as products of British heritage, and which featured the British landscape prominently. As the owner of the largest filmmaking concern in 1930s Britain, Alexander Korda's London Films was the most explicit in this respect. But, despite successful 'historical' films such as *The Private Life of Henry VIII* (1933), it was not until the opening of Korda's Denham Studios in 1936 that British cinema would return to producing a range of lushly photographed films ostensibly set in the British countryside. These locations were promoted as integral to the films' 'Britishness', often in the form of 'filmgrams' – short souvenir booklets for fans that were distributed on the release of a new production. Thus, London Films's pastoral drama *South Riding* (Victor Saville, 1938) would feature in its filmgram a section entitled 'Yorkshire on the Screen', which explained that the fictional location of South Riding was the 'only synthetic part of the picture'.[27] Victor Saville was praised for creating a 'Yorkshire of convincing reality', and the reader was advised that 'this intense realism will come as a refreshing tonic to audiences over the world'.[28]

Similar sentiments were presented throughout the filmgrams, with even films that were not strictly 'rural' legitimised by their connection to an 'authentic' British landscape. The first film produced by MGM-British and recorded at Denham, *A Yank at Oxford* (Jack Conway, 1938), even had the provenance of its artificially created landscapes identified for fans. In a section entitled 'Supplying Turf For Films', its filmgram explained that, in the two years prior to the film's release, 'more than 25,000 pieces of turf [had] been used for garden and woodland settings in British films made at Denham'.[29] In the case of *A Yank at Oxford*, 3,000 turves had been used to create the grass court in the set of the Oxford college quadrangle, and it was made explicit that these had been sourced from a local horticultural firm based in Middlesex. And, just in case the reader was in any doubt as to the authenticity of similar scenes filmed at the studio, they were assured that artificial turf had 'never been used in any Denham production'.[30] This claim to authenticity, once established and reinforced throughout the range of Denham promotional material, could be applied to a number of films produced by the studio and provide its output with an integrity and prestige lacking in other, indoor, studio-bound productions. More importantly, it could also help to assert the 'British' qualities of productions that had an international cast and crew – and hence a controversial position within the British film industry.

This type of promotion would be adopted wholesale by the popular fan magazines, which would also embrace the conflation of femininity with the British landscape that was developed during the teens. For example, the *Film Weekly* supplement promoting MGM's *The Citadel* (King Vidor, 1939) depicted the lead actress, Rosalind Russell, sitting by the banks of the River Colne, her arms held aloft, surrounded by the picturesque beauty of the Denham countryside. Despite

Russell being American, the supplement's profile followed the same format as those regarding her British antecedents: firstly, the establishing of Russell's star status, as in the description of her as possessing 'all the physical qualifications of a glamour queen', and secondly, the suggestion that she 'gladly – even eagerly – shed her customary smartness to play the cheaply dressed village schoolteacher', her character in *The Citadel*. The reader was once again left in no doubt as to Russell's personality, being informed that she was 'that kind of a girl – down to earth, level-headed, free from false ideas'.[31] Actresses were meant to be glamorous, but not too remote from the lives of the average reader, and these down-to-earth qualities were ideally represented by the image of the British countryside, as rendered by Denham Studios and the filmmakers who worked there. But crucially, this also represented the increased blurring of distinctions between reality and film in these publications, and the further merging of the identities of the star and her character.

However, perhaps the most interesting development of this type of portrayal in the late thirties was how it began to be employed for profiles of male British stars too. This is most prominent in the portrayals of Robert Donat and Leslie Howard at the end of the decade. For example, in the *Film Weekly* supplement for *The Citadel*, the reader was presented with an image of Donat knee-high in the River Colne, actively enjoying some fishing, which the reader was told was one of his 'few sports'. This depiction of Donat as an active man of nature, at one with the environment, was integral to the studio's desire to cast him as a dynamic, romantic hero, yet it also served to ground him and make him accessible to the public in much the same way as had been employed with Russell and a number of British actresses previously. Similar to this was the two-page photo-spread dedicated to Leslie Howard in *South Riding*'s filmgram, in which he was shown 'off-duty' outside his countryside residence, tending to his flowers in an inset image and inspecting his horses at their stables. He was portrayed, like Donat, as the active man of the earth, never happier than when at one with nature. Of course, this representation differed from the more passive connection with the pastoral ascribed to actresses in British films, but nonetheless continued to emphasise the equation between the landscape and authentic British life.

The link between male British characters and dynamic British landscapes was also apparent in the promotion of two films from the 1930s that portrayed the literal and metaphorical outskirts of the British Isles: *Man of Aran* (Robert Flaherty, 1934) and *The Edge of the World* (Michael Powell, 1937). Both drew on the notions of authenticity that had been employed by the marketing of other British films, but, in contrast to the Arcadian fantasies of films such as *Comin' Thro' the Rye*, the advertising for *Man of Aran* and *The Edge of the World* depicted humanity in direct confrontation with the landscape. The front covers of the pressbooks for both productions featured images of the rocky cliffs of their respective islands, with *Aran* illustrating violent waves that dwarfed the

3 Filmgram for *South Riding*

protagonist, Colman King, seen in the distance.[32] While Powell's film was a relatively low-key affair and was marketed very simply with a plot description, some
stills and little else, *Aran's* marketing is particularly instructive, as its association
with Gainsborough Studios ensured that the pressbook was especially rich in
detail and differed from the more prosaic approach taken by Powell's independent distributor. In the pressbook's plot synopsis for *Aran*, while the islanders'
lifestyle was described as primitive, the reader was informed that the 'joy of *real
living*, however, was there'.[33] The notion of authenticity was once more directly
linked to the land, yet in this portrayal the relationship with the islander's 'desperate environment' was described as a 'fight from which he will have no respite
until the end of his indomitable days'.[34] Likewise, the American pressbook con-
tinuously referred to the 'conflict between the rugged inhabitants of the rocky
isle of Aran and the raging, unrelenting sea'.[35] While these films were of course
partly about humans conquering inhospitable landscapes, the way these stories
were depicted provided an interesting contrast to the serene countryside of rural
Britain so often portrayed in British cinema, yet retained much of its ideological direction, which emphasised the importance of the landscape to the British
character. The potency of this portrayal can be seen in the later marketing of
imperialistic fantasies, such as Korda's Empire trilogy. It did not take a great

4 Pressbook for *Man of Aran*

leap of imagination to move from representations of humanity defeating natural obstacles in Aran and Foula to the India or Sudan of *The Drum* (Zoltan Korda, 1938) and *The Four Feathers* (Zoltan Korda, 1939) respectively. In the promotion of films of this ilk, the British countryside was always implicit, presented as the calm, tranquil alternative to the wild, uncivilised locales of the British Empire.

Rural landscapes, as portrayed by pre-Second World War British film publicity, consisted of people who lived simply and naturally and to whom material pleasures were inconsequential. While the city was presented as the place to make one's fortune, it was only back in the country where emotional life could be seen to blossom. Likewise, publicists began to conflate these landscapes with similar stereotypes about women, who were seen to embody these sentimental notions and, hence, the enduring qualities of the British character. Once this conception was entrenched, the reverse – that women from the city also embodied the threatening, shallow materialism of the urban environment – was also presented as true, building on the Madonna/whore dichotomy that, while already established in popular culture, was in British film publicity systematically linked to notions of the British countryside. As these depictions began to focus more closely on male protagonists, this environment was reconfigured as less peaceful, which enabled characters to demonstrate their vigour in the process of taming nature. By appealing to the 1930s Hollywood trend for dynamic masculine leads, British film publicists were able to attract a wide audience while adding uniquely British characteristics to this conception. As in its British literary and artistic precedents, it was the qualities of the rural landscape which asserted this 'Britishness'. That the portrayals of this landscape in modern British film publicity maintain much of the character of these early approaches is a testament to the potency of these notions, which, while having a long lineage in British culture, were cultivated and developed throughout the opening decades of the twentieth century.

Notes

1 David Lowenthal, 'British national identity and the English landscape', *Rural History*, 2: 2 (1991), pp. 205–30; p. 213.
2 'The application of animated photography to science and education', *British Journal of Photography* (10 July 1903), p. 26.
3 Ariel, 'The picture playgoer', *Playgoer and Society Illustrated*, 9: 49 (1913), p. 32.
4 Ariel, 'The picture playgoer', p. 32.
5 Ariel, 'The picture playgoer', *Playgoer and Society Illustrated*, 9: 50 (1913), p. 71.
6 British Film Institute: James Anderson Collection, Pressbook for *Ultus, the Man from the Dead* (George Pearson, 1915).
7 British Film Institute: James Anderson Collection, Pressbook for *Ultus and the Grey Lady* (George Pearson, 1917).
8 The National Archives: Public Record Office, HO 45/10955/312971.
9 British Film Institute: James Anderson Collection, Pressbook for *The Manxman* (George Loane Tucker, 1916).
10 British Film Institute, Pressbook for *The Manxman*.
11 British Film Institute, Pressbook for *A Welsh Singer* (Henry Edwards, 1915).
12 British Film Institute: Pressbook for *A Welsh Singer*.
13 'The drama of reality', *Nash's Pall Mall Magazine*, 54: 260 (1914), pp. 342–3.
14 'The divine Sarah on cinema', *Nash's and Pall Mall Magazine*, 55: 261 (1915), p. 572.
15 Marc Silberman, 'Soundless speech, wordless writing: language and German silent cinema', *Imaginations*, https://ejournals.library.ualberta.ca/index.php/imaginations/article/viewFile/9527/7489 (accessed 16 May 2012).
16 British Film Institute, 'The lure of crooning water', *Stoll's Editorial News* (12 February 1920).

17 British Film Institute, 'The lure of crooning water'.
18 British Film Institute, 'The lure of crooning water'.
19 Jill Greenfield, Sean O'Connell and Chris Reid, 'Fashioning masculinity: *Men Only*, consumption and the development of marketing in the 1930s', *Twentieth Century British History*, 10: 4 (1999), pp. 457–76; p. 459.
20 British Film Institute: James Anderson Collection, Publicity material for *Comin' Thro' the Rye* (Cecil Hepworth, 1923).
21 Herbert Howe, 'Close-ups & long shots', *Photoplay*, 25: 4 (1924), p. 54.
22 British Film Institute, Publicity material for *Comin' Thro' the Rye*.
23 M. Mayne, 'The new masters', *Pictures and the Picturegoer*, 7: 37 (1924), p. 41.
24 British Film Institute: Nasreen Kabir Collection, *Publicity Material for A Cottage on Dartmoor* (Anthony Asquith, 1928).
25 British Film Institute, Pressbook for *The Somme* (M. A. Wetherall, 1927).
26 British Film Institute, Pressbook for *The Somme*.
27 Hillingdon Local Studies Archive (HLSA), *Filmgram for South Riding* (Victor Saville, 1938).
28 HLSA, Filmgram for *South Riding*.
29 HLSA, *Filmgram for A Yank at Oxford* (Jack Conway, 1937).
30 HLSA, Filmgram for *A Yank at Oxford*.
31 '*The Citadel*', *Film Weekly Supplement* (4 March 1939), p. 11.
32 British Film Institute, Pressbook for *The Edge of the World* (Michael Powell, 1939).
33 British Film Institute, Pressbook for *Man of Aran* (Robert Flaherty, 1937) (my emphasis).
34 British Film Institute, Pressbook for *Man of Aran*.
35 British Film Institute, American pressbook for *Man of Aran* (Robert Flaherty, 1937).

3

Rural imagery in Second World War British cinema

Tom Ryall

When a 1941 Mass-Observation poll asked the question, 'What does Britain mean to you?' the overwhelming majority of respondents spoke of rural areas, several explicitly identifying these as embodying the nation's essence.

Brian Foss[1]

England is the country, and the country is England.

Stanley Baldwin[2]

Despite the fact that the majority of the British people lived in towns and cities and had done so since the late nineteenth century, the Mass-Observation survey referred to above, conducted early in the Second World War, confirmed the importance of a sense of the rural to the very notion of British and, maybe *or*, English national identity. Such a position received official endorsement in the inter-war period. Alexandra Harris suggests that political 'rhetoric in the 1930s insisted that the English were all still bound together by rural values, the rites of the village green were in the Englishman's bloodstream, and nothing could erase them'.[3] The extent and reach of 'rural-nostalgic "Englishness"'[4] or 'English rural idyllicism'[5] or 'Deep England',[6] to use some recent formulations, is a matter of argument, but there are plenty of cultural examples to support the strength and power of the pastoral in the English if not the British mind, from the landscapes of John Constable to those of Eric Ravilious, from the Romantic poets to the topographical verse of Ted Hughes.

By 1939 and the outbreak of war, the notion of Deep England, 'the idea that within rural England especially there is something ... "incommunicable" or "indivisible" in the national heritage',[7] was a key feature of the ideological landscape and was to be reflected in many cultural and propaganda practices of the time. In 1940, *Recording Britain*, a project devised by Kenneth Clark to make a visual record of the British landscape, resulted in some 1,500 watercolours and drawings mainly of

the English landscape, its farms, fields, cottages, village churches and rolling countryside. Its aims were various and included the provision of employment for artists
and the recording of aspects of British life, of its landscape and of its old buildings,
threatened by neglect and by industrial and commercial development; indeed, the
provisional title for the project was 'A Scheme for Artists to Record Changing or
Vanishing Aspects of Britain'.[8] However, it was also envisaged as a contribution
to the war effort and its significance as propaganda was summarised by art critic
Herbert Read as 'exactly what we are fighting for – a green and pleasant land, a
landscape whose features have been moulded by liberty, where every winding lane
and irregular building is an expression of our national character'.[9]

More overt propaganda deploying pastoral imagery was to be found in one of
the most famous posters of the time, *South Downs*, designed by Frank Newbould,
which depicted a shepherd with his flock amid the rolling English countryside
captioned 'Your Britain – Fight For It Now'.[10] The magazine *Picture Post* often
incorporated images of the landscape as the embodiment of Britain's war aims.
A brief story in a June 1940 issue, entitled 'The Beauty of Britain', was illustrated
with photographs of hay harvesting, a stream running through Ambleside, and
the Welsh hills; a subheading proclaimed, 'under the sunshine of a lovely summer, the fields and woods of Britain – the fields and woods we are all fighting to
protect'.[11] Popular BBC programmes made frequent reference to the countryside. For example, 'ten of J. B. Priestley's seventeen BBC Postscripts from 1941
included references to the joys of rural life'[12] and the Corporation began broadcasting *Country Magazine*, a programme dealing with rural matters, in 1942.[13]
Even popular songs of the time evoked the English countryside, as in 'There'll
Always be an England' (1939) with its lyrics – 'country lane', 'cottage small',
'field of grain' – made famous by Vera Lynn.

Stanley Baldwin, prime minister for much of the inter-war period, often
evoked England's rural heritage, most forcibly in his play on the ambiguity of the
word 'country' quoted above. Such speeches, suggests Alexandra Harris, 'legiti-
mized a culture of country nostalgia almost as Queen Victoria had sponsored a
culture of mourning'.[14] It was in this cultural climate that war-time filmmakers
set about their task of devising the mixture of propaganda and entertainment
required for the industry's key role in the ideological war to sustain British morale
in the face of the privations of war. For various reasons, 'the culture of country
nostalgia' was a key source of sentiment and imagery for war-time Britain. As
Alex Potts has suggested:

> The countryside was, quite literally for many people, a haven from the destruction
> being wreaked in the blitzed cities and could at the same time be seen as a vital
> part of fortress England threatened by alien forces of evil. The countryside could
> even serve as a sign of the beauty of the new order which might rise from the ashes
> of the battered cities, or as a symbol of the permanence of a heritage whose urban
> manifestations might not actually survive.[15]

Landscape and the countryside, of vital practical importance to the war effort in terms of agricultural production and as a safe haven for evacuees from the belea-guered cities, also provided important sources of imagery deployed in a range of media – painting, posters, radio, photo-journalism, popular music. Baldwin's 'The country is England', however mythic and, indeed, oblivious to the national cultures of the Celtic components of the UK, was used as a symbolic focus for national unity. As Sonya O. Rose has argued, while 'urban representation ... depicted the nation at war', the rural landscape 'symbolised its historical per-manence'.[16] Landscape, the countryside and rural life were powerful sources of imagery with a substantial history that could be used to evoke a sense of national community; as Rose suggests, 'the countryside in the national imagination was an aesthetic space that symbolized an enduring way of life'.[17]

Yet, despite the power of the rural vision and its relevance to the propaganda task, it can be argued that the use of pastoral mythology by filmmakers was lim-ited. Indeed, it was 'the ashes of the battered cities' together with other elements of urban life that the cinema drew upon to provide the iconic home-front images of the Second World War: the dome of St Paul's Cathedral, the fire-stricken buildings of London's dockland, firefighters wielding hoses, the devastated ter-races of houses during the blitz and people huddled for shelter and protection in London's underground stations. The drama of Britain at war did not lie in the countryside but in the towns and cities, and also, of course, overseas in the thea-tres of war. It was these that the cinema focused upon in the period.

The rural as idyll

The Lion Has Wings (Michael Powell, Brian Desmond Hurst and Adrian Brunel, 1939) is usually regarded as the first feature film of the war-time period to address the war in a propagandist manner; though set largely in RAF control stations and in the cockpits of RAF bombers, the beginning of the film presents a series of images embodying 'English rural idyllicism'.

The film opens with a shot of the Dover coast followed by a dozen or so rural images including village scenes, ivy-clad cottages, churches, oast houses, rolling hills, sheep and cows grazing in fields and meadows, a hay cart and a windmill. It is a representation compatible with the depiction of the rural to be found in photo-journalism and the visual arts. Indeed, the opening juxtaposes scenes of British life (there are a handful of Scottish images) with images of a regimented militaristic Germany, a contrastive montage technique very similar to that used in an often quoted *Picture Post* story titled 'What We Are Fighting For'. The accompanying text refers to a 'war for the village we live in' and the pictures con-trast images of a relaxed rural Britain – sheep wandering through a village, a darts game in a pub, a cricket match, a two-page spread of oast houses and orchards – with images of a regimented German population listening to Hitler's speeches, and goose-stepping troops.[18] The sentiments of the film's opening images and of the *Picture Post* photostory are echoed in two films set wholly in rural England – *This England* (David MacDonald, 1941) and *Tawny Pipit* (Bernard Miles and Charles Saunders, 1944).

This England, the first of a small number of British films from the period that used history as a vehicle for propaganda, focused upon a small group of characters including Rookeby (John Clements), a farmer, and Appleyard (Emlyn Williams), a farm labourer, setting them in various periods of English history from medieval times to the First World War. The unifying theme of the film is the significance of the land embodied in the poem that precedes the credits ('The earth of England is an old, old earth') and in the opening voiceover, which identifies the country-side with its 'old farms and quiet villages' as emblematic of England.[19] The film effectively follows the contours of the cultural debates about the countryside. In the Elizabethan episode Appleyard, gazing at the landscape, refers to the ways in which his and Rookeby's ancestors are embedded in the land, have cultivated it and have died on it; he comments that their spirits seem to say, 'is not this worth fighting for?' The enemy in the context of the episode is the Spanish Armada, but the war-time resonance of the scene is unmistakeable. The scene evokes 'Deep England' and the film as a whole presents 'the English countryside as an emblem of the birthright of the English in a kind of popularised nature-mysticism'.[20]

The eighteenth-century episode evokes other debates about the bases of the 'rural-nostalgic vision'. The sequence begins with some of the young men of the village departing for London. There is discussion about the lure of the city, 'that monster they call the octopus – London Town', and of the detrimental effects of industry and machinery on the rural economy, an effective embodiment of Martin Wiener's famous thesis about the influence of an anti-industrial strand in British culture and 'the presumed incompatibility of industrial and rural values'.[21] *This England* resolves that tension with the marriage of the industrial-ist's daughter to the farmer, Rookeby, again an illustration of an intellectual the-sis about the relationship between the rural and the industrial. The art historian Paul Street notes that 'between the landed aristocracy and industrial bourgeoisie there was accommodation not revolutionary overthrow', an apt description of the resolution within the fiction.[22] The film suffered somewhat from economic restrictions; it was originally conceived as a Technicolor production with exten-sive location shooting planned, but its presentation of the countryside, the cen-tral theme of the film and the burden of its propaganda power, was confined to a few cursory panoramic shots and some model work, used mainly as links between the episodes.[23]

Tawny Pipit declares its commitment to the rural-nostalgic with its opening credits superimposed upon a series of images – country cottages, a village pond, a river – and the film as a whole depicts 'an idyllic rural community of quaint cottages, leafy lanes, rustic yokels and children playing in the stream'.[24] In the course of his discussion of the idea of 'Deep England', Patrick Wright quotes the naturalist Peter Scott speaking in a 1943 radio broadcast about the way in which his war-time experiences in the Royal Navy intensified his perception of England and its identification with the rural:

> I thought of the Devon countryside lying beyond that black outline of the cliffs, the wild moors and rugged tors inland and nearer the sea, the narrow winding valleys with their steep green sides; and I thought of the mallards and teal which were rearing their ducklings in the reed beds of Slapton Leigh. That was the countryside we were passionately determined to protect from the invader.[25]

Tawny Pipit shows the Scott perspective with a story about the discovery of a pair of rare birds mating in an English field. The wildlife theme condenses the general sentiment – the superiority of rural life and values – that is presented more explicitly in *This England*. The birds are threatened in various ways; a couple of schoolboy evacuees aiming to rob the nest; egg collectors also scheming to steal the eggs; an army tank patrol planning to drive across the field; and the County Agriculture committee's plans to order the ploughing of the field. All the obstacles are dealt with: the schoolboys are co-opted to the conservationist cause, Hazel's (Rosamund John) charms persuade the army patrol to take an alternative route, the thieves are arrested by the army, and the village elder, Colonel Barton-Barrington (Bernard Miles), uses his contacts in Whitehall to thwart the local committee. The colonel mobilises the village with a rousing speech in defence of fair play for the nesting birds, arguing that 'this love of animals and of nature has always been part of the British way of life'. In contrast to *This England*, *Tawny Pipit* did use extensive location shooting (in and around a Cotswold village), presenting the rural – village and landscape – in suitably idyllic images, its sweep and beauty underscored early in the film when Hazel simply gasps at her first sight of the village from an overlooking hilltop.

The dark rural

A darker sense of the rural is evident in *Went the Day Well?* (Alberto Cavalcanti, 1942) and *Great Day* (Lance Comfort, 1945). *Went the Day Well?* was shot on location (an Oxfordshire village and the surrounding countryside) and featured 'quaint cottages, leafy lanes, a windmill on the hillside'[26] among its markers of the rural-nostalgic vision. However, while the extensive rural imagery is evocative, drawing a degree of strength from its 'idyllic' location, the subject of the film, the infiltration of the village by Germans masquerading as British troops, compromises the imagery somewhat.[27] For example, early in the film a series of shots presents the quaint cottages, the leafy lanes and the windmill in a survey of the village. However, the survey of the village is being conducted by the Germans establishing the best way to hold the village, and to set up a communications unit for the impending invasion. Later in the film the Home Guard unit is brutally shot down in the leafy lanes surrounding the village, and the film's violent finale, in which the Germans are defeated, takes place in and around the manor house, a traditional icon of peaceful English village life.

Great Day was released in the summer of 1945, when the war was more or less over. However, it is set during the war in the fictional village of Denley, as the Women's Institute prepares for an official visit from Eleanor Roosevelt, wife of the American president. Indeed, though the film rarely figures in general discussions of war-time British cinema, it does have a significant propaganda dimension, forcibly reflected in Mrs Mumford's (Marjorie Rhodes) impassioned defence of the village's contribution to the war effort. She and the other women of the village have used local resources (fruit and vegetables, rabbit skins, wool from sheep) very effectively to make, among other things, jam for the troops, fur coats for the Russians and blankets for the air force. In this respect, the film, described as 'a masterpiece, which combines radical sexual politics with a ravishing visual style',[28] is an important contribution to the small body of films concerned with the war-time role of women, along with better known titles such as *Millions Like Us* (Frank Launder and Sidney Gilliat, 1943) and *The Gentle Sex* (Leslie Howard and Maurice Elvey, 1943).

The film's rural imagery is a match for other films shot on location in the countryside. The village itself is introduced in the opening credit sequence with a series of shots featuring the local church, a farm wagon, a pony and trap, and children playing in the street. The surrounding countryside is displayed to great effect in a number of scenes featuring members of the Women's Land Army at work, driving tractors, tending to horses and so on, a pony and trap on a drive to the village, and Captain Ellis's (Eric Portman) regular walks through the fields near his home. The sequences involving Captain Ellis, however, illustrate the complexities of the film's stance on country life. The first walk presents the positive dimensions of the rural with shots of Ellis contemplating the beauty of the countryside and watching a hawk through his field glasses. He explains to his daughter, Meg (Sheila Sim), that the bird enjoys freedom. 'That's the only thing that matters, freedom', he says to her, though she challenges this, calling him a 'romantic' and accusing him of being unconcerned with the practicalities of life.

Ellis's subsequent walks are somewhat different in temper. In one he angrily confronts the farmer, Bob Tyndale (Walter Fitzgerald), who has shot a hawk in order to protect the game birds that he rears. The final walk follows an episode in which Captain Ellis, in a drunken state, is arrested for stealing money in a pub and faces disgrace; the walk is a brooding, ominous sequence, shot in a *noir* style, which culminates in his contemplating suicide. However, Meg arrives in time to talk him out of it and he returns to the family home resolving to face the village despite his misdemeanour and disgrace. *Great Day* juggles a number of concerns – women's war work, Anglo–US relationships, the rural community, romance, emasculated males, family tensions, sibling relationships – as well as being a depiction of the vitality and energy of village life. The opening shots of the village, the 'Land Girl' sequences and Ellis's comments on nature and wildlife indicate an idealised sense of the countryside, but the overall tenor of the film is located in its tense, melodramatic quality, which cuts against any sense of rural tranquillity, any sense of the pastoral vision. Indeed, as Brian McFarlane has argued, 'It is hard to think of another film of the period – or later – which so persistently queries the picture-book pleasantness of the (usually southern) English village.'[29]

Great Day's finale – the actual visit of Mrs Roosevelt – is rousing, and the film ends on an high note with shots of the village women, a shot of Ellis and Meg, and a final shot of the redoubtable Mrs Ellis (Flora Robson), all to the strains of Hubert Parry's musical setting of William Blake's 'Jerusalem'. Yet the overall course of the film, the conflicts and tensions it depicts, is not really neutralised by the ending. In terms of a contribution to the depiction of rural life and values, the film has been aptly characterised as possessing 'the echoes of English pastoral with sourly abrasive undertones'.[30] Indeed, both *Great Day* and *Went the Day Well?* mix a visual celebration of the landscape and countryside with darker concerns and interesting contradictions that challenge conceptions of the rural idyll.

Neo-Romanticism: Powell and Pressburger

A Canterbury Tale (Michael Powell and Emeric Pressburger, 1944) is probably the most distinctive and widely discussed of the war-time rural films. It is a complex work that incorporates the familiar war-time convention of disparate characters thrown together, the depiction of a rural community and the rather more unusual activities of the village magistrate. The film is also marked by a mixture of cinematic styles including both a 'flirtation with Expressionism'[31] and several picturesque open-air sequences celebrating the beauty of the Kentish countryside.

In addition, the film is a meditation on history and Englishness that promotes a strong sense of the importance of landscape and the rural to English culture. It has been described as 'a key representation of the Second World War home front, and also as an important expression of Neo-Romanticism or the Romantic Right'.[32] As a film of the 'Romantic Right' it is somewhat at odds with prominent war-time titles such as *Millions Like Us*, *The Bells Go Down* (Basil Dearden, 1943) and *The Gentle Sex*, with their populist, communal, cross-class orientation and largely urban settings.[33] It is also somewhat at odds with the tenor of other rural titles such as *Went the Day Well?* and *Great Day*, with their equivocal delineation of the rural as a context for dark forces. While the 'populist' films looked to the future, Powell and Pressburger's film roots itself very much in the rural past. *A Canterbury Tale*, as Peter Conrad has suggested, 'is a film which enlisted Chaucer in the campaign for national salvation and attempted to recover for England a medieval innocence and a romantic optimism it had

5 *A Canterbury Tale*

lost'.[34] The populist films often emphasised the lessons of war-time co-operation between classes and between sexes in the pursuit of tangible military and industrial war aims – propaganda in a realist sense. *A Canterbury Tale* seems to have a more elusive, philosophical agenda, containing 'mystical and magical qualities which go against the grain of both the British realist tradition and wartime austerity'.[35] Although Powell himself has stated that its aim was 'explaining to Americans, and to our own people, the spiritual values and traditions, we were fighting for',[36] the film was not propaganda in a realist sense. It was propaganda of a different sort, 'a popular romantic picture of Britain'[37] appealing to a specific sense of national identity that emerged from rural traditions. The film 'created a semi-religious mythical landscape'[38] that has prompted Stella Hockenhull and Ian Christie to link it to the neo-Romantic trend in the visual arts during the war years, and to artists such as John Piper and Graham Sutherland, whose work has been described as expressing 'a mystical sense of the numinous in the landscape that corresponded to a personal, religious escape'.[39] Such writing deploys a vocabulary well suited to *A Canterbury Tale*, which has been described as 'a series of rural epiphanies' by Fuller.[40] *A Canterbury Tale* can be located within strong indigenous cultural traditions as 'a pastoral poem to the Kent countryside, a poem which operates a magical Kipling-esque facility to experience the past in the present and to recognise superhuman forces in nature'.[41]

That past is marked in various ways in the film but most strongly in the opening sequence depicting Chaucer's pilgrims on their way to Canterbury. The sequence is elided with the contemporary by way of a bold match cut from a hawk to a spitfire, which moves the narrative forward from the past to the present, from Chaucer's time to the Second World War, implicitly joining the present with the past in philosophical terms. Later in the film, in the course of his lecture to the soldiers, Colpeper (Eric Portman), the village magistrate, makes the bond between the present and the past, between Chaucer's pilgrims and his audience, explicit. It is, however, the intensity of the presentation of the lecture that marks the film out; its stylised silhouetted images of Colpeper are intercut with close shots of a Land Army woman, Alison (Sheila Sim), as she contemplates the somewhat mystical message. The expressionist intensity of this sequence is picked up later when Alison visits Chillingbourne Hill, the place on the Pilgrim's Way that Colpeper has discussed. The sequence of images and sounds presenting her response to the landscape – the distant shot of Canterbury Cathedral, the close-up shots of her face as she responds, the voices and music on the soundtrack – forcibly expresses the 'mystical sense of the numinous in the landscape'[42] that characterises the work of the neo-Romantics. For Stella Hockenhull, the sequence contains a key feature of Powell and Pressburger's film, which she describes as being 'dominated by intensely visual landscape images'.[43] Though a narrative with a procession of interconnected events, the film contains pictorial images, such as the long shot of Canterbury Cathedral, which appears somewhat detached from the narrative, constituting 'an arrested image, a "frozen moment", whereby the formal composition is arranged for spectator contemplation'.[44] Martin Lefebvre has suggested that 'landscape, at least in the visual arts, is *space freed from eventhood*',[45] which seems to fit with the way in which images of the countryside are designed in *A Canterbury Tale* to evoke 'a timeless, mysterious space ... a recurrent feature of war-time neo-romanticism'.[46]

Endthought

During the war approximately 100 feature films with war-time subject matter were made in Britain, about a third of the total number produced in the period.[47] Of these, fewer than 20 can be said to have rural settings and concerns, or to feature the British landscape in any significant way. Sue Harper has argued that 'pastoralism runs like a leitmotiv through most British cultural forms – except the cinema'.[48] Though a provocative sentiment, it does seem to be borne out by war-time British cinema at least. Despite the importance of dream-England, of the rural idyll, to the ideological project of constructing a firm national identity on which the defence of the nation could be based, the cinema's attention lay elsewhere. It lay in the images of fortitude amid urban despoilation to be found in realist home front dramas, and in depictions of the courage and co-operation of the armed forces in many films set in the theatres of war, on the land, in the sea and in the air. It also lay in the lampooning antics of comedians such as Arthur Askey and George Formby, some of which were focused on war subjects, and in Gainsborough's historical melodramas, now regarded as allegorical meditations on sexuality and femininity during the special circumstances of the period.

Where rural settings were used, as in the film examples examined, the representation varied from the magical-mystical imagery of the Kentish countryside in *A Canterbury Tale* to the less idyllic, somewhat darker German occupied village of Bramley End in *Went the Day Well?* What those and the other films share is an idea of rural Britain, of the British landscape, that is basically 'English'. Alan Howkins has argued that the template for 'modern ruralist ideology', traceable back to the early years of the twentieth century, was essentially 'southern' and incorporated 'a model of an ideal landscape type'. Such a landscape, he suggests, can be defined in the following terms:

> It is rolling or dotted with woodlands, and divided into fields by hedgerows. Its hills are smooth and bare, but not wild or rocky. Its streams and rivers flow rather than rush or tumble. Even more importantly its ideal social structure is the village with its green, pub and church clustered together, its ideal architecture stone or half-timbered topped with thatch.[49]

Along with *A Canterbury Tale, This England* is probably the most explicit depiction of the 'modern ruralist ideology' in British war-time cinema. Its 'tactful' re-titling as *Our Heritage* for the Scottish audience[50] indicates an awareness of the specifically southern English character of 'rural nostalgia' but also betrays a project that sought to harmonise national identity across the diverse peoples of Britain on the basis of a set of values that had little to do with their urban lives and, in the case of Celtic people, with a sense of national identity not so intertwined with the English village. Such a harmony was perhaps more easily achieved in the realist 'populist' films and the combat films of the period. Such films often stressed co-operation across class and national boundaries, though in environments – aircraft factories, army training camps, the North African desert, the Atlantic and Mediterranean seas – far removed from the idyllic English countryside and its rolling landscapes.

Notes

1 Brian Foss, *War Paint: Art, War, State and Identity in Britain 1939–1945* (New Haven and London: Yale University Press/The Paul Mellon Centre for Studies in British Art, 2007), p. 89.

2 Baldwin's comment is quoted by several writers on the topic of pastoral ideology and is drawn from his pamphlet *On England and Other Addresses*, published in 1926.

3 Alexandra Harris, *Romantic Moderns* (London: Thames and Hudson, 2010), p. 174.

4 Peter Mandler, 'Against "Englishness": English culture and the limits to rural nostalgia, 1850–1940', *Transactions of the Royal Historical Society*, Sixth Series, 7 (1997), pp. 157–75; p. 164.

5 Brian Short, 'Images and realities in the English rural community: an introduction', in Brian Short (ed.), *The English Rural Community: Image and Analysis* (Cambridge: Cambridge University Press, 1992), pp. 1–18; p. 5.

6 See Peter Wright, *On Living in an Old Country: The National Past in Contemporary Britain* (London: Verso, 1985), pp. 81–7.

7 Alun Howkins, 'Rurality and English identity', in David Morley and Kevin Robbins (eds), *British Cultural Studies* (Oxford: Oxford University Press, 2001), pp. 145–56; p. 148.

8 See Gill Saunders, *Recording Britain* (London: V&A Publishing, 2011).

9 Quoted in Foss, *War Paint*, p. 90.

10 Entitled 'The South Downs', it was an Army Bureau of Current Affairs poster.

11 *Picture Post* (22 June 1940), pp. 16–17.

12 Foss, *War Paint*, p. 88.

13 Sonya O. Rose, *Which People's War? National Identity and Citizenship in Wartime Britain 1939–1945* (Oxford: Oxford University Press, 2003), pp. 214–17.

14 Harris, *Romantic Moderns*, p. 174.

15 Alex Potts, '"Constable country" between the wars', in Raphael Samuel (ed.), *Patriotism: The Making and Unmaking of British National Identity, Vol. III: National Fictions* (London: Routledge, 1989), pp. 160–88; p. 162.

16 Rose, *Which People's War?*, p. 198.

17 Rose, *Which People's War?*, p. 218.

18 'What we are fighting for', *Picture Post* (13 July 1940), pp. 9–38.

19 The film was retitled *Our Heritage* for its Scottish release.

20 Stuart Sillars, *British Romantic Art and the Second World War* (London: Macmillan, 1991), p. 101.

21 Martin Wiener, *English Culture and the Decline of the Industrial Spirit 1850–1980* (Cambridge: Cambridge University Press, 2nd edition, 2004), p. 6.

22 Paul Street, 'Painting deepest England: the late landscapes of John Linnell and the uses of nostalgia', in C. Shaw and M. Chase (eds), *The Imagined Past: History and Nostalgia* (Manchester: Manchester University Press), pp. 68–80; p. 74.

23 See James Chapman, *The British at War: Cinema, State and Propaganda, 1939–1945* (London: I.B. Tauris, 1998), p. 234.

24 Chapman, *The British at War*, p. 241.

25 Wright, *On Living in an Old Country*, p. 85.

26 Anthony Aldgate, '"If the invader comes": *Went the Day Well?*', in Anthony Aldgate and Jeffrey Richards (eds), *Britain Can Take It: The British Cinema in the Second World War* (Edinburgh: Edinburgh University Press, 1994), pp. 115–37; p. 128.

27 A topic previously sketched in the Ministry of Information short *Miss Grant Goes to the Door* (1940).

28 Sue Harper, *Women in British Cinema: Mad, Bad and Dangerous to Know* (London: Continuum, 2000), p. 174.

29 Brian McFarlane, *Lance Comfort* (Manchester: Manchester University Press, 1999), p. 74.

30 McFarlane, *Lance Comfort*, p. 86.

31 Graham Fuller, 'A Canterbury tale', *Film Comment* (March/April 1995), p. 36.

32 Ian Christie, '"History is now and England": *A Canterbury Tale* in its contexts', in Ian Christie and Andrew Moor (eds), *The Cinema of Michael Powell: International*

Perspectives on an English Film-Maker (London: British Film Institute Publishing, 2005), pp. 75–93; p. 75.

33 See Andrew Higson, 'Addressing the nation: five films', in Geoff Hurd (ed.), *National Fictions: World War Two in British Films and Television* (London: British Film Institute Books, 1984), pp. 22–6; p. 22.

34 Peter Conrad, *To Be Continued: Four Stories and Their Survival* (Oxford: Clarendon Press, 1995), p. 23.

35 Stella Hockenhull, *Neo-Romantic Landscapes: An Aesthetic Approach to the Films of Powell and Pressburger* (Newcastle: Cambridge Scholars Publishing, 2008), p. 63.

36 Michael Powell, *A Life in Movies: An Autobiography* (London: Heinemann, 1986), p. 437.

37 Natalie Aldred, '*A Canterbury Tale*: Powell and Pressburger's film fantasies of Britain', in David Mellor (ed.), *A Paradise Lost: The Neo-Romantic Imagination in Britain 1935–55* (London: Lund Humphries/Barbican Art Gallery, 1987), pp. 117–25; p. 118.

38 Aldred, '*A Canterbury Tale*', p. 118.

39 Robert Hewison, *Culture and Consensus: England, Art and Politics since 1940* (London: Methuen, 1995), p. 23.

40 Fuller, 'A Canterbury tale', p. 33.

41 Aldred, '*A Canterbury Tale*', p. 118.

42 Hewison, *Culture and Consensus*, p. 23.

43 Hockenhull, *Neo-Romantic Landscapes*, p. 2.

44 Hockenhull, *Neo-Romantic Landscapes*, p. 2.

45 Martin Lefebvre, 'Between setting and landscape in the cinema', in Martin Lefebvre (ed.), *Landscape and Film* (London: Routledge, 2006), pp. 19–60; p. 22 (emphasis in original).

46 Frances Spalding, *British Art since 1900* (London: Thames and Hudson, 1986), p. 131.

47 A broad indicative statistic based on brief plot synopses of films of the period in Denis Gifford, *The British Film Catalogue* (Newton Abbot/London: David & Charles, 1986).

48 Sue Harper, 'The ownership of woods and water: landscapes in British cinema 1930–1960', in Graeme Harper and Jonathan Rayner (eds), *Cinema and Landscape* (Bristol: Intellect, 2010), pp. 147–60; p. 149.

49 Howkins, 'Rurality and English identity', p. 151.

50 Chapman, *The British at War*, p. 235.

4

'An unlimited field for experiment':
Britain's stereoscopic landscapes

Keith M. Johnston

A stereoscopic tree with branches pointing toward us, or a lanyard hanging down towards us from a flagpole, appears quite different, melodramatically accentuated, from the way it looks in nature.

Ivor Montagu[1]

Between the birth of cinema in the late nineteenth century and the 1950s, there had been several unsuccessful attempts to create a stereoscopic cinema that could add a third spatial dimension to the screen. Three-dimensional experiments in America, France, Germany, Italy and Russia in the first five decades of the twentieth century were intended to enhance the cinema's claims to realism but were more often seen as novelties and gimmicks, with only limited public exhibition. The debut of *In Tune with Tomorrow* (John Norling, 1939), a stereoscopic film advertising the Chrysler Corporation at the 1939 New York World's Fair, has been seen as the first public screening of 3D footage (notably using polaroid glasses rather than the existing red–green anaglyph technology), while during the 1940s Russian filmmakers continued to explore lenticular (non-glasses) screening technology.[2] The first large-scale production, distribution and exhibition of stereoscopic cinema outside Russia, however, occurred in 1950s Britain.

At the 1951 Festival of Britain Telekinema (on London's South Bank), four stereoscopic short films were shown to sell-out audiences. While *Now Is the Time (to Put On Your Glasses)* (1951) and *Around Is Around* (1951) were hand-drawn animations created in association with Scottish-Canadian artist Norman McLaren, *A Solid Explanation* (Peter Bradford, 1951) and *Distant Thames* (Brian Smith, 1951) were live-action films that included studio and location filming in London Zoo and on the River Thames, respectively. These initial films therefore already contained within them a difference in representing the real world: between faux-rural (animals in captivity, performing for urban crowds) and authentically rural (a boat trip down the Thames). Although not the first stereoscopic 3D films to ever be screened in Britain, these were the first films that attempted to capture and project the British landscape through stereoscopic technology.[3] Over the following four years, another seventeen stereoscopic 3D films were produced and exhibited in Britain, projecting 3D representations of a variety of British landscapes. These films offered 3D views of bucolic English countryside, the port of Liverpool, the river banks of Oxfordshire, a Lancashire oil refinery and coronation celebrations in London, Epsom and Edinburgh, and were screened in 3D cinemas throughout Britain, Europe and America.[4]

This chapter will investigate these films and consider how the use of stereoscopic 3D affected the construction and representation of rural landscapes. As such, while the chapter is informed by the spatial turn taken in media and cultural studies since the turn of the twenty-first century, it is more interested in how stereoscopic cinematography challenges and complicates those debates. As Steve Chibnall and Julian Petley have noted, 'place in British cinema ... was rarely simply somewhere seen by the eye of the camera, but rather a site of rhetorical claims and ideological connotations ... a crucial part of film's signifying system'.[5] The addition of the third dimension to that signifying system, the creation of added layers of visual information and the enhancement offered to what the camera saw, suggests an important development in filmic representation that has yet to be fully explored, despite a recent increase in academic interest in this field.[6] Exploring this aspect of the 3D aesthetic, then, will expand debates around stereoscopic imagery more generally, but with a firm focus on how these British stereoscopic rural landscapes complicate existing work on the representation of landscape on screen.

Of the 21 British stereoscopic 3D films produced between 1951 and 1955, this chapter will focus on four specific examples: *Distant Thames/Royal River* (Brian Smith, 1951), *Northern Towers* (Roy Harris, 1952), *Sunshine Miners* (J. D. Chambers, 1952) and *Vintage '28* (Robert M. Angell, 1953).[7] These films offer the most concerted engagement with British rural landscapes, covering a range of different locations and suggesting potent links to wider debates around immersion, gimmickry and realism in stereoscopic filmmaking (debates that were as potent in the 1950s as they are in the twenty-first century). Given that gimmickry and spectacle are terms rarely associated with the British documentary impulse, these films work to complicate broader understandings of stereoscopic media in this time period. Following the lead of what has been dubbed the 'New Film History', close analysis of the *mise-en-scène* of these stereoscopic 3D landscapes will be combined with contemporary interviews and articles by the stereoscopic filmmakers involved, and the critical reception of these short films.[8] This allows the chapter to examine how these British pioneers attempted to redefine the traditional landscape of the social realist documentary through the visual spectacle of 3D imagery and composition.

Stereoscopic landscape

The Stereoscope presents to the eye all the objects in solid relief, as perfectly as if the landscape itself were spread before it.

C. and E. Bierstadt, *Stereoscopic Views among the Hills of New Hampshire* (1862)[9]

The presentation of stereoscopic films at the 1951 Festival of Britain was as much a celebration of the past as it was a portent for the future: David Brewster had introduced his version of a photographic stereoscope a hundred years earlier, at the 1851 Great Exhibition, a display of the British Empire's scientific, manufacturing and engineering progress that the Festival of Britain hoped to emulate.[10] The commercialisation of the stereoscope throughout the 1850s and 1860s had included within it a belief that the stereoscope could capture and represent reality to the individuated viewer.[11] Despite scientific studies on the stereoscope's construction of visual reality, and its creative arrangement of the objects it captured, the promotion of Victorian stereoscopic photography was dominated by ideas of transparent reflection and reliable authenticity, 'truthful depictions of lifelike solidity'.[12] This led to an expanding stereoscopic industry – in both stereographs and stereoscopes with which to view them – where famous and exotic landscapes and natural wonders were dominant and popular stereoscopic options. The stereoscopic display of landscape was so dominant in this period that 'many people's first glimpses of such wonders as Niagara Falls or the Grand Canyon were through the stereoscope'.[13]

The 1950s British stereoscopic pioneers, led by scriptwriter and documentarian Raymond Spottiswoode, disputed this claim of transparent authenticity and went to great pains to stress the constructed nature of their 3D images. Spottiswoode, in a treatise on stereoscopic filmmaking, noted that the 'parallel with the human eye is simple and attractive; but … the viewing of a stereoscopic image cannot at present be made to resemble human vision at all closely … it is a mental construction from data supplied solely by overlapped images on a flat screen'.[14] Spottiswoode was the driving force behind the Telekinema 3D films and the specialist stereoscopic company Stereo Techniques, which pursued British 3D filmmaking as a creative tool throughout the 1950s. Spottiswoode and his Stereo Techniques colleagues (including Jack Ralph and Charles W. Smith) were convinced 3D films could be the next step for cinema. Yet achieving this would require major changes in production methods and attitudes, not something that could simply be added to existing practices. The British 3D films were, therefore, not designed to be simple reflections of reality but can best be seen as experiments in stereoscopic production and aesthetics, as an attempt to find 'new visual ideas … which would be ineffective in the ordinary flat film … [but] which take on a new vitality in the more real world of 3D'.[15] Central to that new vitality would be the representation of stereoscopic landscapes and the ability of filmmakers to establish what, to adapt John Grierson's phrase about documentary filmmaking, could be called the stereoscopic treatment of actuality.

The link to the British documentary movement is particularly apt, given that all Stereo Techniques films were co-productions with existing commercial and documentary producers: the likes of Anglo-Scottish, Associated British-Pathé, International Realist and the Shell Film Unit. The sponsored or commercial documentary route was inspired by the work of the 1930s documentary pioneers, who developed two particular forms of film: 'those instructional films which stand back from their subject matter and offer a public, social gaze at a place, a process, a people; and ... the story documentary which begins to ... offer a private, personal look from the point of view of an individual member of "the people", from within the place that he or she inhabits'.[16] The 1950s Stereo Techniques 3D films contain examples of both of the forms that Andrew Higson identifies here, as well as other more experimental approaches, but the application of stereoscopic technology to such forms, and to the treatment of existing documentary subjects such as realism and landscape, problematises traditional notions of documentary realism through the foregrounding of spectacular imagery in otherwise realistic settings.

The terms 'realism' and 'spectacle' loom large in discussions of landscape in British cinema, from the influence of the 1930s British documentary movement to the British 'New Wave' of the 1960s, which created 'images that became shorthand for the Northern industrial working-class community ... shots of canals, street scenes, the pub, the fairground, the bus journey, the visit to the nearby countryside'.[17] This last category, featuring brief depictions of rural areas, is described as offering 'contradictory meanings and pleasures' by Andrew Higson, who reads them as spectacular, visually pleasurable moments for the audience.[18] Yet the focus of both Lovell and Higson is the relationship of such iconography to the larger narrative world being created, the use of historical place as a space for fictional activities. Such spaces are never ideologically neutral: in the British New Wave, as in later social realist films, landscape can be politically contested or defined through social class. Yet those films tend to prioritise urban spaces over rural ones, where pre-lapsarian views of the countryside tend to promote traditional ideas of 'England', a trend that is more pronounced in the heritage films that are almost wholly based in and around rural locations (albeit largely upper-class ones). Existing work on the rural countryside landscapes found in British cinema, therefore, has focused on how such films draw on 'well-established cultural traditions', and 'embody the nation' and how 'a particular picturesque version of rural England is frequently offered as an alternative to the England of modernity'.[19]

The stereoscopic films analysed here, however, sit between the 1930s documentary movement and the New Wave of the 1960s (and pre-date the Free Cinema movement that fed into it) and exist on the brink of British modernism: their representation of the rural and the urban necessarily moves beyond these dominant ideas of landscape in British cinema, not least because they drew

6 *Northern Towers*

from industrial documentary roots and experimented with innovative technology that offered new aesthetic and representational possibilities. That is not to say that these films do not engage in mythologising both urban and rural spaces, but the circumstances of production and the use of new cinematic technologies complicate the cultural traditions they draw on.

The 1950s growth of widescreen filmmaking (in Britain and elsewhere) expanded 'the space of the cinema screen … [where] the filming of vast geographic spaces was increasingly used to signify the very spectacle of cinema itself'.[20] This focus, however, elides the earlier geographical spectacle offered by widescreen's 1950s competitor, stereoscopic 3D. *Northern Towers*, for example, opens with a still image, composed in depth: a tree dominates the foreground, a dark silhouette that stretches up the right-hand side of the screen, with branches extending almost all the way across the top of the image; a series of fence posts runs horizontally along the bottom of the screen; a white gate and gatepost lurk near the bottom of frame; and the cooling towers and gleaming metal spires of Stanlow Refinery dominated the centre and background.[21] Each of these exists in its own slice of screen depth, offering a sense of distance between them while the image remains coherent and interlinked, designed to contrast old and new, tree and tower, nature and technology. The decision to hold the image, without cutting, also ties the composition back to traditional ideas of landscape painting, wherein the viewer has time to understand the 'visual ordering' of the image.[22] Then movement is added, as a horse and cart travels across screen, left to right, passing in front of almost all the other screen elements and stressing the depth cues on screen. In one sense, then, the addition of depth could be claimed to enhance the realism on offer; but the layering of imagery is caught between the desire for immersion and for viewers to observe the spectacle on display, a return to Montagu's concept of melodramatic accentuation within the stereoscopic frame.

Equally, in *Sunshine Miners*, a slow camera pan across a wide field contains hedgerow, fences and trees in the middle distance and farm buildings further back: the physical space offers a suggestion of the actual filmed location, but the stereoscopic effect works to make the landscape spectacular. The tension 'between proximity and distance, body and mind, sensuous immersion and detached observation' found within discussions of landscape art is equally valid within these stereoscopic films.[23] In the opening sequence of *Sunshine Miners*, each level of imagery is designed to draw the viewer into the image, an artificial depth that retreats into the screen at the same time as the film's titles (which appear over part of this sequence) hang in front of it, a spectacular addition. Later scenes show fence posts lined up either diagonally across the screen or in a line that stretches back into the image: in both cases, those lines lead the eye across and into the image. While similar techniques can be seen in 2D 'flat' filmmaking, the stereoscopic process here uses rural landscape images as technological spectacle, an attempt to expand the space of the cinema screen not, as in widescreen, to the left and right (a widening of the image ratio) but where imagery can emerge and retreat into the screen. As Raymond Spottiswoode claimed, Stereo Techniques stereographers were keen to find 'visual material which will enhance the sense of forward and backward movement, or nearer and further away'.[24]

This use of positive (where images appear to exist in depth behind/beyond the screen) and negative (where images seem to pop out of the screen) parallax offers another challenge to existing concepts of how the rural landscape has been represented in cinema, most notably the claim that such rural depictions 'can be said not to take us *toward* but rather to take us *away* from the land'.[25] In 3D landscapes, elements can, quite literally, be used to bring the landscape to the audience or to draw the eye into that landscape: as Montagu noted, the ability to move 'towards and away from the spectator' was 'a gigantic, a tremendous, an immeasurable new power' for cinema.[26] While this remained an artificial and heavily constructed process, the impetus of many stereoscopic filmmakers was precisely to bring the audience into the rural landscape being depicted. As noted above, *Sunshine Miners* delivers strong examples of positive parallax with slow panning shots of fields and quarries and compositions that aim to pull the viewer into the scene; equally, it highlights negative parallax in images that emerge out of the screen, most notably the arm of the biggest mechanical digger, which swings towards and past the camera several times. Extending out from the traditional flat surface of the screen, this giant metal arm is a spectacular intrusion into the space of the audience.

Given that landscape has been theorised as 'not only something we see ... [but] also a *way of seeing things* ... not just about *what* we see, but *how we look*', these stereoscopic landscapes present a unique challenge to 'how' films look at landscapes and how the audience is positioned to look at them.[27] One intrinsic difference here is what, elsewhere, I have termed a 'cinema of projections': uses of negative parallax within stereoscopic 3D that attempt to extend on-screen elements towards the audience.[28] With landscape, this negative parallax is often more subtle but still exists to push parts of the landscape out at the viewer: a breaking down of traditional artistic assumptions that present landscape as something to be viewed at a distance rather than something that is capable of approaching, or poking out, at them. In the first of the 1950s British films that deals specifically with landscape, *Royal River* features tree branches that hang 'off' screen, water that laps at the edge of the screen and flowers in bloom that emerge out of the screen. Moving landscape imagery into and out of the screen expands the space of the cinema screen along the z-axis yet also highlights the artificial construction of what, with the application of positive parallax, has been presented as a real and knowable space.

That is not to say that such landscapes are purely there for realist or spectacular effect: these rural stereoscopic spaces also inform the narratives being constructed. Landscape is an essential narrative and iconographical element in *Sunshine Miners*, where a farmer agrees to his fields being dug up and mined for coal. From the opening images of fields and hedgerows, the film takes great delight in showing the landscape being pulled apart, reduced to mounds of dirt in a makeshift quarry. Here, the spectacle is based around the shocking change in landscape from rolling fields to quarries surrounded by mountains of earth, but also the scene provided by the machines that cause that narrative shift. The middle of the film is dominated by these mechanical diggers and earth-moving equipment as they trundle across the screen, the stereoscopic effect separating them from the landscape they are destroying. As in *Northern Towers'* celebration of a new oil refinery, the stereoscopic narrative exists as a contrast between old and new, both at the level of narrative (modernity and progress within rural spaces) and at the level of production (technology representing natural beauty and making it spectacular).

Northern Towers also stresses Higson's instructional approach, the gaze at a place or process. Propagandist in nature, it features a stentorian male voiceover explaining the virtues of the stereoscopic science-fiction landscape of engineering marvels, sleek metal, sheer heights and unfamiliar machinery. Its spectacular views and stereoscopic fetishisation of cooling towers does not offer any sign of the people running the terminal, or their lives: technology and modernity are spectacular in their own right. *Sunshine Miners* offers a balance of instructional film and story documentary, visually featuring the farmer (whose voiceover narrates portions of the film) who exists within its rural landscape; yet the stereoscopic depiction of the spectacle of destruction and rebuilding rarely overshadows that personal point of view (the farmer is never highlighted in a similarly stereoscopic manner). However, outside these two examples, which foreground sponsored documentary approaches, the 1950s stereoscopic movement also produced work that featured other celebrations of the rural landscape: monarchy and poetic ruralism in *Royal River* and eccentric rural tradition in *Vintage '28*.

Royal River opens with a spectacular single stereoscopic colour image: a carpet of green grass and a fallen brown tree trunk, stark against the blue sky. The camera, mounted on a boat, is carried round this location, allowing the dimensions of the image to become clear – each element layered and separate but combining to give a rounded sense of the scene. The producers at Stereo Techniques noted the film was designed around such 'scenic views ... making best use of overhanging trees and bridges for 3-D effect', with the Technicolor adding 'a pictorial quality never seen before'.[29] As one of the first British stereoscopic experiments, *Royal River* was restricted to more stately, mannered long shots due to technical restrictions caused by the twin three-strip Technicolor cameras being used (this also appears to have been the first, and last, six-strip colour stereoscopic movie). These restrictions emphasise single well-composed images, such as the opening shot or those scenes that draw the eye across the river, through inlets to stone bridges, tree trunks and beyond, or through overhanging willow branches to stone cottages and villages. As noted above, occasionally negative parallax is used, notably with tree branches that appear stark against the blue sky, underwater images of fish swimming 'into' the camera and a series of brightly coloured flowers blooming in the parks around Windsor.

Raymond Spottiswoode regarded the film as 'a cameraman's picture, made almost without benefit of direction, and showing how complex movements of planes can lend a new beauty to scenery when viewed through the twin lenses of the stereocamera'.[30] It is true that this stately river travelogue demonstrates one great power of the stereoscopic image – the illusion of depth heralded since Victorian stereoscopic photography – but there remains a central ideological purpose to the film. Unlike the use of landscape in *Northern Towers* or *Sunshine Miners*, the emphasis here is on presenting the spectacle of stereoscopic rural landscape as the source of English heritage and history: the open fields, small villages and churches lead inexorably to the majesty of Windsor Castle (and then, to London). As the accompanying voiceover notes, the 'sweet Thames' flows 'between the pastures and the parishes ... through their enduring, ever changing English heritage' and this 'river of royal swans' glances 'upon a Norman keep of kings' in Windsor. The stereoscopic imagery here tells a story about the journey from the rural to the urban but also about the place of heritage within that 3D journey. The final scene of the film, a cut that links Windsor to the Festival of Britain site, reinforces that continuity, visually placing 1951 modernity in direct relation to rural and royal heritage.[31]

7 *Vintage '28*

The final film being considered for this chapter, *Vintage '28*, contains less of the instructional tone found in *Northern Towers* or *Sunshine Miners*. It is equally distinct from the poetic and travelogue aesthetic of *Royal River*, and it continues the stereoscopic films' focus on technology, heritage and visual spectacle. A story documentary about an American serviceman, Hank (Desmond Montgomery), and his discovery of classic car racing, this film features a more playful use of stereoscopic material than the previous examples. Rural landscapes and technology remain at the heart of the stereoscopic spectacle: the various motor cars that emerge from those landscapes are the most obvious examples of negative parallax here, driving 'into' the camera and 'off' the screen with a regularity not seen in the other Stereo Techniques films (there is also an obvious use of negative parallax when one character leans into the camera to reattach a lead to the engine). Although Raymond Spottiswoode had noted that audiences will 'become weary of these tricks' (a component of the pre-war anaglyphic films), it is possible such moments were seen as more acceptable in a dramatic form than in the sponsored documentaries, which had a more immediate desire to connote realism.[32] Alternatively, the later production date of this film (it was produced in the third batch of stereoscopic films made by Stereo Techniques and its partners) might simply demonstrate a more confident 3D aesthetic within the company.[33]

Such moments are combined with attempts to draw the film's audience 'into' the film: several images show cars racing towards the camera down a long road, with telephone poles arranged along the right of screen, receding into the distance from which the cars appear, leading the eye into and beyond the screen. Similarly to the opening images of *Northern Towers* and *Royal River*, which emphasised the stereoscopic spectacle of landscape, *Vintage '28* contains several moments that linger on the cars and the space of the countryside they race within, constructing images that place those elements at different places within the stereoscopic image. Such moments also reinforce the connection between rural landscape, tradition and technology: Hank describes the stereoscopic roads he drives along as 'funny little English lanes' and thinks the British classic car enthusiasts 'sure do live in the past'. Yet these landscapes are not purely agrarian: several scenes of the car meetings show encroaching suburban housing and cooling towers in the background. These elements are never made spectacular (that remains the purview of the bushes and trees along the country lanes, the roads that stretch to the horizon and the cars that speed along them) but they suggest that the rural can never completely be removed from the growing process of urbanisation (a theme that, as seen, runs through many of these stereoscopic films).

Like the other 3D films studied here, then, *Vintage '28* creates stereoscopic spectacle through elements of its rural landscape but also relies on external elements (mainly the classic cars) to enhance and create narrative events within that landscape. By using 3D technology and stereoscopic aesthetics, the Stereo Techniques films problematise the way in which rural landscape has been described in 2D film analysis: rather than simply being the site of 'cultural tradition and heritage', which can be opposed to an urban landscape defined 'in terms of technology, progress and forward development', these stereoscopic landscapes attempt to combine technology and tradition, new and old, urban and rural.[34] It is perhaps fitting that *Vintage '28*, the last of Stereo Techniques' stereoscopic films that directly engages with the British rural landscape, does so by depicting a world on the fringes of urbanisation. From *Royal River*'s bucolic rural world to *Vintage '28*, these films offer a stereoscopic alternative to depictions of the rural landscape as a place of tradition and continuity.

Critical response

Critical commentary on 3D and the use of landscape within stereoscopic filmmaking in the 1951–3 period was cautious, often debating the merits of the technology and the potential addition to claims of realism. Of the Festival of Britain films, *The Times* described *Distant Thames/Royal River* as 'an exciting experience' and a 'stereoscopic spectacle' of landscape: 'The quiet water of the Thames flowed over into the laps of the audience, the branches of the riverside trees jabbed at their eyes, and, all the time, the sight and the imagination were being drawn into depths and perspectives, the screen has never before possessed the secret of revealing.'[35] Despite that claim of 'jabbing' the audiences' eyes, critical opinion remained focused on the issue of realism. The *Daily Mirror* claimed, 'You might be gliding along in a canoe, so perfect is the "depth" effect of the countryside scenes' and the *Daily Mail* described the film as having 'a depth and realism never before seen, with river views of Windsor Castle in which the loveliness of the English land is really captured'.[36] The importance of the rural landscape is clear in these (and other) responses, which highlight how stereoscopic filmmaking has enhanced the realism of traditional elements such as the countryside and riverside.

Yet, as *The Times* review noted, 'if stereoscopy can do so much with landscape, what could it not do with scenes deliberately constructed with the aim of violent dramatic effect?'[37] Many critics felt that the question of 'how many dimensions does a feature film need?' remained unanswered by the Festival of Britain films.[38] Later Stereo Techniques films did little to fulfil that query for critics: *Northern Towers* was seen as a novelty that lacked 'sufficient foreground detail', while *Vintage '28* was described as an 'acceptable novelty' and 'moderate material enlivened by one or two effective 3-D tricks'.[39] The increase in negative parallax described above was picked up by several critics, who noted that 'the temptation to push out various objects into the audience in order to "exploit" the medium is not entirely resisted'.[40] While reporting of the British short films in the popular press faded after the initial flurry of interest in 1951, it is clear that the celebratory tone of the Festival of Britain films had been replaced by uncertainty around technology and aesthetics. Indeed, as I have demonstrated elsewhere, terms such as 'novelty' and 'gimmick' are rarely absent from critical response to 3D films in Britain. The initial flurry of excitement around the possibilities of stereoscopic landscape and enhanced realism in the Stereo Techniques short films was soon challenged with the introduction of full-length American commercial features, with critics focusing more on complaints about polaroid glasses and negative parallax.[41] Critically, 3D became regarded as an intrusive American technology, not one linked to British technicians, directors or landscapes. However, despite this move, it is clear from the original critical responses that landscape remained a key element within British stereoscopic production, and one where the 3D aesthetic had potential to contribute something new to cinema's future.

Conclusion

In unskilled hands this may easily degenerate into a trick.

Raymond Spottiswoode[42]

The stereoscopic short films produced by Stereo Techniques remain important experiments in 3D filmmaking, albeit ones that have been overshadowed by the American feature films that followed. As this chapter has demonstrated, the use of stereoscopic composition and construction was designed as a creative tool, one that could provide enhanced verisimilitude but also impressive spectacle both in front of and behind the screen. This places stereoscopic filming within a continued cultural geography tradition of tension between landscape as something to be subjectively immersed within or objectively distanced from. The stereoscopic treatment of actuality is most obviously displayed in the films analysed here, with unique representations and uses of British rural landscapes that allowed those locations to move towards an audience or draw the audience into the space on screen. While the 1950s British 3D films were not purely focused on landscape above all other elements (*Eye on the Ball* (Peter Bradford, 1952) featured several vignettes of sporting activities; *Around and About* (Danny Carter, 1952) was split between scenes of Liverpool and square dancing in Hammersmith), the stereoscopic scenes of Britain and British locations were a central part of their appeal.[43]

These stereoscopic experiments demonstrate that the filmmakers struggled to revise 2D filmmaking practices around landscape for the new 3D world they were promoting. Stereoscopic film presents a different look at landscape, a creative composition that requires the artificial placement of images both in front of and behind the flat surface of the screen. The process inevitably affects how audiences see the landscape being represented: the scene itself (what is seen) but also the aesthetic representation of that scene (how it is shown). Filming in 3D necessitates longer shot length, slower editing and slower panning (allowing the eyes to assess the full image), and requires careful composition: Raymond Spottiswoode noted that stereoscopic films had to do more than just place 'some meaningless post or tree … in the foreground of each shot' in order to emphasise the stereoscopic scene.[44] Despite this, the Stereo Technique films do feature that technique (the fence post in *Sunshine Miners*; poles and flags in *Vintage '28*), and such moments point up the illusion of three-dimensionality and the constructed nature of the landscape being presented.[45]

However, while aesthetic and production elements may have restricted the scope of the British 3D films, they nevertheless make clear that the addition of stereoscopic technology altered the production, presentation and use of landscape imagery beyond simple claims to increased realism. Stereoscopic filmmaking offers the possibility of spectacularising landscape in a similar way that colour and widescreen filmmaking once did. The evidence of these four Stereo Techniques films has demonstrated that a more concerted focus on the construction and representation of stereoscopic landscapes is an essential step to developing a wider understanding of how the 3D aesthetic can engage with existing debates around realism, spectacle, narrative and space, both in the 1950s and in the more recent expansion of digital 3D production and exhibition.

Notes

1 Ivor Montagu, 'The third dimension: film of the future', in Roger Manvell (ed.), *The Cinema 1950* (Harmondsworth: Penguin, 1950), pp. 132–9; p. 136.
2 Ray Zone, *Stereoscopic Cinema and the Origins of 3-D Film* (Lexington: University Press of Kentucky, 2007), pp. 153–9.
3 Short American 3-D films promoted as 'Audioscopiks' were shown in Britain in the 1930s, and recycled for the 1953–5 US 3D boom, and featured 'the usual stereo novelties of baseballs thrown at the camera, jugglers with flaming torches, and so on': Charles W. Smith, '100 years of 3-D movies … and the second 100 years', *Cinema Technology* (April 1996), p. 8.
4 For more on the creation of a British 3D exhibition circuit, see Keith M. Johnston, 'Now is the time (to put on your glasses): 3-D film exhibition in Britain, 1951–55', *Film History*, 23: 1 (2011), pp. 93–103.
5 Steve Chibnall and Julian Petley, 'Introduction', *Journal of British Cinema and Television*, 4: 2 (2007), pp. 213–18; p. 213.
6 On 3D aesthetics see, for example, Miriam Ross, 'Spectacular dimensions: 3D dance films', www.sensesofcinema.com/2011/feature-articles/spectacular-dimensions-3d-dance-films (accessed 25 May 2012); Philip Sandifer, 'Out of the screen and into the theatre: 3-D film as demo', *Cinema Journal*, 50: 3 (2011), pp. 62–77. On 3D studies more broadly, see Thomas Elsaesser, 'James Cameron's *Avatar*: access for all', *New Review of Film & Television Studies*, 9: 3 (2011), pp. 247–64; R. M. Hayes, *3-D Movies: A History and Filmography of Stereoscopic Cinema* (Jefferson, NC: McFarland & Company, 1989); Michael Kerbel, '3D or not 3D', *Film Comment*, 16: 6 (1983), pp. 11–20; Hal Morgan and Dan Symmes, *Amazing 3-D* (Boston: Little & Brown, 1982); Ray Zone, *3-D Filmmakers: Conversations with Creators of Stereoscopic Motion Pictures* (Oxford: Scarecrow Press, 2005); Ray Zone, *Stereoscopic Cinema and the Origins of 3-D Film* (Lexington: University Press of Kentucky, 2007).
7 *Distant Thames* was the title given to the incomplete stereoscopic river journey down the Thames that premiered at the Festival Telekinema. However, the film was completed, and re-titled *Royal River*, in time for its premiere at the 1951 Edinburgh Film Festival. It is this fuller version that this article makes reference to.
8 James Chapman, Mark Glancy and Sue Harper, *The New Film History* (London: Palgrave, 2007).
9 C. and E. Bierstadt quoted in Laura Burd Schiavo, 'From phantom image to perfect vision: physiological optics, commercial photography, and the popularisation of the stereograph', in Lisa Gitelman and Geoffrey B. Pingree (eds), *New Media, 1740–1915* (London: MIT Press, 2003), pp. 113–37; p. 129.
10 Schiavo, 'From phantom image to perfect vision', p. 122.
11 Schiavo, 'From phantom image to perfect vision', p. 113.
12 Schiavo, 'From phantom image to perfect vision', p. 121.
13 Morgan and Symmes, *Amazing 3-D*, p. 13.
14 Raymond Spottiswoode, N. L. Spottiswoode and Charles Smith, 'Basic principles of the three-dimensional film', *Society of Motion Picture and Television Engineers Journal*, 59: 4 (1952), pp. 249–86; p. 276.
15 Spottiswoode et al., 'Basic principles of the three-dimensional film', p. 266.

16 Andrew Higson, 'Space, place, spectacle: landscape and townscape in the "kitchen sink" film', in Andrew Higson (ed.), *Dissolving Views: Key Writings on British Cinema* (London: Cassell, 1996), pp. 133–56; p. 151.

17 Terry Lovell, 'Landscapes and stories in 1960s British realism', in Andrew Higson (ed.), *Dissolving Views: Key Writings on British Cinema*, pp. 157–77; p. 169.

18 Higson, 'Space, place, spectacle', pp. 133–4.

19 Andrew Higson, 'A green and pleasant land: rural spaces and British cinema', in Catherine Fowler and Gillian Helfield (eds), *Representing the Rural: Space, Place, and Identity in Films about the Land* (Detroit: Wayne State University Press, 2006), pp. 240–55; pp. 252–3.

20 Chibnall and Petley, 'Introduction', p. 214.

21 As Miriam Ross has noted, writing about the stereoscopic aesthetic and effect without being able to regularly access 3D versions of the chosen films poses an issue for scholars. The following analysis is necessarily based on an initial viewing of 3D footage and a subsequent re-viewing of 2D copies of the same films to confirm details from initial notes. See Ross, 'Spectacular dimensions'.

22 John Wylie, *Landscape* (Abingdon: Routledge, 2007), p. 4.

23 Wylie, *Landscape*, p. 1.

24 Spottiswoode et al., 'Basic principles of the three-dimensional film', pp. 265–6.

25 Catherine Fowler and Gillian Helfield, 'Introduction', in Catherine Fowler and Gillian Helfield (eds), *Representing the Rural: Space, Place and Identity in Films about the Land* (Detroit: Wayne State University Press, 2006), pp. 1–14; p. 9.

26 Montagu, 'The third dimension', p. 136.

27 Wylie, *Landscape*, p. 7.

28 Keith M. Johnston, ' "The action was so real I thought I was cheating on my wife": the stereoscopic sex films of the 1970s', in Eylem Atakav and Andy Willis (eds), *From Smut to Softcore: Sex and 1970s World Cinema* (Manchester: Manchester University Press, forthcoming).

29 Charles W. Smith, '3-D: the British foundations', *Eyepiece: Journal of the Guild of British Camera Technicians*, 8: 1 (1987), pp. 26–7.

30 Raymond Spottiswoode, 'Three dimensions – or two?', Films in 1951 supplement, *Sight & Sound* (1951), pp. 44–5.

31 With three separate films focusing on royal events, including *Royal River, Royal Review* (Angell, 1953, about the Coronation) and *London Tribute* (Angell, 1953, a 3D newsreel on Queen Mary's funeral), the link between stereoscopy and the monarchy (given Queen Victoria's connection to the original stereoscope) is something that would merit further investigation.

32 Spottiswoode at al., 'Basic principles of the three-dimensional film', p. 283.

33 Its May 1953 release date suggests it was produced before or during the release of the first US 3D films in March 1953, but there is no evidence to suggest the feature films had any direct impact on the later stereo techniques films.

34 Fowler and Helfield, 'Introduction', p. 2.

35 'The telecinema: stereoscopic films', *The Times* (1 May 1951), p. 6.

36 Donald Zec, 'Specs make these films come to life', *Daily Mirror* (1 May 1951), p. 6; 'What to see at the South Bank – 4', *Daily Mail* (11 May 1951), p. 3.

37 'The telecinema: stereoscopic films', p. 6.

38 Review of *Distant Thames*, *Monthly Film Bulletin*, 18: 209 (1951), p. 283.

39 'Short subjects', *Today's Cinema* (27 May 1952), p. 8; 'Short Subjects', *Today's Cinema* (12 June 1953), p. 5.

40 Review of *Vintage '28*, *Monthly Film Bulletin*, 20: 234 (1953), p. 114.

41 Keith M. Johnston, '"A technician's dream?" The critical reception of 3D films in Britain,' *Historical Journal of Film, Radio and Television*, 32: 2 (2012), pp. 245–65.

42 Spottiswoode et al., 'Basic principles of the three-dimensional film', p. 266.

43 Stereoscopic landscapes were equally important to many US 3-D feature films: the African plains of *Bwana Devil* (Oboler, 1952); the Western settings of *Hondo* (Farrow, 1953) and *Wings of the Hawk* (Boetticher, 1953); the expanse of the Mojave Desert in *Inferno* (Baker, 1953); or the jungle of *Creature from the Black Lagoon* (Arnold, 1953), for example.

44 Spottiswoode et al., 'Basic principles of the three-dimensional film', p. 283.

45 For more on this restriction to the 3D effect, see Sandifer, 'Out of the screen and into the theatre'.

5

The figure (and disfigurement) in the landscape: *The Go-Between*'s picturesque

Mark Broughton

The prominence of the country estate as a setting in British cinema suggests that it would be fruitful to consider the aesthetic history of the landscape garden on screen. Yet, while a number of publications on landscapes in cinema have emerged, landscape gardens have received little attention, perhaps because of 'heritage' criticism's refusal to address the roles played by country-estate imagery and locations' historical associations in films' narratives.[1] This chapter seeks to situate *The Go-Between* (Joseph Losey, 1971) at a turning point in the history of the country estate on screen and to demonstrate how Joseph Losey and his collaborators deployed a location rhetorically to comment on the history of landed power. The film represented a new kind of country-estate cinema, for it was shot entirely on location in Norfolk, at sites unusually close to one another.[2] No previous country-estate film was grounded to such an extent in local geography. Most of the interiors and exteriors of the fictional country estate – Brandham Hall – were shot at Melton Constable Hall. Apart from those set or shot in Norwich, all other sequences were shot within a ten-mile radius of Melton Constable Hall.[3] *The Go-Between*'s detailed exploration of a wide variety of landscapes around one main estate location was unprecedented. This exploration was purposeful, for the film thereby articulated various ways of understanding the estate's socio-cultural structure.

More than any country-estate film before it, *The Go-Between* established a congruence between its narrative and a location. The film's landscape fiction is best understood, then, as an adaptation of *both* the 1953 source novel by L. P. Hartley and Melton Constable Hall. Adaptation theory has moved away from the notion of a single 'original' source and towards a consideration of ways in which, for example, a film or television programme may draw on multiple texts.[4] It is thus worth considering the deployment of locations as a key part of the adaptation process, and locations as sources in their own right, particularly when a film engages with their aesthetics and historical associations.

This chapter traces the genesis of *The Go-Between*'s screen landscapes, from Hartley's novel and contemporaneous debates about stately homes, through Losey's development of a new approach to filming the country estate, to the production of the film itself. It then analyses a key sequence in which the protagonist Leo (Dominic Guard) makes a fateful journey from the country house, Brandham Hall, to Black Farm, where he meets the farmer Ted Burgess (Alan Bates), a sequence in which the estate's spatial and ideological span is mapped. The chapter concludes with a consideration of how *The Go-Between* both echoed emerging forms of landscape historiography and paved the way for other country-estate films and television programmes. I am therefore concerned not only with the origins and aesthetics of the on-screen estate but also with how the novel and the film can each be situated in terms of both modes of practice in landscape culture and approaches to landscape historiography.

There has been little discussion of *The Go-Between*'s landscape gardens or its position in the history of country-estate cinema.[5] Indeed, the film's representation of rural landscape has been dismissed as antithetical to its politics. For instance, a reviewer in *Sight & Sound* argued that, 'despite the picture-postcard imagery, the filmmaker's real preoccupations – snobbery, sex, betrayal and violence – are always apparent'.[6] D. I. Grossvogel was more severe, contending that 'the picture's visual beauty distracts … from its sociological intent'.[7] In contrast, this chapter argues that the film's landscape shots are integral to its social commentary.

The Go-Between's tale of a boy who is mentally harmed by his experience of secretly carrying notes between Marian (Julie Christie) at the hall and her lower-class lover Burgess is indissoluble from the landscape in which this experience takes place, since the social structure that defines the relationship as illicit is shaped by landownership and embedded in the owned land. Back and forth, Leo goes between the rarefied aesthetics of the country house and the functional rural world of Black Farm. But the film does more than simply contrast the 'second nature' of agriculture with the 'third nature' of landscape gardens; Leo's journey reveals their interrelationship through the picturesque space that links them.[8]

Likewise, the fractured remembrance of the older Leo (Michael Redgrave), which is reflected in the disjointed intercutting of scenes from 1900 with his return to the area around Brandham in the 1950s, is inseparable from the setting. The remembrance appears to spring from the sight of the landscape through a car window in the film's first shot, which precedes the first line of the older Leo's voiceover: 'The past is a foreign country: they do things differently there.' This line derives from the first sentence of the source novel, with which L. P. Hartley not only points towards memory's spatial organisation (that is, the past as a country) but also denies the continuity of national history, by suggesting that the England of the past is a foreign land.[9] Indeed, the novel goes on to relate how the older Leo's exploration of his mind's hinterlands reveals a chasm between the optimism of the Victorian era and the disillusionment of mid-twentieth-century England.[10] At the same time, the process of regaining lost memories is reflected in the experience of viewing the country estate: it is only at the end of the novel that 'the south-west prospect of the Hall, long hidden from my memory, sprang into view'.[11] Is the 'view' ocular or mental? The older Leo has returned to Brandham, but it is not clear whether this sentence describes a literal sight of the forgotten prospect or an unearthed recollection: if the former, his memory has been refreshed by visiting the estate; if the latter, he has regained access to part of the estate through the release of a suppressed memory. Either way, it is evident that his explorations of his memory and of the geography of the estate are inextricable.

Hartley's geographical psyche: the country estate in print, 1927–53

How can we contextualise Hartley's conflation of the psyche, the country estate and national history? His novel resembles Evelyn Waugh's *Brideshead Revisited* (1945), which also contrasts the past and present of a country estate from the point of view of a middle-class outsider who recalls his visits to the house and, at the same time, reflects on social changes in England. Both novels end with a narrator struggling to come to terms with a downfall caused by his emotional investment in the house and its family, and with parts of the house under occupation (by the army in *Brideshead Revisited* and a girl's school in *The Go-Between*). The influence of Marcel Proust is evident in Waugh's and Hartley's treatment of remembrance as a spatial experience, but their explorations of country-estate aesthetics and history were, more specifically, part of a growing trend in England, which included Christopher Hussey's book *The Picturesque: Studies in Point of View* (1927) and Nikolaus Pevsner's 1940s articles on the picturesque.[12]

As Peter Mandler shows, while Hussey's aesthetic theory argued in favour of the aristocracy's continued residence in country estates, Pevsner's claim was that he 'could separate the houses from the vanished way of life they had once embodied'.[13] The emerging professional historiography of the country house and its gardens was initially characterised by these disparate political perspectives. The aesthetics of the country estate thus became a contested ideological ground, both in architectural historiography and in national politics; during 1949 and 1950, a Labour-initiated committee considered the preservation of country houses and discussed whether continued residence was desirable from the point of view of architectural maintenance.[14]

Hartley's reflection on the country estate and the conduct of its past inhabitants can, therefore, be seen as part of a tendency that became prominent in the 1940s, the era in which the preservation and democratisation of the stately home began to be seen as a concern of the welfare state. But his view of the estate also derived from personal experience. At least some elements of his novel were drawn from a visit he made as a teenager to Bradenham Hall, in Norfolk. How much of the book is autobiographical is open to conjecture,[15] but Hartley rooted the story in a recognisable geography and mobilised a toponymy of Norfolk to imbue the novel with local colour. The name Trimingham came from a Norfolk village, while the Beeston Castle to which Mrs Maudsley proposes a visit on Leo's birthday is most likely a reference to a village called Beeston, just north of Bradenham Hall.[16]

The name of the novel's house, 'Brandham Hall', bears a close orthographical resemblance to 'Bradenham Hall'. However, it also fulfils a proleptic role, anticipating the 'branding' of various characters by the events that unfold, including Leo's knee injury and his psychological trauma. This combination of an actual place name with symbolism is characteristic of the book's hybridisation of landscape writing. On the one hand, the novel contains large amounts of description of the estate's grounds and farmland. For instance, Leo's first walk alone, which ends in his accident sliding down the haystack at Ted's farm, is charted with detailed, positivist rural observation. Leo as narrator remarks on the distinctive features of the area, such as the corn stooks, whose shape is different from that of the stooks in Wiltshire, where he grew up. He also describes the physical sensations of walking through the landscape, such as the way he feels the sharp edges of the corn stubble against his ankles.[17]

On the other hand, Leo has a tendency to look superstitiously beyond appearances and contingency to try to find meaning and determinism. This 'magical thinking' leads him to see the Zodiac not only as a system that shapes and determines character, emotion and events but also as a schema that specifically corresponds to the world of Brandham Hall, so that Marian, for example, *is* the Virgin, or Virgo, in his eyes. His desire to find ordered meaning in events also affects his descriptions of the landscape, so that he often transforms metonyms into metaphors: at one point, he has a 'fancy' that Ted is a sheaf of corn 'the reaper had forgotten and that it would come back for him'.[18] Ted's contiguity to the harvested corn provides a metonym (in which the 'reaper' is a harvesting machine), which Leo translates into a metaphor that foreshadows Ted's suicide (in which the 'reaper' is death); contingency and contiguity become 'fate' in his eyes.

The younger Leo's inclination to find design and intention in events at Brandham can be seen as a desperate attempt to make sense of a world in which he often feels bewildered and powerless as a double outsider: a member of the middle class and a child. With his destruction of the deadly nightshade, Leo makes what he sees as a symbolic and magical intervention in the landscape, an attempt to remove illicit desire. That the older Leo as narrator reports every such 'fancy' his younger self had suggests that this inclination persists even as he tries to rationalise events that happened half a century ago. Consequently, the older Leo never manages to fully distinguish between his psychic landscape and the actual landscape of Brandham; his tendency towards metaphor and prolepsis to evoke fate is pathological, as it prevents the older Leo (and Hartley) from fully analysing the true determinant of tragedy at Brandham: the power of landowner-ship and its attendant hierarchies of class, culture and propriety.

The novel's emotive account of Leo's attempt to come to terms with the his-tory of the country estate nevertheless resonated with readers at a time when art historians and the welfare state were also attempting to come to terms with that history and its legacy in the form of surviving houses and gardens. Like Waugh's *Brideshead Revisited*, Hartley's novel became a bestseller and almost immediately attracted the interest of the film industry, which had also begun to revisit the country estate as a setting.[19]

Losey and the country estate on screen after 1945

Several country-estate films emerged in the 1940s, including *The Wicked Lady* (Leslie Arliss, 1945), *Jassy* (Bernard Knowles, 1947) and *Kind Hearts and Coronets* (Robert Hamer, 1949). All of these films were set in the past and foregrounded lav-ish period set and costume design, but their tales of outsiders struggling for power over and/or independence within country estates echoed contemporary concerns about the relationships between aristocrats and the lower classes, and about the potential role of country estates in post-war England: were they monuments to greed, violent oppression and snobbery or works of art worth preservation and democratisation? Many of the country-estate films have had it both ways, by pre-senting period aesthetics to audiences through plots about avarice and murder.

As was conventional at the time, the 1940s country-estate films were shot mainly in studios and included only a few location sequences, for exteriors only. These films thus only engaged to a limited extent with actual country estates; they were more concerned with the country estate's place in the social imagi-nary than with specific locations. Plans were made to adapt *The Go-Between* for cinema soon after the novel's publication, when Alexander Korda bought the rights.[20] Had these plans borne fruit, it is likely that the film would have con-sisted of a combination of studio sets and some exterior location shots. With such an approach, it would have been difficult to achieve anything that resembled Hartley's novel's grounding in local rural observation or its juxtaposition of Leo's objective description of the estate with his magical thinking. Director Anthony Asquith, who most likely became involved in the film after 1956, when Robert Velaise acquired the rights, had planned to use Wilbury Park, near Salisbury in Wiltshire, as a location for Brandham Hall.[21] This suggests that situating the events within the distinctive geography and architecture of Norfolk was not a high priority for Asquith. There is no evidence, either, to suggest that he intended to map Brandham precisely onto Wilbury Park by using the location's interiors as well as its grounds and facade.

While location shooting became much more widespread in the late 1950s and 1960s in Britain, in the wake of Free Cinema and the 'kitchen sink' films, studio–location combinations continued to be used in country-estate films. *The Grass Is Greener* (Stanley Donen, 1960) and *The Innocents* (Jack Clayton, 1961) both joined exterior location shooting with interior sets constructed at Shepperton Studios. The exception is Joseph Losey's first country-estate film, *The Gypsy and the Gentleman* (1958). Bringing the fresh perspective of a left-wing, émigré director to the country house, Losey shot not only exteriors but also some of the interiors at Shardeloes, Buckinghamshire, retaining where possible the location's dialogue between Robert Adam's interior decoration and Humphrey Repton's landscape gardens. Where the interiors were sets, production designer Richard Macdonald drew heavily on Adam's style to ensure architectural unity. The film is largely ignored now, but, despite weaknesses in its plot and performances, it is noteworthy for the rhetoric of place Losey constructed through innovative location work. *The Gypsy and the Gentleman* was the first country-estate film to be grounded in the kind of attention to architectural detail popularised by Nikolaus Pevsner.

By shooting as many of the interiors and exteriors as possible at one site, and basing set designs on the *oeuvre* of the location's architect, Losey and production designer Richard Macdonald replaced the eclectic pastiches that characterised studio set designs in the 1940s Gainsborough melodramas with a new emphasis on the materiality and integrity of historical architecture *in situ*. This historical-materialist approach culminates in a particularly striking shot linking the gardens with the house's interior. This shot is focalised by the gypsy Belle (Melina Mercouri), who gazes out of the house's windows and surveys the landscape garden she covets. At first, only the landscape is visible, but then the camera pulls back to show that we have been looking through a window with Belle. She is holding a riding crop, with which she strikes the window pane (and hence the landscape) as if to discipline it, before moving away. David Caute argues that Losey made Belle 'an undeviating bitch', but at this moment we are drawn into empathising with her desire to own the estate by the way the shot begins with an aesthetically pleasing view and then reveals that we have been sharing her gaze. This moment suggests that, despite (or perhaps because of) her immorality, she is the only character who seems to appreciate the estate as an aesthetic entity rather than simply as property or a home. The shot implies (and exploits) the attraction of landscape design, an aesthetic system that displays but also mystifies the power of landownership.

Scripting *The Go-Between*: time out of place

Joseph Losey had wanted to make *The Go-Between* as his second country-estate film as early as 1963, but legal problems delayed production by seven years.[22] In the intervening period, Losey developed his working partnership with Harold Pinter on *The Servant* (1963) and *Accident* (1967), both of which deconstructed

British hierarchies of wealth, class and culture. With *Accident*, Pinter, Losey and editor Reginald Beck began to experiment with flashbacks, intercut scenes and the separation of dialogue and image. These temporal experiments were extended in *The Go-Between*, also edited by Beck, and Pinter's 1972 script for an unrealised film of Proust's *À la recherche du temps perdu*.[23]

In adapting Hartley's novel, Pinter omitted all but the first line of the prologue and interspersed parts of the epilogue throughout the plot, so that between the sequences set in 1900 there are flashforwards to the 1950s.[24] We can tell one era from the other not by sequencing, in this case, but by how the same area looks different in each era: cars replace horses, clothes are different, and the weather is bad in the 1950s, whereas 1900 is sunlit until Leo's fateful birthday. By intercutting the two eras and using production design and the pathetic fallacy rather than chronological order to orientate the viewer, the filmmakers achieved a form suitable for what was just a theme in Hartley's novel: the spatialisation of memory.

As he revised his script, Pinter removed Hartley's description of the social position of the Maudsleys and their financial relationship with Trimingham (Edward Fox) as tenants: the film is not interested in how the Maudsleys have come to live in the house or whether the house is Trimingham's ancestral seat. Pinter also removed all but two references to the name of the hall. 'Brandham Hall' is never spoken in the dialogue and only appears in the letterhead above the note from Marian to Ted, which Leo reads and cries over, and on the envelope of the letter from his mother telling Leo that he cannot come home earlier when he is desperate to escape the world of the house. Marian's affair with Ted and Leo's mother's coldness are thus both implicated in the 'branding' that Leo is subjected to. However, by limiting references to the house's fictional name to these two shots, and removing exposition about ownership and tenantry from the dialogue, Pinter left Melton Constable Hall relatively unadorned. The on-screen landscape, then, is more than the setting for events remembered by Leo; it is a location, whose own aesthetics, materiality and place in history we are encouraged to dwell on. As well as the double articulation of time through Leo's experiences in 1900 and the 1950s, the film draws on the historical associations of the location, so that the imbrication of the story's two different eras reflects and adds more temporal layers to the location's traces of different epochs.

Adaptation by landscape

From the moment he began to devote himself to preparatory work on *The Go-Between* in early 1969, Losey was resolved to film entirely on location.[25] The decision to place so much visual emphasis on a small area in Norfolk, however, was taken as pre-production progressed. Losey and production designer Carmen Dillon initially considered at least twenty estates as possible locations, some of them outside Norfolk, including Asquith's intended chosen site, Wilbury Park.[26]

They solicited advice from Norfolk's major landowners and, by the autumn, Losey had decided to shoot in north-east Norfolk.[27]

One of the reasons for choosing this region was to document the area described in Hartley's novel. Indeed, Losey considered filming at Bradenham Hall, the house Hartley had stayed at, but decided against it: he recalls that 'the house and gardens had obviously been re-done and it was not the place my imagination searched'.[28] Instead, the production team selected Melton Constable Hall, about fifteen miles north of Bradenham. The house was dilapidated: the interior had to be redecorated. Outside, Dillon made plaster reproductions of the garden's statues, which were falling apart, and the crew sprayed the ailing lawns with green paint.[29] Because the house was not occupied and was in a state of neglect, Dillon and Losey could add the décor they felt was appropriate. They chose to preserve the estate's geography on screen as far as possible, though, rather than editing shots of several gardens together to give the impression of a whole.[30]

There were two exceptions: editing was used to link the estate's furthest woods with Ted's Black Farm, shot nearby at an old dairy farm on Hanworth Hall's grounds, where a corn field was also specially planted so that a period sail cutter could be filmed harvesting it.[31] The scene in which Mrs Maudsley (Margaret Leighton) interrogates Leo was shot at Blickling Hall's flower garden, nine miles east of Melton Constable Hall, because the latter's flower garden was no longer

8 Melton Constable Hall, in *The Go-Between*

extant.[32] Apart from these additions, Melton Constable Hall's integrity as a location was preserved. Indeed, one of the attractions of shooting there was that its interiors were suitable, so that Dillon and Losey would not have to compromise by combining exteriors and interiors from different locations. Above all, they could film through the house's windows and thus link the garden outside with the décor inside, as well as the characters' behaviour indoors and outdoors. For instance, when Leo and Marcus (Richard Gibson) stand at a window, through which we see figures formally arranged in a croquet game, the camera pans left, lingering on the formally arranged silverware. Etiquette and refined deportment make the adults in this world become like the objects they own. Such shots occur throughout the film.[33] Furthermore, by linking indoors and outdoors, the window shots establish the interiors as the centre of the estate, which is shown to stretch across a series of different landscapes towards Ted's farm. For Losey, who claimed his preoccupation with location filming was informed by the documentary tradition, Melton Constable Hall was almost a found object, in a found county:[34] 'Norfolk helped me a lot because Norfolk hasn't changed. The house was there, there was very little to adapt.'[35] Losey's words point to *The Go-Between*'s geographical discourse, but the film itself shows that Norfolk *has* changed.

History in the landscape: the picturesque

Landscapes in cinema are usually audio-visual and *The Go-Between*'s sound designer, Peter Hanford, was concerned to use a range of techniques to document the difference in the Norfolk countryside between 1900 and the present: in particular the ambient silence of an era before car ownership was widespread. He offset silences with occasional sounds of animals and train engines. He was also aware that the *raison d'être* of the town of Melton Constable had in 1900 been the railway and that the local railway was not in use by the late 1950s, so he made train whistles and engines evident in the 1900 sequences, adding historical context to the older Leo's journey to Marian's house by car from Norwich in the 1950s.[36] The sound design thus contributes to Losey's historical-materialist impulse. However, that impulse is balanced by an emphasis on narrative symbolism in the landscape, conveying how Leo feels. Thus, the black car he travels in is also a metaphorical hearse, suggesting he is mourning what he lost when he became 'all dried up inside', as Marian puts it. Drawing on Hartley's mixture of positivism and superstitious metaphor, the film sustains a dual rhetoric, weighing emotive symbolism against materialism.

This dual rhetoric extends to Losey's portrayal of the fate of the country house in the post-war era. At the very end of the film, when Leo's car drives away from the hall, the road curves around the house's terrace garden. The road, not visible in the 1900 scenes, is clearly a public road, separated from the estate by a fence. If the road demarcates the estate's border, a large part of

the landscape has been sold off since 1900. The loss is both historically plausible and figural.[37] The grounds look far less overbearing now they have been
diminished. The view of the estate from the car window contrasts diametrically with the high-angle 1900 shots of the landscape, which imply both Leo's
awe and the threat the estate and family pose to him. As he drives away, the
final message apparently undelivered, Leo's 1950s car window now frames and
contains the estate: only at the very last moment does the older Leo appear
to achieve a different perspective on and, therefore, a different power relation
with the estate.

The aforementioned contrasts between the 1900 and the 1950s Norfolk
reinforce the film's double articulation of time. However, evidence of a changing
landscape is also to be found within single 1900 sequences. The estate, as found
by Dillon and Losey, combined landscape designs from different periods. Next
to the house was a mid-nineteenth-century terrace garden.[38] Surrounding this,
there was a park, whose layout was largely as Capability Brown had landscaped it
between 1764 and 1769.[39] Typical of Brown's work, the park contained clumps
of trees and, in contrast with the formal terrace garden, was picturesque in its
contrived naturalness.[40] It also included a deer park, dating back to the enclosure
of the estate in 1290 but reshaped by Brown.[41] Beyond the park were neglected
areas, woodier and more picturesque, which Beck edited together with the area
around the farm at Hanworth.

Parts of the estate appear several times in the film, but there is one central
landscape sequence, during which Leo discovers Black Farm and injures his
knee. The sequence charts Leo's journey from the house to the farm, so all of
the above areas of the estate are shown. The sequence begins with Leo's returning to his room to incant a spell and ends with his being helped by Ted into
the farmhouse. It consists of a montage that is disjunctive in part, as the temporal and spatial relationships between five consecutive shots are unclear: Leo's
incantation; his (silent) reading of the thermometer; Marian lying in the grass;
Leo walking (shot in a high-angle zoom-out); and the deer park. We have no
indication whether the shots of Marian and the deer park are from Leo's optical
point of view or not.[42] However, connections between the shots are implied; it
seems as if the reading of the thermometer continues the incantation, which
conjures up Marian. We could infer that Leo makes the traditional equation of
female body with landscape and imagines his exploration of the grounds as an
exploration of Marian's body.[43] On the other hand, Marian's relaxed pose suggests confident possession of the grounds, cuing a zoom-out that makes Leo
become minuscule. The historical process of enclosure, alluded to in the next
shot, which is of the deer park, is re-enacted by the zoom-out, as Leo is effectively enclosed by the 'improved' landscape. Leo's desire for control through
casting a spell – his magical thinking – is at odds with the long history of power
relations embedded in the landscape

These five shots and the sequence as a whole are lent cohesiveness by Michel Legrand's ominous non-diegetic music, which begins before the spell and ends as Leo arrives at Black Farm, implying a causal relationship between the spell and what follows, including the knee injury and Leo's encounter with Ted, which will lead to the message-carrying and, ultimately, Mrs Maudsley's discovery of the illicit relationship and Ted's suicide. The emotive bridge supplied by the music thus suggests the older Leo's belief that the spell led to the injury. Later in the film, when the aged Marian mentions her grandson's conviction that he is 'under some sort of spell or curse', the older Leo averts his eyes, his nod, in agreement to her 'that's just plain silly', clearly forced; the older Leo still believes in his curse and its supposed consequences. We have to read the older Leo's feelings from such gestures and the mood conveyed by the score, because, unlike the novel, the film is not explicitly narrated by him. We hear a couple of maxims spoken by him, but they are more commentary than narration. The images from 1900 seem to emerge from his memory or subconscious: in conversation with Michael Ciment, Losey describes the film's double articulation of time as 'subliminal'.[44] Later in the interview, Ciment resurrects the term to characterise some of the film's shots, including those featuring deer.[45] The term is appropriate for this sequence's dual logic of staccato editing and implied causality, which suggests at once fragments of memory and a sublimated attribution of coherent meaning to the remembered events.

However, the landscape sequence that links the incantation with the injury also separates the two, distancing them. The staccato editing and Leo's non-chalant walking pace stress this ironic distance. If the sublimated implication is that Leo's spell is responsible for the injury, the interpolation of the landscape scenes suggests, on another level, that the landscape is in fact the precondition of Leo's injury. The shot that implies a relation between Marian's body and the landscape significantly precedes the shot in which Leo's body is effectively enclosed by a zoom-out, implicating Marian (and her position in the estate) in this symbolic enclosure of Leo and, by association, the historical enclosure of the countryside. The hidden axe and the haystack are the results of a cultivation that is both determined by and maintains enclosure. Leo treats the farm as a playground and is consequently punished when the tools of cultivation are unveiled. An alternative causal chain therefore subtly links the sequence: from Marian in the landscape, to the process of enclosure, to Black Farm, to Leo's injury and finally to Ted's arrival on the scene. Losey thus deconstructs the picturesque's historical function of naturalising land-ownership: to make landscapes look like 'natural' spaces rather than controlled property. The landscape conceals its design and its violence, along with the power relations that create them: the very conditions that lead Leo to become harmed physically and emotionally, so that, in Leo's eyes, it is his curses that cause harm, including his own injuries and, ultimately, Ted's suicide. However, it is Leo's misguided linking of curse and knee injury, across the intervening landscape, that makes available the alternative: a materialist representation of landscape power relations.

The landscape that we see Leo wander through, from the house towards Black Farm, is increasingly picturesque. The historical picturesque, with its 'natural' excess, roughness and concealments, often acted as a screen, hiding boundary lines of estates and thereby obfuscating the differences between labour and leisure, between poverty and property, while the natural appearance of the landscape gardens hid their status as private culture, thus naturalising ownership. The most picturesque part of Brandham separates the park from the farm and blurs the distinction between the farm's functional landscapes and the emphatically aestheticised design of the park. Closer to the house, away from prying eyes, the openly artificial formal terrace garden more overtly signifies control of the land and provides an appropriately refined setting for upper-class deportment.

By following a trajectory across the estate – from the house's interior, through windows, across the terrace garden and the Brownian park, and through wooded areas – Losey could trace an aesthetic and ideological chain across the landscape. Towards and through the picturesque, he reveals the violence (animal blood, Leo's injured knee, Ted's suicide) and cultivation that seem beyond the estate's gardens but that in fact underpin the whole estate. The 'Old Garden', played by Melton Constable Hall's pre-Brownian kitchen garden, where Ted and Marian have sex, acts as a picturesque enclave near the house's terrace garden: a reminder that the violence and differences concealed by picturesqueness are at the heart of the estate as well as at its periphery.

In the film's ironic symbolism, Leo, the figure in the landscape, emerges as a new, human incarnation of the *genius loci* of the picturesque tradition: he performs within and takes on elements of the landscape but in turn alters the landscape.[46] That is, he is wounded in the landscape but in the process unwittingly exposes its apparatus of cultivation. In this way, *The Go-Between* presents its historical landscape as a socio-economic construction that is ultimately instrumental in the downfall of its *genius loci*. Leo is reconstituted in a disfigured form in the 1950s, as an old man whom Marian describes as being 'all dried up inside': Leo's knee wound anticipates this later disfigurement, the hidden axe serving as a symbol for the dangers concealed beneath the country estate's aesthetics.

The spell/axe sequence implicates Marian in the trauma Leo suffers. However, the film also positions her as a victim in the socio-economic structure of the estate. In a later scene, we see a deer herd race through the park and then a reverse shot of Marian and Leo, watching through a window. An exchange follows:

Leo: Why don't you marry Ted?
Marian: I can't. I can't – can't you see why?
Leo: Why are you marrying Hugh?
Marian: Because I must. I must. I've got to.

Marian's 'can't you see why?' can be seen as a reference to the deer park she and Leo are gazing at. Marian cannot marry Ted because she would lose her privileged place in the landscape. Like the deer, whose freedom is illusory, Marian is enclosed as part of the demesne's aesthetics, a marriageable asset prepared for Trimingham's consumption. She must choose between this closed existence and one beyond the estate's comfortable confines, in a space she might well imagine as like the one in the painting hanging behind them: an unyielding sublime landscape utterly unlike the view from the window.

Conclusion

The Go-Between uses the narrative arc of its figure in a landscape to expatiate on the power relations of the country estate. If Hartley's geographical psyche reflected to some extent the place of the country estate in both architectural history and the post-war social imaginary, Losey's film foreshadowed and complemented the revisionist landscape historiography that emerged in the 1970s and that formed the first major Marxist contributions to the field: the television series and book *Ways of Seeing* (1972);[47] John Barrell's *The Idea of Landscape and the Sense of Place 1730–1840: An Approach to the Poetry of John Clare* (1972) and *The Dark Side of the Landscape: The Rural Poor in English Painting 1730–1840* (1980);[48] and Raymond Williams's *The Country and the City* (1973).[49] These texts all discussed representations of figure and landscape from a socio-economic perspective.

Meanwhile, the film's focus on one country-estate location set a precedent that was followed by *Brideshead Revisited* (Michael Lindsay Hogg and Charles Sturridge, 1981) and *The Draughtsman's Contract* (Peter Greenaway, 1982), although these films could also exploit tourist knowledge of locations whereas *The Go-Between* democratised landscapes that no member of the public had seen in such great detail.[50] Heritage criticism has tended to see shots of country estates in British film and television as ideological extensions of the tourist industry, but *The Go-Between*, *Brideshead Revisited*, *The Draughtsman's Contract* and later films and programmes not only explore locations extensively but also offer critical commentaries on those locations' histories, through narratives about characters who are harmed by their visits to estates.

Leo, the figure in *The Go-Between*'s landscape, moves through the estate as no other character in the film does and, indeed, as no character had walked through a location in any country-house film before *The Go-Between*. It has been argued that causality plays only a minor role in the film,[51] but Leo's movements unveil the socio-economic links across the setting and location. Through Leo, the film comments on the ideological causalities at work in a country estate in 1900. The estate's span, both spatial and ideological, is documented via his meandering. At the same time, Leo's perception is wounded; as an old man he still imagines that a mystical causality underpins the events on the estate and therefore fails to realise the full truth, until perhaps the last moment, when his car takes him away from the hall. The film opposes his mysticism with naturalistic rural observation and historical-materialist social commentary, using innovative location work to achieve a new cinematic perspective on the country estate.

Notes

1 Heritage critics have often argued that shots of country houses and gardens inter-rupt and distract from narrative, but this actually applies to very few – if any – films. For an archetypal heritage approach, see Andrew Higson, 'Re-presenting the national past: nostalgia and pastiche in the heritage film', in Lester D. Friedman (ed.), *Fires Were Started: British Cinema and Thatcherism* (London: Wallflower, 2nd edition, 2006), pp. 91–109. For a persuasive attack on this kind of approach, see Sheldon Hall, 'The wrong sort of cinema: refashioning the heritage film debate', in Robert Murphy (ed.), *The British Cinema Book* (London: British Film Institute, 2nd edi-tion, 2001), pp. 191–9. The few essays that discuss gardens in British film include Mark Broughton, 'Landscape gardens in *The Ruling Class*', in Paul Newland (ed.), *Don't Look Now: British Cinema in the 1970s* (Bristol and Chicago, IL: Intellect, 2010), pp. 241–51; Kenneth Helphand, 'Set and location: the garden and film', in Marc Treib (ed.), *Representing Landscape Architecture* (London and New York: Taylor Francis, 2008), pp. 204–23.

2 The only exceptions were some inserts of the deadly nightshade, filmed at Elstree stu-dios rather than at Melton Constable Hall, because re-takes of the plant were needed after the shoot had ended: Christopher Hartop, *Norfolk Summer: Making The Go-Between* (Cambridge: John Adamson, 2011), p. 55.

3 'Programme for the Royal Norfolk Première of The Go-Between, ABC Cinema, Norwich, 29 October 1971' (Norwich: Friends of the Norwich Churches and the Norfolk Branch of the Council for the Protection of Rural England, 1971), p. 6; this programme is item JWL/1/18/7 in the BFI's Joseph Losey Special Collection. Hereafter, codes with the prefix JWL/1 indicate that sources are from this collection.

4 See Sarah Cardwell, *Adaptation Revisited: Television and the Classic Novel* (Manchester and New York: Manchester University Press, 2002), pp. 25–8.

5 Charles Shiro Tashiro's article on the film's production design considers the way in which Losey uses windows and doors to symbolise thresholds between binary oppo-sitions but does not comment in any detail on the gardens: Charles Shiro Tashiro, '"Reading" design in *The Go-Between*', *Cinema Journal*, 33: 1 (1993), pp. 17–34.

6 'The Go-Between', *Sight & Sound*, 10: 9 (2000), p. 61.

7 D. I. Grossvogel, 'Losey and Hartley', *Diacritics*, 4: 3 (1974), p. 56.

8 On the origin of the terms 'second nature' (functional landscapes shaped by human intervention) and 'third nature' (gardens), see John Dixon Hunt, *The Picturesque Garden in Europe* (London: Thames & Hudson, 2003), pp. 3–4.

9 L. P. Hartley, *The Go-Between* (London: Penguin, 1997), p. 5.

10 See Douglas Brooks-Davies, 'Introduction', in L. P. Hartley, *The Go-Between* (London: Penguin, 1997), pp. xi–xxix.

11 Hartley, *The Go-Between*, p. 261.

12 Christopher Hussey, *The Picturesque: Studies in a Point of View* (London and New York: G. P. Putnam's Sons, 1927); Nikolaus Pevsner, 'Price on picturesque

planning', *Architectural Review*, 95 (1944), pp. 47–50; Nikolaus Pevsner, 'The genesis of the picturesque', *Architectural Review*, 96 (1944), pp. 136–46.

13 Peter Mandler, *The Fall and Rise of the Stately Home* (New Haven and London: Yale University Press, 1997), p. 332.

14 Mandler, *The Fall and Rise of the Stately Home*, pp. 341–2.

15 James Lees-Milne, *Diaries, 1971–1983* (London: John Murray, 2007), p. 320; Adrian Wright, *Foreign Country: The Life of L. P. Hartley* (London: André Deutsch, 1996), pp. 30–3.

16 Douglas Brooks-Davies, 'Notes', in L. P. Hartley, *The Go-Between* (London: Penguin, 1997), p. 274 n. 35 and p. 291 n. 6.

17 Hartley, *The Go-Between*, p. 71.

18 Hartley, *The Go-Between*, p. 93.

19 Robert Murray Davis, *Mischief in the Sun: The Making and Unmaking of 'The Loved One'* (Troy, NY: Whitson Publishing Company, 1999), *passim*; Brooks-Davies, 'Introduction', p. xii.

20 David Caute, *Joseph Losey: A Revenge on Life* (London: Faber and Faber, 1994), p. 254; Hartop, *Norfolk Summer*, p. 18.

21 Letter from Joseph Losey to the Dowager Lady St. Just, 17 February 1969, JWL/1/18/13.

22 Caute, *Joseph Losey*, p. 254.

23 Paul Newland and Gavrik Losey, 'An involuntary memory? Joseph Losey, Harold Pinter and Marcel Proust's *À la recherche du temps perdu*', in Dan North (ed.), *Sights Unseen: Unfinished British Films* (Cambridge: Cambridge Scholars Publishing, 2008), pp. 33–51.

24 The film's conception of time is a complex issue and has been dissected at length. See, in particular, Colin Gardner, *Joseph Losey* (Manchester and New York: Manchester University Press, 2004), pp. 134–79; Edward T. Jones, 'Summer of 1900: *A la récherche* of *The Go-Between*', *Literature/Film Quarterly*, 1: 2 (1973), pp. 154–60; James Palmer and Michael Riley, 'Time and the structure of memory in *The Go-Between*', *College Literature*, 5: 3 (1978), pp. 219–27; James Palmer and Michael Riley, *The Films of Joseph Losey* (New York: Cambridge University Press, 1993), pp. 90–116.

25 Letter from Joseph Losey to Lord Dyvenor, 4 February 1969, JWL/1/18/13.

26 Joseph Losey and Carmen Dillon, '*The Go-Between*: suggested locations' (n.d.), JWL/1/18/13.

27 Letter from Dillon to Lady Nichols, 21 November 1969, JWL/1/18/13.

28 Joseph Losey, 'Norfolk jackets: the making of *The Go-Between*', in Angus Wilson (ed.), *Writers of East Anglia* (London: Secker & Warburg, 1977), pp. 3–8; p. 5.

29 Edith de Rham, *Joseph Losey* (London: André Deutsch, 1991), p. 266; Hartop, *Norfolk Summer*, p. 29.

30 By the 1970s, creative geography was, in country-estate films, something directors either avoided whenever possible or drew attention to. Two later films, *The Ruling Class* (Peter Medak, 1972) and *Barry Lyndon* (Stanley Kubrick, 1975) used combinations of locations reflexively, making a virtue of atomism. See Broughton, 'Landscape gardens in *The Ruling Class*', pp. 241–51.

31 Pressbook for *The Go-Between* (London: Columbia Pictures, 1971); Hartop, *Norfolk Summer*, pp. 27–8, p. 39.

32 Caute, *Joseph Losey*, p. 256. The British Film Institute's Joseph Losey Special Collection contains his copy of Blickling Hall's tourist guide: James Lees-Milne, *Blickling Hall* (Stoke Ferry, Norfolk: National Trust, 1970), JWL/1/18/6.

33 Much has been written about the ubiquitous windows in *The Go-Between*: their role in the film's treatment of subjectivity and voyeurism, as well as their metaphoric values as 'thresholds' and/or 'barriers': see Thomas Elsaesser, '*The Go-Between*', *Monogram*, 3 (1972), p. 18; James Palmer and Michael Riley, 'Time and the structure of memory in *The Go-Between*', *College Literature*, 5: 3 (1978), pp. 220–1; Tashiro, ' "Reading" design in *The Go-Between*', pp. 19, 33.

34 Caute, *Joseph Losey*, pp. 256, 323; Losey, 'Norfolk jackets', p. 7. The village scenes were shot at locations (Thornage and Heydon) only a few miles from Melton Constable: Hartop, *Norfolk Summer*, pp. 7, 45. Heydon was also something of a 'found' location: the village was privately owned, preserved as if part of an estate. For Marian's dower house, seen in many of the 1950s sequences, as well as in the 1900 sequence during which Leo goes to church and is given his first message to carry by Trimingham, Losey used the village's actual Dower House.

35 Michael Ciment, *Conversations with Losey* (London and New York: Methuen, 1985), p. 154.

36 Letter from Peter Handford to Joseph Losey, 9 August 1970, JWL/1/18/13.

37 As Mandler points out, most of the houses that were not sold off or demolished in the 1950s were maintained only by auctioning off significant parts of the estate's art collections and land. Mandler, *The Fall and Rise of the Stately Home*, pp. 356–68.

38 Nikolaus Pevsner and Bill Wilson, *The Buildings of England, Norfolk I: Norwich and North-East* (London: Penguin, 1997), p. 615.

39 Pevsner and Wilson, *The Buildings of England, Norfolk I*, p. 612; Dorothy Stroud, *Capability Brown* (London: Faber and Faber, 1975), p. 112.

40 Brown's work was often criticised by theorists of the picturesque, but, on the extent to which Brown's work was picturesque, see Hunt, *The Picturesque Garden in Europe*, pp. 38–40.

41 On Capability Brown and the deer park at Melton Constable, see Roger Turner, *Capability Brown and the Eighteenth-Century English Landscape* (Chichester: Phillimore, 1999), p. 184.

42 In general, the sequence plays with point of view, sometimes following Leo, sometimes anticipating him, sometimes focalised by him. On the film's ambiguous articulation of point of view, see Tashiro, ' "Reading" design in *The Go-Between*', pp. 19–20.

43 As Karen Lang points out, there is a long history, evidenced in male writing associated with the emergence of the British picturesque garden, of the passive woman seen as corresponding to the landscape: Karen Lang, 'The body in the garden', in Jan Birksted (ed.), *Landscapes of Memory and Experience* (London: Spon Press, 2000), pp. 107–28; p. 107.

44 Ciment, *Conversations with Losey*, p. 304.

45 Ciment, *Conversations with Losey*, p. 311.

46 Alexander Pope urged Lord Burlington to 'Consult the genius of the place' – that is, its intrinsic character – when designing 'improvements'. Different versions of this idea appeared throughout the eighteenth century, in, for example, Capability Brown's evaluation of the estate's 'capabilities' and Uvedale Price's avowed belief that buildings should be designed to match their surroundings. Nikolaus Pevsner had modernised the idea of the spirit of the place in his 1940s and 1950s work on the picturesque, arguing that this and other principles of English landscape-garden design were apparent in British modern town planning: Nikolaus Pevsner, *The Englishness of English Art* (London: Penguin, 1997), pp. 178, 181.

47 John Berger and the series' director, Mike Dibb, deconstruct and historicise Gainsborough's *Mr and Mrs Andrews*, a painting which, thirty years later, was still at the heart of debates about the Marxist analysis of the power relations between landed figures and eighteenth-century country estates. See *Ways of Seeing* (Mike Dibb, BBC, 1972); John Barrell, 'Mr and Mrs Equivalent', *Times Literary Supplement* (8 November 2002), p. 21; John Berger, *Ways of Seeing* (London: BBC and Penguin, 1972), pp. 106–8; Michael Rosenthal and Martin Myrone (eds), *Gainsborough* (London: Tate Publishing, 2002), pp. 62–3.

48 John Barrell, *The Idea of Landscape and the Sense of Place 1730–1840: An Approach to the Poetry of John Clare* (Cambridge: Cambridge University Press, 1972); John Barrell, *The Dark Side of the Landscape: The Rural Poor in English Painting 1730–1840* (Cambridge: Cambridge University Press, 1980).

49 Raymond Williams, *The Country and the City* (London: Hogarth Press, 1973).

50 Unlike Castle Howard (the main location for *Brideshead*) and Groombridge Place (the main location for *Draughtsman*), Melton Constable Hall has never been open to the public.

51 Palmer and Riley, *The Films of Joseph Losey*, p. 93.

6

'Here is Wales, there England': contested borders and blurred boundaries in *On the Black Hill*

Kate Woodward

Ynom mae y Clawdd a phob ymwybod,
y tir hwn a godwyd
rhyngom a'r gwastadedd blin.

The dyke is within us, and all consciousness;
this land has been raised
between ourselves and the threatening plain.[1]

It is dawn. The moon is still visible, and rolling hills thick with morning mist emerge through the twilight, stretching back as far as the eye can see. The camera slowly pans, revealing miles of ethereal hills bathed in a soft pink glow, accompanied by a slow crescendo of the dawn chorus. It settles firmly on one hill, and the titles 'ON THE BLACK HILL' are inserted, visually mapping the space in which the narrative of the film will be played out and highlighting the importance of the geographical specificity of the location. Despite this seemingly bucolic and verdant opening to *On the Black Hill* (Andrew Grieve, 1987), the film quickly resists simple categorisation in terms of how it represents rural landscape. Moments later, the camera swoops above green hills, the word 'WALES' appearing on the screen, before turning 180 degrees and ascending a mountain ridge, revealing the land lying beyond and beneath it: 'ENGLAND'.[2] In the course of this chapter I will argue that *On the Black Hill* opposes the idea that rural films use land 'as a metonymy for national territory'.[3] It is not the nation that is this film's primary concern but rather a tantalising space where contradiction and ambiguity reign: the ambivalent territory lying both between and within two nations – specifically, the borderscape between England and Wales. Employing post-colonial ideas concerning spatiality and reflecting on ways of thinking that are specific to the Welsh language, such as *cynefin*, I will demonstrate the ways in which *On the Black Hill* seeks not to enunciate the national but instead to interrogate the concept of borders, both geographical and physical, both external and internal.

Andrew Grieve's adaptation of Bruce Chatwin's celebrated novel, funded by the British Film Institute, British Screen and Channel 4, depicts the rural lives of the identical twin brothers Lewis and Benjamin Jones (Robert and Mike Gwilym) over a period of 80 years.[4] Shot in seven weeks in Llanfihangel Nant Brân, near Sennybridge, and around the Black Mountains, Hay-on-Wye and Crickhowell, the narrative takes place within a square mile of The Vision, the farmhouse where the twins live all their lives. The family home sits on the border between England and Wales, and therefore the legal, administrative border runs, literally, through the film: through the lives of the brothers and through the community in which they live. Crucially the brothers are signified by name, accent and culture as being Welsh, and therefore the film offers a specifically Welsh perspective on the border.

On the Black Hill could be described as falling within the parameters of rural cinema as defined by Catherine Fowler and Gillian Helfield. For them, the three prominent features shared by rural cinema are the importance of the land, the connection to a way of life and cultural traditions associated with the land and the past, and the films function as an ideological hub that allows for the intersection of socio-political issues and conflicts.[5] Indeed, it is generally accepted that the countryside, when represented in films located in the rural milieu, operates as an embodiment of the nation, as national identities are often largely defined by landscapes.[6] As I will demonstrate, in *On the Black Hill* the iconography of the land and of the rural way of life has very strong ties to 'the national' in a Welsh context. But, although it alludes to ideas about the Welsh landscape, the main concern of *On the Black Hill* is engaging imaginatively with ideas of the border, to the extent that the film is fuelled by the tension between visions of cartographic and material certainty and the phenomenological experience of lives lived in an ambiguous, liminal space.[7]

Landscape and national identity

'Landscape creates nations', said Jan Morris, 'and nowhere is this truism truer than in Wales, *Cymru*. Almost everything about Wales has been decreed by its terrain; certainly if the countryside had been different the Welsh people as we know them would never had existed.'[8] For the cultural geographer Denis Cosgrove, 'landscape is not merely the world we see, it is a construction, a composition of that world. Landscape is a way of seeing the world.'[9] In suggesting that landscape is a construction but also a way of seeing the world, Cosgrove draws attention to landscape as a product of human perception. This 'way of seeing' interprets landscape as a visual ideology that plays a crucial role in the invention and imagining of nations. Jan Penrose talks of a 'mystical bond' that is formed between people and place, to create an 'immutable whole' that is the nation.[10] In their work on the national construction of social space, Colin Williams and Anthony D. Smith claim that, 'Whatever else it may be, nationalism is a struggle for control of land; whatever else the nation may be, it is nothing if not a mode of constructing and interpreting social space.'[11] The ideology of nationalism transforms land into national territory. Far from producing a static and fixed space, this is a dynamic process in which images are perpetually constructed and contested. Particular features of the landscape may become emblematic of national identity, achieving, as Stephen Daniels has put it, 'the status of national icons'.[12] These are special spatial communities where inhabitants can trace their roots to ancestral landscapes.[13] National identity is therefore linked to a particular territorial space with specific geographical features. Another important factor in the creation of nations is the formation of boundaries and the delimitation of maps, which play a crucial role in defining those who belong and those who are 'Other'. Wales, without the political apparatus of the traditional nation-state and with a border (partially straddled by the Black Mountains) that remained legally unconfirmed until 1972, has long been considered an 'imagined' and 'invented' nation, and the Welsh landscape has sat at the heart of discourses of philosophy, politics, painting and poetry in Wales.[14]

The border and imaging the Welsh landscape

The act of traversing the Welsh–English border has played a pivotal role in the imaging of the Welsh landscape. Following the Acts of Union in 1536, Wales was opened up to tourists from England who were equally fascinated and appalled by the Welsh mountains.[15] In an early travelogue in 1770, Wales was described as 'the fag end of creation' by Daniel Defoe, who later noted the way that Wales almost jeopardised his plans to tour the whole of Britain, describing it as 'so full of horror that we thought to have given over the enterprise, and have left Wales out of our circuit'.[16] The hills encountered at Brecknockshire were 'horrid and frightful'; Glamorganshire he considered 'mountainous to an extremity' with names 'seem'd as barbarous to us, who spoke no *Welch*, as the Hills themselves'.[17] Snowdon, England and Wales's highest peak, was 'a monstrous height' over which 'even Hannibal himself wou'd have found it impossible to march his army'.[18] In 1740 Archbishop Thomas Herring described Wales as being 'like the rubbish of creation'.[19]

Later, the two volumes of Thomas Pennant's *A Tour in Wales* (published in 1778 and 1783 respectively) were 'perhaps the single most important textual influence upon English attitudes toward travel in Wales'.[20] For the first time, a favourable picture of north Wales was presented, with Pennant's narrative replacing the 'horrid' vision of Defoe's work with a 'romantic' version, reimagining Wales in ways that were alluring to burgeoning Romantic sensibilities. The perception of the Welsh landscape therefore changed, with its romantic craggy mountains and lush waterfalls proving a magnet for artists and its topographical and cultural differences appealing to tourists, writers and painters alike.[21] Following William Gilpin's influential volume *Observations on the River Wye* (1782), parts of Wales became known as the cradle of the picturesque. Lured by the landscape described in Pennant's volume, and his interest in myths and history, a young J. M. W. Turner visited Wales and painted the best-known example of the picturesque in the Welsh landscape, the Hafod estate in Ceredigion, which was developed by Thomas Johnes, an advocate of the movement. The interaction between those from both sides of the border has therefore heavily influenced the way that the Welsh landscape has been perceived.

Welsh landscape on film

The advent of cinema continued and cemented the Romantic way of seeing Wales. Twenty-six fictional films, including at least fourteen features, were set or part-set (not merely shot) in Wales between 1912 and 1927, as technological advances led to British- and Hollywood-based crews venturing to outside locations.[22] Despite this coinciding with an explosion of industrial prosperity that subsequently ignited political and social struggles in Wales, it certainly was not the urban south that drew the attention of filmmakers. It was rather Wales's more photogenic locations, its rugged mountains and its rolling hills that captured their imaginations, and therefore they perpetuated the traditional 'way of seeing' Wales that had developed earlier in the field of visual art.[23] *A Welsh Singer* (Henry Edwards, 1915), starring Florence Turner, the famous Vitagraph girl, *By Berwen Banks* (Sidney Morgan, 1920) and *Torn Sails* (A. V. Bramble, 1920) were all adapted from the romantic rural novels of Allen Raine. Others clearly reflected the locations in their titles, such as *The Pedlar of Penmaenmawr* (Sydney Northcote, 1912), *The Belle of Bettwys-y-Coed* (Sydney Northcote, 1912), *The Smuggler's Daughter of Anglesea* (*sic*) (Sydney Northcote, 1912), *The Witch of the Welsh Mountains* (Sydney Northcote, 1912), *Gwyneth of the Welsh Hills* (Floyd Martin Thornton, 1921) and *Love in the Welsh Hills* (Bernard Dudley, 1921). Even when Hollywood's eye was turned to Wales's mining communities during the 1940s and 1950s with films such as *Proud Valley* (Pen Tennyson, 1940), *How Green Was My Valley* (John Ford, 1941) and *Valley of Song* (Gilbert Gunn, 1953), the representation of Wales continued to be that of an unknown, exoticised 'Other'. In later films it was a land in need of mapping – in *An Englishman Who Went Up a Hill and Came Down a Mountain* (Christopher Monger, 1994) – or a peripheral land, geographically distant from the political and economic 'centre', as in *A Run for Your Money* (Charles Frend, 1949) and *Very Annie Mary* (Sara Sugarman, 2001).

Cynefin and cognitive mapping

On the Black Hill offers a very different representation of landscape to the entrenched romantic vision that operates merely as a picturesque backdrop to the characters' lives in many of the aforementioned films. Indeed, *On the Black Hill* engages with 'spatial notions' that are specific to Wales, which articulate the relationship between people and place that are distinct to the Welsh language. *Cynefin, milltir sgwâr* and *bro* are terms that signify specifically Welsh ways of engaging with spatiality. These are words that evoke Welsh cognitive maps that are 'not precise territorial zones, rigorously defined, delineated and patrolled'.[24] The farm (The Vision) and its immediate surrounding area operate as the characters' *cynefin*. Bedwyr Lewis Jones locates *cynefin* in the place where we were brought up, the area that impresses itself on us during the formative period between five and fifteen years old.[25] The word itself implies a dwelling place, or a family seat, but it has far wider connotations than that of a building.[26] *Cynefin* is not defined by clearly demarcated borders, nor is it fixed territorial space. It varies from person to person. Neither is its interest in the picturesque. It is a Welsh concept that describes lived landscape, not scenery; it is 'the Welshman's first and foremost window on the world'.[27] This then is a habitat or territory with people at its core, where Wales is seen as a tapestry of *cynefinoedd* where men and women have lived out their lives, where the landscape is a major component of the drama of human life.[28] Bedwyr Lewis Jones sees land and language as the two forces that tie Welsh speakers to their *cynefin*, and his argument that place is constructed by a community through language is taken further by the philosopher J. R. Jones. In his thesis on land and language, *Prydeindod* (Britishness, 1966), he roots the national community within the Welsh landscape.[29] Jones's concept of 'cydymdreiddiad tir ac iaith' (the interpenetration of land and language) 'suggests that a thousand secret chords bind a people to the land, and that centuries of continuous occupation confirm the land as the vessel which safeguards and nurtures all cultural traditions'.[30]

The narrative of *On the Black Hill* takes place within 'a few square miles', with the family hardly ever leaving the farm.[31] D. J. Williams referred to the power of the *milltir sgwâr* (the square mile) in his memoir *Hen Dŷ Ffarm* (1953), in which he speaks of the area in which he grew up:

> Dysgais ei charu, mi gredaf, cyn dysgu cerdded. Ni theithiais y darn yma o wlad erioed … heb deimlo rhyw gynnwrf rhyfedd yn cerdded fy natur – cynnwrf megis un yn teimlo penllanw ei etifeddiaeth ddaearyddol ac ysbrydol yn dygyfor ei enaid. Dyma wlad fy nhadau mewn gwirionedd. Fe'm meddiannwyd i ganddi; ac, yn ôl y gynneddf syml a roddwyd i mi, fe'i meddiannwyd hithau gennyf innau. … Y brogarwch *cyfyng* hwn, os mynner, a'i ganolbwynt yn y 'filltir sgwâr', yn Hen Ardal fach fy mebyd.[32]

> I learnt to love it, I believe, before I learnt to walk. I have never travelled this part of the country … without feeling strangely stirred in my nature, like one who feels the

full tide of his terrestrial and spiritual inheritance surging through his soul. This, actually, is the land of my fathers. It took possession of me, and I have taken possession of it in accordance with that simple property of my nature that responds. ... This close homeland love, if you will have your way, concentrated upon the square mile in the old locality of my boyhood.[33]

The renowned poet T. H. Parry-Williams in his poem 'Hon' (This One) addressing his place of birth, felt that:

Ond wele, rhwng llawr a ne'
Mae lleisiau a drychiolaethau ar hyd y lle.

But see, between earth and sky,
There are voices and phantoms in all these places.[34]

Later, in 'Bro' (a neighbourhood, district or *Heimat*), he imagines the landscape around Snowdonia – his *cynefin* – responding to news of his death and claims that 'Mae darnau ohonof ar wasgar hyd y fro' (There are bits of me scattered all over that land).[35]

On the Black Hill depicts such a landscape, one that cannot be separated from the lives lived there. Amos Jones (Bob Peck) is a man of the soil. His flesh bears the marks of a life toiling on the land. He is seen early in the film ploughing the fields with horses in the mist and running freely and wildly through the landscape to reach Mary Latimer (Gemma Jones) when he hears that her father has died. Raymond Williams argued that 'a working country is hardly ever a landscape. The very idea of landscape implies separation and observation.'[36] There is no such separation and observation for Amos. Indeed, his relationship with Mary is one that arises from his relationship with the land. On a walk early in their courtship, she is distressed when she accidentally steps on a lark's nest, breaking the tiny eggs inside. He consoles her by telling her that 'there will be other nests' and promises her that he knows where to find them. He gently whispers into her ear his intimate knowledge of the surrounding land, and his intention to show her its riches, including 'badgers, berries in the heather and mushrooms standing in rings', and it is this that seems to seal their relationship. It is alone to the mountains he goes to profess his love, by shouting her maiden name to the skies, and then her would-be married name, which echoes powerfully around the hills. Ned Thomas describes this intimate, almost sensual relationship with landscape when he talks of places 'where fields and rivers and hills and villages conserve old and human feelings, and where the consciousness of these things is still widespread and can move one like the contour of a loved face'.[37]

Despite the fact that the narrative is rooted in the soil and terrain within a very limited geographical space and a specific landscape, The Vision is also essentially a worldly place, culturally connected to the global. For example, Mary is an educated English daughter of a vicar who spent many years doing missionary work in India, and she travelled extensively to Nazareth, Bethlehem, Jerusalem and the

Sea of Galilee. Many traditions and influences were brought back with her, and as a result the tiny farmhouse is adorned with a watercolour of the Pool of Bethesda, a photograph of the Sphinx and a colourful portrait of a Native Canadian sent by the twins' Uncle Eddie from Canada. But these external influences brought by Mary from beyond the immediate *milltir sgwâr* highlight her alterity in relation to both nationality and class, and are a cause of friction, frequently firing Amos's ferocious temper. When Mary cooks a meal of rice one evening, Amos furiously smashes it to the floor, claiming that he doesn't want to eat her 'filthy Indian food'. He mocks her intention to grow asparagus, scoffing that she did not marry into the gentry. When she falls asleep with a copy of *Wuthering Heights* on her lap (an aptly ironic text, dealing as it does with generations of a family inhabiting a specific rural landscape) he strikes her with it cruelly, and berates her for reading to the twins, claiming that she is 'mollycoddling' them. Her middle-class Englishness jars with the people of the locale, who laugh at her desperate her attempts to fit in by talking about farming. A neighbour sighs that the twins attend church 'like their mother', as opposed to chapel. Amos resents her worldliness, but it is this, her inherent difference and otherness, and the very fact that she is from beyond both the border and the *milltir sgwâr*, that helps the family time and again. Mary is a confident, educated and articulate woman, whose connections to the Bickertons – the landowners who own The Vision – is key in ensuring that her family secures the place as a home. This fuels Amos's resentment, and results in this cross-border marriage between a dark, weather-beaten Welsh man and pale English woman, which is played out literally on the border, being tempestuous, brutal and full of suffering. The initial gentle tenderness played out in the landscape is a distant memory once they move to The Vision.

The Vision as dwelling place

When thinking about the depiction of The Vision in *On the Black Hill*, it is illuminating to consider Heidegger's concept of 'dwelling' and its influence on other thinkers and human geographers. In *The Poetics of Space*, phenomenological philosopher Gaston Bachelard considers the house as a human being's first world. This is a primitive space that acts as a 'first universe' and that frames the way people understand and think about the wider universe.[38] His notion of the home is overwhelmingly positive: 'life begins well, it begins enclosed, protected, all warm in the bosom of the house'.[39] In *Being and Time* (1927), Heidegger maintains that the relationship between humanity and space takes the form of dwelling. It is a building that creates a sense of place for dwelling to occur, and for Heidegger this dwelling is the very essence of existence – the way humans exist in the world.[40] Heidegger famously used the example of a farmhouse in the Black Forest to illustrate the way that dwelling is rooted in having a sense of place: 'here the self-sufficiency of the power to let earth and sky, divinities and mortals enter *in simple oneness* into things ordered the house'.[41] For Heidegger, dwelling is the basic character of 'being'.[42] A properly authentic existence is one rooted in place, and his detailed description of the farmhouse rooted in the soil is reminiscent of The Vision: 'on the wind sheltered slope … among the meadows close to the spring' and 'the different generations under one roof'.[43] The 'fourfold of existence', which, for Heidegger, is at the basis of all dwelling – the earth, the sky, mortals and divinities – are all present at The Vision, and Amos, Mary, Lewis and Benjamin physically and spiritually dwell in a Heideggerian home. Cloke and Jones have noted that 'dwelling cannot be happily represented or understood in terms of a fixed gaze upon a framed landscape. Rather it should suggest an embodied, practised, contextualised melange of experience within that landscape'.[44] Although Heidegger's notion of dwelling has been criticised for being rooted in a 'sinister … rustic romanticism', it continues to be influential.[45]

Tim Ingold has further aligned ideas of dwelling with those of landscape in a manner that reflects the relationship between people and nature in *On the Black Hill*. In an attempt to move beyond what he sees as the Cartesian dualism implicit in the work of cultural geographers such as Cosgrove and Daniels, which he accuses of making a fundamental distinction between the 'ideas of culture' and the 'matter of nature', Ingold has developed what he terms 'the dwelling perspective'.[46] For Ingold, landscape is not 'land' in the sense that it can be an area 'mathematically described, quantified and measured'.[47] Rather than being an amount of something, place is a 'quality of feeling … an emotional investment'. For Ingold, landscape is not 'nature' in the Western sense, in which it is external to human life and thought. Contrasting landscape with 'space', Ingold equates 'space' as a cartographic representation of the earth's surface. By contrast, landscape is 'anchored in human, embodied perception'.[48] This is precisely the relationship between landscape and people articulated in *On the Black Hill*, which evokes a *cynefin* where 'the boundaries between person and place, or between the self and the landscape, dissolve altogether'.[49]

Physical and psychological borders

The highly complex nature of landscape as bordered space is explored in *On the Black Hill* through the development of the relationship between Lewis and Benjamin, who are locked in what seems to be an incestuous embrace with each other. They dress identically throughout their lives. In a sequence that highlights the strangely close relationship between them, Lewis is sent to another farm to work in the hope of avoiding conscription, despite the fact that Amos is concerned that being apart from him will kill Benjamin. During his time away from The Vision, Lewis for the first time feels physical pain when it is inflicted on Benjamin. In this instance, Benjamin, pining for his brother, attempts to walk through a blizzard to reach him. When Benjamin is eventually conscripted,

Lewis continues to feel the physical pain that Benjamin suffers. Even their father considers them to be 'one person'. In some senses the borders between them – between self and the other – are seen to break down. But this dependence is not entirely mutual. Lewis clearly desires to form a meaningful relationship with a woman, but opportunities are snatched from him time and again due to Benjamin's intense rage and jealousy. There is clear attraction between Lewis and Rosie, a local girl, and she invites him to her house. Nevertheless, when Lewis finally manages to arrive, he spies her in the throes of a sexual act with a man, and runs away aghast. This is swiftly contrasted with a graphic scene of two horses mating, the positions of both couple and horses drawing a connection between Lewis's ease with fornication and the animalistic, despite his apparent inexperience and unease at engaging in any meaningful intimacy himself. Lewis is forced to leave The Vision due to Benjamin's apoplectic reaction when he notices lipstick on Lewis's cheek. He only returns when Mary is on her deathbed. Following the deaths of their parents, Lewis and Benjamin share their parents' bed, which sits in a room surrounded with family photographs. With the arrival of Lotte Zons (Catherine Schell), a German woman who researches twins who have never separated, the blurred physical boundaries between Lewis and Benjamin become ever more apparent. Benjamin reveals to her that he believes that he and his brother transcend their physical boundaries and that they have one soul. But Lewis reveals that sacrificing his own dreams – of a wife and a family of his own – has been an intensely painful experience. His lifelong obsession with flying and his collection of cuttings about aeroplanes and aviation accidents can be read as a desire to break free from his ties to his brother, the oppressive farmhouse and the *cynefin* that anchors him to it. On the twins' eightieth birthday their great-nephew, Kevin, arranges for them to take a flight in an aeroplane. Seeing the rural landscape and The Vision from a starkly different perspective is a transformative experience of intense joy for Lewis. As he stares at The Vision, tiny and unassuming beneath him, he has transcended all boundaries, and he now sees the landscape in which he has long been located from a different point of view, from above, from a map-maker's perspective. After spending his whole life bearing a futile desire to escape, he is, at the close of the film, offered a perspective he has not experienced before, and the connection between himself and the land recedes into temporary cosmic insignificance.

The visibility and ambivalence of the English–Welsh border

For Heidegger, a space cannot exist until a site has been cleared or had room made for it, and, crucially, a space cannot exist until there is a boundary: 'A boundary is not that at which something stops, but … the boundary is that from which *something begins its presencing*'.[50] In *The Location of Culture* (1994), Homi K. Bhabha draws on Heidegger's ideas when he advocates that the border

9 *On the Black Hill*

is a boundary in which this 'presencing' begins.[51] Bhabha relates this 'presencing' to literal and metaphorical borders and articulates it as a series of dynamic negotiations between conflicting cultures that constitutes a liminal, hybrid space that provides 'the terrain for elaborating strategies of selfhood – singular or communal – that initiate new signs of identity, and innovative sites of collaboration, and contestation, in the act of defining the idea of society itself'.[52] For Bhabha, then, the border represents an ambivalent space between two fixed identifications that holds the possibility for non-hierarchical cultural hybridity.[53] Bhabha argues for the 'beyond' and the 'Third Space', where new forms of cultural identity are a possibility and where there is 'a complex, on-going negotiation that seeks to authorize cultural hybridities'.[54] This has been echoed by the geographer Edward W. Soja, who, when reinvestigating the ideological constructions of space, built on Henri Lefebvre's spatial trialectic and coined the term 'thirding-as-Othering', which draws 'selectively and strategically from the two opposing categories to open new alternatives'.[55] Borders therefore might not always be constraining but might instead represent opportunity, newness and boundless possibilities for identities to flourish.

Nevertheless, for Wales, the history of the Welsh–English border is certainly not associated with flourishing new possibilities. On the contrary, as well as being a highly visible escarpment in some locations (particularly in the locale of *On the Black Hill*), it is a powerful cultural symbol attached to a narrative of continual retreat and overwhelming loss of land and language.[56] After the post-Roman era, when the Welsh language evolved, its speakers came under attack and rapidly lost ground to the Saxons. The border has been relatively fixed since the eighth century, when Offa's Dyke was constructed by Offa, King of Mercia, around 770–80. This huge linear earthwork remained the frontier between Wales and England for centuries. The boundary as it is known today was strengthened by the Laws in Wales Act (commonly known as the Acts of Union) in 1535 and 1542 under Henry VIII, where Wales was effectively annexed into England, creating a single state. As historian John Davies points out, despite the border being strengthened by the acts, their purpose meant that the border's specific route had little significance:

> Thus was created the border between Wales and England, a border which has survived until today. It did not follow the old line of Offa's Dyke nor the eastern boundary of the Welsh dioceses; it excluded districts such as Oswestry and Ewias, where the Welsh language would continue to be spoken for centuries, districts which it would not be wholly fanciful to consider as *Cambria irredenta*. Yet, as the purpose of the statute was to incorporate Wales into England, the location of the Welsh border was irrelevant to the purposes of its framers.[57]

Thus the administrative border of Wales was established and has continued to exist ever since, apart from the ambiguity attached to Monmouthshire, which lasted between the sixteenth and twentieth centuries, with some, including the *Encyclopaedia Britannica* of 1911, placing the county firmly in England. This anomaly was not resolved until the Local Government Act of 1972, which legally incorporated Monmouthshire into Wales. The present-day border stretches about 160 miles from the Dee estuary in the north to the Severn estuary in the south. It is only since the 1970s that the Welsh borders have been confirmed, although Offa's Dyke represents a true, visible demarcation and is one of the oldest national borders in the world between two nations whose rivalries are very much alive.[58]

The materiality of this border – a looming, undisputed ridge, dominating and tearing through the landscape in the opening sequence of *On the Black Hill* – stands in stark contrast to the more ambiguous ways in which the borderland is represented through the lives of the characters in the film. This is a mysterious place. It is uncertainly mapped. This tension between the idea of the fixed cartographic border and the lived experience of the borderland propels the narrative. Gloria Anzaldúa once wrote that 'a border is a dividing line, a narrow strip along a steep edge. A borderland is a vague and undetermined place created by the emotional residue of an unnatural boundary. It is in a constant state of transition.'[59] As Horsman and Marshall have stated, 'There has always been a tension between the fixed, durable and inflexible requirements of national boundaries and the unstable, transient and flexible requirements of people.'[60] Raymond Williams, writing about the area of his birth (close to the location of the film), argued, 'Within the Black Mountains, these lines on the map mean nothing.'[61]

When Mary visits the solicitor Arkwright (James Bree) to express interest in renting the farmhouse, he pleads ignorance and has to turn to a large map of the area on a wall in an attempt to locate it, and immediately describes the location in negative terms. A bitter border dispute regarding The Vision's land with the neighbour, Watkins (Eric Wyn), leads to a cycle of revenge that threatens to destroy Amos completely. Watkins claims that he owns a field and allows his sheep to graze there, despite Amos's contention that the field belongs to the estate and is part of The Vision. Amos produces a map to prove this, but even in the face of cartographic evidence Watkins continues to deny the location of the border. In this liminal border space, then, nothing is certain. The revenge culminates in the burning of the farm's rickets and the brutal killing of the family's beloved dog, which leaves Amos physically and mentally ruined, leading ultimately to his death.

The fact that the Jones family are marked as culturally Welsh is highly significant when we consider the ways that discourses of land and power are played out in the film. In an early sequence in the hills the twins' grandfather asks them to name the surrounding hills and makes connections with the past. Williams and Smith have highlighted the importance of the national homeland being imbued with memory: 'Its mountains are sacred, its rivers are full of memories, its lakes recall distant oaths and battles.'[62] Pointing to the hills he educates them about 'Prince Llywelyn of Wales who fought the English. Up out of England they came and stole the good land of the Valleys. But the Welshmen kept the hills and stopped them from coming any further.' Later, due to death duties, the Bickertons are forced to sell their farms, and, although the tenants are originally informed that they will be offered them for a fair price, they are ultimately put up for public auction. The auction sequence demonstrates the political nature of land ownership and its centrality to discourses of power, and, specifically in Wales, to the innate connection between land and nationalism. This auction scene quickly acknowledges discourses of colonialism and power. One farmer asks, 'Should I not die on the farm I was born in?' and the English auctioneer retorts, 'Of course you shall, by making the appropriate bid.' The outraged response results in Arkwright claiming, 'This is a public auction, not a political meeting,' to which a farmer responds powerfully, 'It will turn political soon enough. You Englishman! You think you have troubles enough in Ireland, well I can tell you there's a room full of Welshmen ready to make trouble for you right here!' The packed room of farmers stand as one and sing *Mae Hen Wlad fy Nhadau*, the Welsh national anthem, in its entirety. The scene thus makes a clear link between land, power, politics and identity explicit, especially by referring to Northern Ireland. So, despite the ambiguous nature of the border here, the nature of power and politics in terms of national identity is not ambiguous at all. As Pyrs Gruffudd has pointed out, 'the whole notion of landscape is one that has … been politicized in Wales', and 'landscape became a crucial proponent of political identity within Wales, invested with significant emotional importance'.[63] In *On the Black Hill*, due to the border dispute, Watkins drives the price of The Vision ever higher by continually bidding against Amos, dramatically inflating the price. Amos is keenly aware of the discourse of power of which he is a player: 'Bloody English, who do they think they are? It's me that farms the land not them … I'm the one who's scraped and saved and ruined his health, me, a Welshman.' But it is this dispute that leads to the breakdown of his health and subsequent death. It is again left to Mary to write to the Bickertons and use her awareness of the subtleties of class and power to beg for the price to be lowered.

Focusing on nation-building and the geographical imagination in the first half of the twentieth century, Pyrs Gruffudd demonstrates how a particular version of Welsh identity was negotiated that was 'fundamentally geographical in that it located Welshness within a particular rural environment' and that 'exhibited a profound territorial sense in its defence of "national space"'.[64] In discussing an example of this defence, Gruffudd focuses on the establishment of an aerodrome at Porth Neigwl, on the Llŷn Peninsula, in 1936, in an area considered a heartland of the Welsh language and culture. The farmhouse of Penrhos, a site of cultural significance, was to be demolished to make way for the construction of the bombing school at Penyberth. Saunders Lewis, D. J. Williams and Lewis Valentine set fire to the bombing school, and the Tan in Llŷn (Fire in Llŷn) has attained iconic status as the first example of national resistance to the appropriation of rural land by the London government for the benefit of England (or Britain). It certainly was not the last. There were numerous examples of the London government's perceived disregard of rural Wales and its culture.[65] Three years later, the Ministry of Defence acquired Mynydd Epynt for military training purposes, requiring 219 residents of the farming community to leave in order to establish the Sennybridge Training Area. The most famous example of the English appropriation of Welsh land remains the drowning of the village of Capel Celyn to provide a water reservoir, Llyn Celyn, for the residents of Liverpool and the Wirral in 1965. These events, and the protests or direct action in response to them, are powerfully evocative symbols in Welsh history, their power continuing to this day.

In *On the Black Hill*, the relationship between landscape and people, and the complex relationship between borderlands and borders, is richly explored. Despite the film's closing credits, where the characters are divided into 'The Welsh' and 'The English' – a pertinent echo of how these binary oppositions are set up in the opening shots – the film actively destabilises such simplistic divisions. This is a film not about the national, *per se*, but instead interested in the ambiguous nature of all borders and in ways of living that disrupt and transcend them. Due to their existence on the borderland, the Jones family reside both within and outside two nations, without truly belonging to one or the other. The ambivalence and ambiguity of such spaces is not only acknowledged but also deeply probed, as is the potent colliding that occurs in such furrows, fissures, clefts and cleavages on the periphery of nations. The film demonstrates that these characteristics belong not just to the borderlands but to the whole nation. The borderland experience is, in fact, an integral part of the Welsh national experience.

Notes

1 'Y Clawdd' (Cyfres o Gerddi), in *Cerddi Bryan Martin Davies: Y Casgliad Cyflawn* (Llandybie: Cyhoeddiadau Barddas, 2003), p. 132. The translation is by Grahame Davies and appears in Grahame Davies, 'Borders in the Mind', *Agenda* (Spring 2004), pp. 4–9; p. 5.
2 The quote in the title of this chapter is taken from the poem 'The Boundary' by Gladys Mary Coles, in Dewi Roberts (ed.), *Both Sides of the Border: An Anthology of Writing on the Welsh Border Region* (Llanrwst: Gwasg Carreg Gwalch, 1998), p. 37.
3 Catherine Fowler and Gillian Helfield (eds), *Representing the Rural: Space, Place, and Identity in Films about the Land* (Detroit: Wayne State University Press, 2006), pp. 1–14; p. 12.
4 The brothers are also played by Aled and Rhys Baker (aged six) and by Lewis and Huw Toghill (aged twelve).
5 Fowler and Helfield, *Representing the Rural*, p. 6.
6 Stephen Daniels, *Fields of Vision* (Cambridge: Polity Press, 1993), p. 5.
7 Daniels, *Fields of Vision*, p. 12.
8 Quoted in *Cymru Wledig / Rural Wales* (Spring 2013), p. 2.
9 Denis Cosgrove, *Social Formation and Symbolic Landscape* (London: Croome Helm, 1984), p. 13.
10 Jan Penrose, 'Reification in the name of change: the impact of nationalism on social constructions of nation, people and place in Scotland and the United Kingdom', in Peter Jackson and Jan Penrose (eds), *Constructions of Race, Place and Nation* (London: University College London Press, 1993), pp. 27–49; p. 29.
11 Colin Williams and Anthony D. Smith, 'The national construction of social space', *Progress in Human Geography*, 7 (1983), pp. 502–18; p. 502.
12 Daniels, *Fields of Vision*, p. 5.
13 Anthony D. Smith, 'When is a nation?', *Geopolitics* 7: 2, pp. 5–32; p. 22.
14 Tony Curtis, *Wales: The Imagined Nation* (Bridgend: Poetry Wales Press, 1986); Gwyn A. Williams, *When Was Wales?* (London: Black Raven Press, 1985).
15 Stewart Mottram and Sarah Prescott, *Writing Wales: From the Renaissance to Romanticism* (Farnham: Ashgate, 2012), p. 2.
16 Quoted in Mike Parker, *Neighbours from Hell?* (Talybont: Y Lolfa, 2007), p. 77; quoted in Mottram and Prescott, *Writing Wales*, p. 2.
17 Quoted in Mottram and Prescott, *Writing Wales*, p. 2.
18 Mottram and Prescott, *Writing Wales*, p. 2.
19 Parker, *Neighbours from Hell?*, p. 77.
20 Shawna Lichtenwalner, *Claiming Cambria: Invoking the Welsh in the Romantic Era* (Newark: University of Delaware Press, 2008), p. 97.
21 Lichtenwalner, *Claiming Cambria*, p. 98.
22 David Berry, *Wales and Cinema* (Cardiff: University of Wales Press, 1994), p. 66.
23 Berry, *Wales and Cinema*, p. 66.
24 Mike Pearson and Michael Shanks, *Theatre/Archaeology* (London: Routledge, 2001), p. 138.
25 Bedwyr Lewis Jones, 'Cynefin: the word and the concept', *Nature in Wales*, (1985), p. 121.
26 Lewis Jones, 'Cynefin', p. 121.

27 Lewis Jones, 'Cynefin', p. 121.

28 Lewis Jones, 'Cynefin', p. 122.

29 See Colin H. Williams, *Called Unto Liberty! On Language and Nationalism* (Clevedon, Avon: Multilingual Matters, 1994), p. 129.

30 Williams, *Called Unto Liberty!*, p. 129.

31 Andrew Grieve, 'Revisiting the Black Hill' (DVD booklet), *On the Black Hill* (1987).

32 D. J. Williams, *Hen Dŷ Ffarm / The Old Farmhouse* (Llandysul: Gomer Press, 2001), p. 67.

33 Williams, *Hen Dŷ Ffarm / The Old Farmhouse*, p. 68.

34 T. H. Parry-Williams, 'Hon' / 'This One', in R. Gerallt Jones (ed.), *Poetry of Wales 1930–70* (Llandysul: Gomer Press, 1974), pp. 60–1.

35 T. H. Parry-Williams, 'Bro' / 'Locality', in R. Gerallt Jones (ed.), *Poetry of Wales 1930–70* (Llandysul: Gomer Press, 1974), pp. 58–69.

36 Raymond Williams, *The Country and the City* (London: Oxford University Press, 1973), p. 120.

37 Ned Thomas, *The Welsh Extremist: A Culture in Crisis* (Talybont: Y Lolfa, 1991), p. 31.

38 Gaston Bachelard, *The Poetics of Space* (Boston: Beacon Press, 1994), p. 4.

39 Bachelard, *The Poetics of Space*, p. 7.

40 Tim Cresswell, *Space: A Short Introduction* (Oxford: Blackwell, 2004), p. 22.

41 Martin Heidegger, 'Building, dwelling, thinking', in David Farrell Krell (ed.), *Martin Heidegger: Basic Writings* (London: Routledge, 1993), pp. 343–64; p. 362 (emphasis in original).

42 Heidegger, 'Building, dwelling, thinking', p. 362.

43 Heidegger, 'Building, dwelling, thinking', p. 362.

44 Paul Cloke and Owain Jones, quoted in John Wylie, 'Landscape, performance and dwelling: a Glastonbury case study', in Paul Cloke (ed.), *Country Visions* (Essex: Pearson Education, 2003), pp. 136–57; p. 145.

45 Wylie, 'Landscape, performance and dwelling', p. 144.

46 John Wylie, *Landscape* (London: Routledge, 2007), p. 154.

47 Wylie, *Landscape*, p. 160.

48 Wylie, *Landscape*, p. 160.

49 Tim Ingold quoted in Wylie, *Landscape*, p. 161.

50 Homi K. Bhabha, *The Location of Culture* (Routledge: London, 1994), p. 1 (emphasis in original).

51 Bhabha, *The Location of Culture*, p. 1.

52 Bhabha, *The Location of Culture*, p. 2.

53 Bhabha, *The Location of Culture*, p. 2.

54 Bhabha, *The Location of Culture*, p. 2.

55 Henri Lefebvre, *The Production of Space* (Blackwell: Oxford, 1991). See also Edward W. Soja, *Thirdspace: Journeys to Los Angeles and Other Real-and-Imagined Places* (Cambridge, MA: Blackwell, 1996), p. 5.

56 Jane Aaron, 'Border blues: representing the Welsh borders in twentieth-century Anglophone literature', in Johan Schimanski and Stephen Wolfe (eds), *Border Poetics De-limited* (Hanover: Wehrhahn Verlag, 2007), pp. 199–215; p. 199.

57 John Davies, *The History of Wales* (London: Penguin, 1994), p. 233.

58 Davies, 'Borders in the mind', p. 5.

59 Gloria Anzaldúa, *Borderlands/La Frontera: The New Mastiza* (San Francisco: Aunt Lute Books, 1999), p. 25, quoted in Siwan Rosser, ' "Ynom mae y Clawdd?" Croesi Ffiniau Ieithyddol' ('The dyke is within us?' Crossing literary borders), *Transactions of the Honourable Society of Cymmrodorion*, 14 (2008), pp. 188–212; p. 201.

60 Mathew Horsman and Andrew Marshall, *After the Nation-State: Citizens, Tribalism and the New World Disorder* (London: HarperCollins, 1995), p. 45.

61 Raymond Williams, 'Black mountains', in Daniel Williams (ed.), *Who Speaks for Wales? Nation, Culture, Identity* (Cardiff: University of Wales Press, 2003), pp. 73–8; p. 76.

62 Williams and Smith, 'The national construction of social space', p. 509.

63 Pyrs Gruffudd, 'Prospects of Wales: contested geographical imaginations', in Ralph Fevre and Andrew Thompson (eds), *Nation, Identity and Social Theory* (Cardiff: University of Wales Press, 1999), pp. 149–67; p. 151.

64 Pyrs Gruffudd, 'Remaking Wales: nation-building and the geographical imagination, 1925–50', *Political Geography*, 14: 3 (1995), pp. 219–39; p. 220.

65 Kirsti Bohata, *Postcolonialism Revisited* (Cardiff: University of Wales Press, 2004), p. 81.

7

Where the land meets the sea: liminality, identity and rural landscape in contemporary Scottish cinema

Duncan Petrie

Introduction

In *I Know Where I'm Going!*, Michael Powell and Emeric Pressburger's classic 1945 film, the headstrong English protagonist, Joan Webster (Wendy Hillier), has her journey to the fictional Hebridean Isle of Kiloran interrupted by the forces of nature. The short crossing by boat from Mull to Kiloran is blocked, firstly by thick fog and then a storm, stranding our heroine and preventing her from fulfilling her narrative trajectory: reunion with and marriage to a wealthy industrialist, Sir Robert Bellinger. This tiresome interruption allows the strange and remote environment to begin working its magic on Joan, sowing the first seeds of doubt in someone whose entire *raison d'etre* has been characterised by a clear and unwavering sense of purpose and direction.

Gradually, the enchantment of landscape segues into the unruly forces of desire as Joan begins to falls in love with the dashing Torquil McNeil (Roger Livesey), Laird of Kiloran and thus a physical embodiment of the seductive and elemental power of the place. In this way *I Know Where I'm Going!* contributes to an enduring tradition of cinematic representation that I have examined elsewhere, in which Scotland is constructed as a wild and untamed environment, a rural periphery geographically distant but also far removed from the rules, conventions and certainties of contemporary metropolitan society.[1] But it also provides a rich example of the productive intersection of cinema studies and cultural geography, offering as it does a demonstration of how questions of subjectivity and identity can be explored through the creative use of space, place and landscape. In Powell and Pressburger's film this includes picturesque and highly atmospheric shooting on the Isle of Mull by cinematographer Erwin Hillier. But this material is juxtaposed with studio work and process shots, in part a consequence of the

10 *I Know Where I'm Going!*

unavailability of Roger Livesey for the location shoot, a pertinent reminder of the essentially constructed nature of all films, whatever the relationship of their images to 'real' places.

This representational viewpoint of *I Know Where I'm Going!* comes from outside the physical and cultural space of Scotland and so corresponds with Cairns Craig's identification of a recurring narrative figure in such films being akin to a 'visitor from the stars'.[2] Sometimes the consequence of this encounter is the awakening of desire through an unanticipated and overwhelming sense of connection to the landscape and its inhabitants. In addition to *I Know Where I'm Going!* this is the dominant theme of films such as *Brigadoon* (Vincente Minnelli, 1955) – a film made entirely in the studio – *Local Hero* (Bill Forsyth, 1983) and *Loch Ness* (John Henderson, 1996). But in other cases the strangeness of environment generates unease or even fear, prompting rather darker and even destructive consequences for the incomer. This is the case in the Gainsborough melodrama *The Brothers* (David MacDonald, 1947); the Ealing comedies *Whisky Galore!* (1949)[3] and *The Maggie* (1954), both directed by Alexander Mackendrick; and the cult horror *The Wicker Man* (Robin Hardy, 1973). But the shared connection across all of the above examples, positive and negative, is that Scotland – as space, place and landscape – functions as essentially a projection of the desires, fears and fantasies not only of their (outsider) protagonists but also of the metropolitan

British and American filmmakers who made them – and by extension their audiences.

Now this phenomenon has deeper roots stretching back beyond the cinema. One can find a similar set of associations in nineteenth-century literature and painting, which similarly depended on fixing Scotland as a particular kind of place: wild, remote and rural. We find this in the 'Waverley' novels of Walter Scott and in the landscape paintings of Edwin Landseer and Skeoch Cummings (with their picturesque images of noble stags and dashing plaid-wearing soldiers), and it provides an ideological underpinning to the establishment by Queen Victoria and Prince Albert of a Scottish residence at Balmoral on Deeside. Thus a particular romanticised vision of Scotland came to be constructed, an empty land, conveniently purged of the dissenting elements that supported the ill-fated Jacobite uprising of 1745 through the infamous 'clearances' and reconstructed as a site of leisure for the 'British' establishment, a playground where they could indulge in sport ('hunting, shooting and fishing') and tourism.[4] Moreover, with the threat of actual rebellion removed, the highlands were also recuperated as the setting for romantic tales of Scottish heroism and (depoliticised) resistance, which proved a gift for the cinema through adaptations of Scott and Stevenson that reinforced the association of Scottish history with romantic heroic Jacobites and brutal Redcoats in films such as *Bonnie Prince Charlie* (Anthony Kimmins, 1948), *Kidnapped* (Robert Stevenson, 1959) and *Rob Roy: The Highland Rogue* (Harold French, 1953), the last remade in 1995 by Michael Caton Jones. The familiar topography of the highlands also recurs in Mel Gibson's Oscar-winning *Braveheart* (1996), the tale of the medieval warrior William Wallace, whose military struggles against the English took place primarily in the central belt and borders.[5] In this way landscape functions as 'habitat', the natural environment of a Scottish variant of the noble savage, which gives him the edge over his English (and therefore outsider) antagonists.

This (necessarily limited) repertoire of national representation was subsequently challenged by the emergence of a 'new Scottish cinema', fuelled by new sources of finance for independent film production, from the 1980s onwards. This not only saw the proliferation of film production in Scotland but also crucially facilitated a new creative viewpoint from within the culture. The resulting decolonised cinematic vision prompted a marked shift away from the tourist gaze of rural and the romantic landscapes and towards a new engagement with urban stories, experiences, spaces and places. This was not only a reflection of the everyday 'reality' of the majority of Scots whose lives were in towns and cities but also drew on another potent tradition of cultural representation – that of Clydesidism[6] – rooted in the masculine culture of industrial labour, hard drinking and violence. This also provided a different kind of emblematic physical location: notably the shipyards, factories, pubs, streets and tenements of Glasgow and Edinburgh. Thus, Scottish space and place in cinema were reoriented towards the representation of a more modern, industrial and urban social experience and were also to be central to the contemplation of the psychological and social consequences of the process of wholesale deindustrialisation, well under way by the time the new Scottish cinema began to emerge, and central to key films such as *Trainspotting* (Danny Boyle, 1996), *My Name is Joe* (Ken Loach, 1998), *Orphans* (Peter Mullan, 1998) and *Ratcatcher* (Lynne Ramsay, 1999).

Despite this fundamental shift in perspective, some filmmakers continued to engage with rural Scotland. But they did this in new ways that provided an interesting challenge to both the external construction of the highlands and islands and the new orthodoxy of an urban and the masculine Scottish imaginary. In this essay I will examine some of these more recent cinematic representations, focusing on *Another Time, Another Place* (Michael Radford, 1983), *Blue Black Permanent* (Margaret Tait, 1993) and *The Winter Guest* (Alan Rickman, 1997). While all three films feature rural settings, the cultural and narrative perspective is resolutely internal, avoiding replaying the traditional encounter involving a protagonist from outside the environment. But there is another point of novelty in that the three films are located not in the familiar topography of the western highlands and islands but on the north-east coast of Scotland, – a region hitherto limited to a handful of documentaries such as John Grierson's films *Drifters* (1929) and *North Sea* (1938), which focus on the fishing fleet and the coastguard respectively, and John Eldridge's *North East Corner* (1946), a depiction of farming and community life. But the most significant factor from the point of view of the concerns of this essay is the way in which these three features explore that relationship between the land and the sea, creating a different order of 'territoriality' – in Martin Lefebvre's use of the term as 'space seen from the "inside", a subjective and lived space'.[7] Thus, in place of a sense of identity provided by material solidity of *terra firma*, the seashore signifies a zone of uncertainty, indeterminacy or liminality, and consequently these films use landscape to question as much as to confirm identity and belonging. This has links with strands of feminist theory, which is interested in how such zones of liminality serve to unsettle and challenge established identities and power relations. For example, Susan Triesman identifies a recurring feature in the work of the playwright Sharman MacDonald (author of *The Winter Guest*): 'the wild Scotland at the edge of the sea – where nature offers a meeting place for a new understanding'.[8] Indeed, the films discussed here notably eschew the preoccupation with masculinity and maleness that links so many recent Scottish films (and novels), providing a new focus on the female dimension of experience, consciousness and subjectivity.

In different ways *Another Time, Another Place, Blue Black Permanent* and *The Winter Guest* introduce new ideas and pose different kinds of questions appropriate to a changing sense of national self-determination and identity – a cultural process that was also to manifest itself in political terms with the return of a devolved parliament to Edinburgh in 1999. Collectively they serve to challenge the legacy of a pre-devolutionary external view in which the Scottish landscape and its inhabitants function as projections of the fantasies, desires and fears of metropolitan filmmakers and their audiences, reasserting a perspective resolutely from within the culture and with it posing different kinds of questions and generating different kinds of meanings in relation to cinematic constructions of space, place and landscape.

Dreams of fulfilment: *Another Time, Another Place*

One of the early films commissioned by Channel 4, *Another Time, Another Place*, is the debut feature of writer–director Michael Radford. Based on the autobiographical novel by Jessie Kesson, it also serves as a sequel to Radford's earlier adaptation of Kesson's *The White Bird Passes*, made for the BBC in 1980. The earlier drama is set in Elgin during the 1920s and depicts the impoverished childhood of Janey, the eight-year-old daughter of a local prostitute, who is taken into care when her alcoholic mother is deemed unable to look after her. The narrative is recounted in flashback from the point of view of a teenage Janey (played by Phyllis Logan), on the verge of leaving the orphanage and making her way in the world. *Another Time, Another Place* moves the story on to 1944 with Janey (again portrayed by Logan) now the young wife of a tenant farmer, eking out a living on the Black Isle, to the north-east of Inverness. In *The White Bird Passes*, Janey's literary talents and ambition to be a writer had been suppressed by the trustees of the orphanage, and it is clearly signalled from the very beginning of *Another Time, Another Place* that she continues to yearn for more than the hard life of a cotter's wife can possibly offer. Janey embodies a youthful vivacity that marks her out in the community: contrasting sharply with the demeanour of her rather dour and taciturn husband, Dougal (Paul Young), and the similarly joyless temperament of the other wives whom she labours alongside in the fields. Janey's restless curiosity and yearning for experience are continually signalled – in the way she watches the Mosquito bomber on training manoeuvres, in her suggestion to Dougal that they buy bikes. But Janey's subjectivity is given a more direct dramatisation with the arrival of a group of Italian prisoners of war, who constitute a rather different kind of interruption from the world outside. The POWs are housed in the rude bothy next door and are forced to work alongside the community in the fields. In this way, *Another Time, Another Place* reaffirms two key tropes in rural cinema noted by Catherine Fowler and Gillian Helfield: establishing a fundamental relationship of the local people to the land that provides their livelihood while at the same time evoking a connection to the past through the physical and temporal rhythms of cultivation.[9] However, as I have noted, Janey stands apart from the community, and this theme is developed through her fascination for the exotic foreigners in her midst, who struggle to master the rudiments of even basic agricultural labour – a significant shift of emphasis from the tradition of the outsider's fascination with the Scots. Moreover, her curiosity has a palpable erotic charge; but, while Janey seems initially attracted to the tall, handsome Roman Paolo, it is the short Neapolitan Luigi with whom she has a brief and ill-fated love affair.

Janey's subjectivity is also conveyed through her relationship to the landscape of the Black Isle. On one hand, the physical environment clearly inhibits and confines her, just as she is confined by her class and her gender. The film opens with a shot of a bleak, grey seascape before the camera pans left to reveal a lonely figure on the shore gazing outwards and contemplating the world beyond. The images are underscored by John McLeod's melancholic music, evoking further Janey's emotional state. But lurking behind the isolation and ennui is her yearning for new experiences and encounters – 'Other Times, Other Place' – beyond the horizon. The fact that the physical topography of the Black Isle is actually a peninsula provides a landscape where the sea is continually glimpsed in the background, a continual reminder of the dual sense of limitation and possibility it signifies. This sense of ambivalence is also suggested by the way in which Radford films Janey within the landscape and her participation in the quotidian activities taking place within it. On the one hand the undulations of the land and the furrows of the fields seem to hem in and define the emotional outlook of the inhabitants – the harsh, unforgiving climate mirrored by their resignation and dourness. This link between mentality and environment is thrown into sharp relief by the Mediterranean temperament of the Italians, who pine for the sunshine and warmth of their own home and land, causing Umberto, the Milanese intellectual, to mutter in despair that their life in captivity seems to consist of 'tatties, neeps, wind and rain'. Just as Janey's aspirations for a more fulfilling existence are constrained, so these outsiders are markedly denied any transformative and life-affirming encounter with Scotland familiar from films such as *I Know Where I'm Going!*, *Brigadoon* or *Local Hero*.

Yet at the same time the landscape also underpins the life-sustaining rhythms of nature and of the agricultural year. Radford and his cinematographer Roger Deakins explicitly depict the seasonal cycles of cultivation beginning with the autumn harvest followed by the harsh interlude of winter, the spring planting, the brightness and new growth of summer. In this eternal natural progression, *Another Time, Another Place* evokes Lewis Grassic Gibbon's novel *Sunset Song*, whose chapters and narrative are similarly structured. And, just as that book's heroine, Chris Guthrie, is closely linked with the elemental landscape of the Mearns, Janey – in spite of her distance from the other locals and her yearning for alternatives – is similarly connected to the life-affirming qualities of her environment. Not only does she make love with Luigi in the spring heather (her uninhibited orgasm contrasting starkly with an earlier passionless coupling she had instigated with Dougal) but also her youth, vivacity and sexuality are associated with the fertility of the land and the livestock. This is confirmed by the scenes in the film where she is naked. In the first, Janey unselfconsciously washes the dirt and chaff from her supple flesh before climbing into bed and initiating sex with Dougal; in the second, she is milking a cow and, while pressed up against its flank, fantasises herself naked in front of the leering gaze of the Italians while milking the cow, this time conveying her vulnerability and shame.

While the correspondence of landscape, nature and the female body may be a rather familiar and even clichéd trope – as Jane Sillars and Myra MacDonald have argued[10] – in *Another Time, Another Place* the association does not carry the same burden of mystical enchantment as it does in, for example, a contemporaneous production like *Local Hero*, where the two main female characters, Marina and Stella, are explicitly linked to the sea and the stars. Moreover, contrary to John Brown's assertion that the film disappoints because it fails to explore 'the resonances – social, religious, historical – which could have been thematically gathered around the Janey/Luigi relationship',[11] Radford's concern with Janey's subjectivity offers a critical contemplation of identity and the limits of experience, creating in the process a film in which the (Scottish) woman becomes the active and desiring subject. This is in no small part a consequence of the way in which these issues are evoked and explored in relation to space, place, and landscape or seascape.

'Torn between languages': *Blue Black Permanent*

An even more profound link is made between identity and fate, land and sea in *Blue Black Permanent*, the first and only feature directed by Margaret Tait, made when she was 71 and approaching the end of a 40-year career, primarily as an experimental, avant-garde filmmaker. The narrative of *Blue Black Permanent* interweaves the life of Barbara (Celia Imrie), a professional photographer living in Edinburgh, and that of her mother, Greta (Gerda Stevenson). Barbara is haunted by Greta's death by drowning some 30 years previously, when the latter had apparently walked into the sea while sleepwalking – the tragedy therefore tempered by the uncertainty of whether this was an accident or suicide. The potency of loss is further complicated by the revelation that Greta's own mother had also been claimed by the sea, swept off a rock during a storm. The cumulative weight of this legacy bears down on Barbara, who in recounting the stories of her family to her lover Philip is clearly struggling to assert her own sense of identity. Barbara's own connection to the sea is signalled at the start of the film when we see her as a child learning to swim on an East Lothian beach, watched by a rather anxious Greta.

The significance of the sea is also directly linked to landscape in *Blue Black Permanent*. The story is located in both Edinburgh and Orkney, which establishes a tension or duality between the urban and the rural. This is central to Greta's predicament: she is introduced as a wife and mother living in 1950s Edinburgh and, like Janey in *Another Time, Another Place*, she yearns for more – in her case through her poetry, which is encouraged by a local artist, Andrew Cunningham. But Greta's artistic sensitivity also reveals an emotionally fragile individual; her ecstatic response to being caught in a storm causes a profound sense of disorientation and she has to be rescued by her friend. Greta is a native of Orkney and her apparently greater sensitivity to the natural elements (in comparison to the accumulated historical and cultural resources of the Scottish capital) suggests that the rural landscapes of her childhood retain a strong pull on her. As a poet, she processes this dilemma in a particular way, admitting to Andrew her desire for both a domestic and an artistic life, and more significantly being 'torn between languages' – a new twist on the perennial theme of Scottish duality[12] that references both ways of living and the tension between bourgeois Edinburgh and the rich Orcadian dialect that her father and his friends use. When Greta returns to visit her father, we discover just how much she misses the environment that she grew up in – a remote landscape of wild beauty and elemental power. When visiting the cliff top where her mother died, Greta discovers a rare flower that can only grow in that locale – 'try to transplant it and it just dies', she muses – clearly a corollary of her own difficult situation.

But, if her attachment to and identification with the land is certain, Greta's relationship to the sea is unsurprisingly much more ambivalent. She may not be upset – let alone traumatised – by a visit to the cliff top where her mother died, and earlier she had told Andrew of her recurring dreams in which the sea seems to connect everything and give her peace. Yet there is a continual reminder of the sea's potentially destructive power in the film – for example in the sequence in which the young Greta visits the mermaid's pool (another magical place), which suddenly becomes a site of danger as the tide begins to advance, threatening to trap her. This is revealed to have been a defining experience, triggering Greta's recurring dreams of the sea. It is also the prelude in the film to the revelation that Greta's own mother had been a victim of the sea, which happens during the visit to the cliff top. Significantly, Barbara also has dreams – of a white cat and mouse and of flying – which symbolise a desire to break free from her own fears of the past. Significantly, her father hails from the borders and is thus symbolically connected to the land. She also photographs the older Andrew Cunningham for a retrospective of his work – which consists primarily of urban roofscapes, a sharp contrast to the elemental forces that inspire Greta.

The tensions at the heart of *Blue Black Permanent* have a personal resonance, for Margaret Tait's own creative life was split between city and island. On returning to Scotland in 1952 after studying at the Centro Sperimentale di Cinematografia in Rome, Tait began making films in Edinburgh. But by the 1960s she had relocated back to Orkney, where she had been born and raised. The distinction is encapsulated by two striking montage sequences in the film that provide examples of what Sarah Neely refers to as the filmmaker's 'artistic concerns with the detail of the everyday'.[13] The first sequence is short and follows a conversation between Barbara and Andrew in which she reminds him of his 'guru' status for Greta. The subsequent shots of the Edinburgh cityscape, in which church spires and towers feature prominently, are accompanied by a lone pier on the soundtrack, suggesting an elegiac and rather sombre evocation of the sadness and loss that Barbara and Andrew feel. The second montage, nearly four minutes in length, forms the film's final moments and consists of a series of images of the sea shore: water, rocks, pebbles, driftwood, sand, weeds and fishing net. But, significantly, unlike the paintings of the wild sea we glimpse in Barbara's apartment and in the home of her grandparents, these shots do not convey wildness or danger but rather provide a comforting sense of timeless equilibrium and peace, a sensation reinforced by the natural soundscape, replete with noises of water gurgling, sucking and splashing. For Ian Goode, in providing a coda to Greta's life and her tragic death, this montage 'suggests that what remains is the relative *permanence* of creative endeavour'.[14] Greta had left a poem on her writing desk when she died, and it is read silently by her husband but remains unseen or unspoken to the audience, suggesting that the closing series of images are offering a visual version of the poet's words. Thus *Blue Black Permanent* leaves us not with a sense of resolution – Barbara is still coming to terms with the legacy of her past – but rather with the (reassuring) idea that the world continues to turn, nature endures and place remains fundamentally connected to concepts of identity, life and death. As such, Tait's film also provides a much more emphatic example than *Another Time, Another Place* of the interconnection between people and place and the way in which the latter serves to underpin and sustain not only subjectivity – as a felt sense of self – but also creative agency – the active articulation of self.

Venturing out onto the ice: *The Winter Guest*

The third film under discussion relates more directly and explicitly to the overarching thematic concerns of liminality introduced at the start of this chapter. Adapted by Sharman MacDonald from her stage play and directed by Alan Rickman, *The Winter Guest* was shot on location in the Fife fishing villages of Pittenweem and Elie during winter. And, if the relationship between the fixity of the land and the fluidity of the sea in the two films I have already discussed is complex but clearly defined, in this film that relationship is deliberately obscured by the fact that the sea is frozen over, making it impossible to discern where one ends and the other begins. Significantly, compared with *Another Time, Another Place* and *Blue Black Permanent*, *The Winter Guest* is less directly concerned with national identity – posed through the respective contrasts of Scottish/Italian and Edinburgh/Orkney – than with existential anxiety. This is partly a consequence of its contemporary – and essentially bourgeois – setting, which gives it a more

overt connection to European modernism. Indeed, the visual intensity, austerity and introspection of *The Winter Guest* invokes the distinctive aesthetic and
thematic sensibility of Scandinavian masters such as Carl Theodor Dreyer and
Ingmar Bergman.

Rickman and MacDonald explore a range of themes through the interactions
of the eight main characters, deployed as four distinct dyads. The central pairing
is that of Elspeth and Frances (played by real-life mother and daughter Phyllida
Law and Emma Thompson) – the latter is struggling to come to terms with the
death of her husband while the former, who is elderly and beginning to deterior-
ate physically, fears that this will drive her daughter to live far away in Australia
at just the point she is beginning to need her. Frances's teenage son Alex is also
haunted by the memory of his father – given physical presence via the many
photographs taken by his mother – and his encounter is with Nita, a lively and
precocious young girl, who provides a welcome distraction but who confronts
the boy with his own fears of moving on and of expressing his sexual desire. The
other characters are Tom and Sam, two pubescent boys who are taking advantage
of the bad weather to skip school and whose fears relate to the uncertainties of
growing up – notably, living up to expectations, physical maturation and having
to take responsibility for things. Then there is the elderly duo, Lilly and Chloe,
who spend their time in the rather morbid pursuit of attending other people's
funerals and who, rather inevitably, are forced to confront their own mortality.
Linking the four pairs is a shared preoccupation with questions of courage and
fear, life and death – the latter providing the 'winter guest' metaphor of the film's
title – but each of the conflicts involves a resolution that requires the summoning
of courage to overcome fear.

But the other overarching feature is the physical landscape in which the drama
is set – and notably the recurring images of the frozen sea, which completely
erases the shifting space where the solidity of the land encounters the fluidity of
the water. This astonishing sight is introduced at the very beginning of the film
via a magisterial crane shot that moves from the sea front to the vast expanse of
whiteness. The frozen sea is also a focal point in the various interactions; it presents a very specific kind of challenge – a test of courage or nerve on the part of
those who walk out onto the ice. Indeed, all of the characters in the film either
contemplate or physically explore the frozen shoreline, with some venturing out
onto the 'debatable land' itself. The fearless Nita – who first encounters Alex
while building a snowman on the shore, throwing snowballs to attract his attention – dares Alex to follow her onto the ice. 'Don't you want to know what it feels
like?' she asks. But he is clearly too frightened to follow where she leads and his
uncertainties end up with him getting his feet wet. Despite being the most pen-
sive and uncertain of the two young boys, it is Tom who musters the courage to
walk out onto the ice towards the end of the film – disappearing into the fog in
the process. A prelude to this had been the discovery of two abandoned kittens,

which the boys rescue and look after, but the walk onto the ice is confirmation that Tom is prepared to embrace life, and he is subsequently followed by Sam, who is anxious not to be left behind.

Tom had previously encountered Frances and Elspeth on the shore, inadvertently providing a means of reconnection between mother and daughter. Elspeth had earlier chided her daughter for using her camera on their walkabout (like Barbara in *Blue Black Permanent* she is a professional photographer), suggesting this is a form of evasion of the world through taking images of 'dead' buildings or people – the numerous portraits of her husband. But here it has become a way of seeing her mother and reconnecting with life in the process – a moment that is reinforced when Frances gives Elspeth her arm to help her up the frozen and slippery pathway from the shore, a recognition of the mutual bond and shared need for support between the two. Lilly and Chloe on the other hand spend much of the film attending a funeral in a neighbouring town, but when the bus arrives back home Chloe has a moment of panic and runs for the shore. Her fall is saved by the railings on the harbour-side (a repetition of a similar moment at the beginning of the film when Elspeth also stumbles and is forced to grab hold of the railings). But Lily quickly comes to her aid, in a reaffirmation of their bond of mutual support and friendship.

Thus *The Winter Guest* connects with some of the ideas raised in relation to the other two films, but it is also very different in tone and style. The constant talk may be a reminder of its theatrical origins, but the exquisite cinematography by Seamus McGarvey ensures a palpable cinematic rendering. Indeed the placing of characters in the winter landscape, coupled with the cold, clear light, recalls the beautiful austerity and psychological intensity of many of Bergman's films in which the physical place (notably the recurring topography of the island of Faro) serves to mirror the emotional and psychological landscapes of his often troubled protagonists. Unlike the other two films under consideration here, *The Winter Guest* is set in the present and has a different relationship to human mobility and the world beyond north-east Scotland. Frances may gain the courage to remain and face her demons rather than running away to Australia, but she arguably wears her identity more lightly so that her sense of 'home' is notably less portentous than Janey's Black Isle of war time or Greta's Orkney of the 1950s.

Conclusion: connections beyond the national

The construction and use of rural landscape in recent Scottish films poses a number of questions relevant to the wider contemplation of identity. Within an explicitly Scottish frame, these films present challenges to some of the dominant traditions of cultural representation. In rejecting the pervasive colonised view of Scotland, its landscape and inhabitants, they assert an internal or de-colonised perspective that poses new questions for how cultural identities can constituted and function in relation to a changing sense of Scottish nationhood and self-determination. These films also offer a welcome corrective to the urban, masculine and realist discourse of subjectivity and place that came to dominate representations of Scotland in the 1970s and 1980s. In foregrounding the rural, the feminine and the fantastical, *Another Time, Another Place, Blue Black Permanent* and *The Winter Guest* provide important alternatives to the more common topographies and geographies of Scottish cinema. But perhaps even more importantly they beg questions that reach beyond the space of the nation in new ways. The juxtaposition of land and sea invokes a point of new possibility that also entails connections to other places beyond. If the traditional colonised perspective had privileged an external gaze that constructed Scotland as a fantasy projection, in different ways these films use space and place to look outwards to places over the sea that provide potentially liberating alternatives (Janey), points of connection that affirm identity and belonging (Greta and Barbara) or metaphors for the dialectic between fear and courage, stasis and purposeful action (Frances and Alex).

But there is a literal dimension to this outward momentum and here the most obvious point of connection is to Scandinavia, suggested in the emotional and visual properties of *The Winter Guest*. The shared north-east setting of the three films provides an important historical link via Viking invasion and subsequent trade and other contacts between Scotland and Scandinavia, including the role of Scottish mercenaries in the wars between Sweden and Denmark. But other significant points of contact can be made. The shared heritage of landscape and climate, coupled with Presbyterian and communitarian ideologies, can be discerned in terms of similar aspects of cultural expression including dour introspection, black humour and bouts of garrulous excess. This may be why productive links have been formed in more recent years between Scottish and Scandinavian – notably Danish – filmmakers, leading to a number of co-productions including *Breaking the Waves* (Lars von Trier, 1996), *Wilbur Wants to Kill Himself* (Lone Scherfig, 2002), *The Last Great Wilderness* (David Mackenzie, 2002) and *Red Road* (Andrea Arnold, 2006). As Jonathan Murray argues, this 'still ongoing process of collaboration between individuals and institutions working within the Scottish and Danish production sectors represents perhaps the most visible example of contemporary Scottish cinema's systematic move beyond a single set of borders in both industrial and representational terms'.[15]

In a different way that predates this current development of what Mette Hjort has called 'affinitive transnationalism',[16] the three films considered in this essay challenge certain assumptions about cinematic representation and Scottish national identity. They do this by laying bare and probing the tensions that exist between familiar categories of analysis: tradition and modernity, male and female, inside and outside, responsibility and freedom, the domestic and the artistic. In all three films the relationship between subjectivity and landscape is crucial: offering possibility, identity and belonging while simultaneously imposing limits, provoking anxieties and reflecting fears. But what emerges is a sense of complexity and pluralism in which the nation may be privileged but never all encompassing: Janey's Scottishness in *Another Time, Another Place* is experienced as oppressive in both emotional and legal terms (in the legal aspect, her liaison with Luigi transgresses not only marital fidelity but also the rules governing the behaviour of POWs); Gerda's Orcadian identity ensures her dislocation in Edinburgh; and Frances's anchor is provided by her familial relations. And, in terms of the key concerns with space, place and landscape, this complex subjectivity is underpinned by a key trope running through all three films: that zone of liminality, of uncertainty but ultimately of possibility, where the determinate solidity of terra firma intersects with the indeterminate fluidity of the sea.

Notes

1 See Duncan Petrie, *Screening Scotland* (London: British Film Institute, 2000).
2 Cairns Craig, 'Visitors from the stars: Scottish film culture', *Cencrastus*, 11 (New Year 1983), pp. 2–11.
3 While the main outsider – the pompous English army office Captain Waggett (Basil Radford) – is undermined by the anarchic forces of the islanders of Todday, his college Sergeant Odd (Bruce Seaton) falls in love with a local girl and is integrated into the community. Thus the film embodies both narrative tendencies.
4 See Peter Womack, *Improvement and Romance: Constructing the Myth of the Highlands* (London: Macmillan, 1989).
5 The most recent manifestation of this tradition is the animated feature from Pixar *Brave* (Mark Andrews, Brenda Chapman, 2012), which, in addition to incorporating this digital simulation of iconic highland landscapes of untamed wilderness punctuated by jagged peaks and cascading waterfalls, breaks with tradition by having a female central protagonist, albeit one reminiscent of other fiery red-headed highland maidens, notably Jessica Lange's portrayal of Mary Macgregor in the 1995 version of *Rob Roy.*
6 The representational trope of Clydesideism is discussed by Colin McArthur in his chapter 'Scotland and cinema: the iniquities of the fathers', in Colin McArthur (ed.), *Scotch Reels: Scotland in Cinema and Television* (London: British Film Institute, 1982), pp. 40–69. But, for a more detailed discussion of the urban tradition, see Ian Spring, *Phantom Village: The Myth of the New Glasgow* (Edinburgh: Polygon, 1990).
7 Martin Lefebvre, 'Between setting and landscape in the cinema', in Martin Lefebvre (ed.), *Landscape and Film* (London and New York: Routledge, 2006), pp. 19–60; p. 53.
8 Susan C. Triesman, 'Sharman MacDonald: the generation of identity', in Aileen Christianson and Alison Lumsden (eds), *Contemporary Scottish Women Writers* (Edinburgh: Edinburgh University Press, 2000), pp. 53–64; p. 54.
9 See Catherine Fowler and Gillian Helfield, 'Introduction', in Catherine Fowler and Gillian Helfield (eds), *Representing the Rural: Space, Place and Identity in Films about the Land* (Detroit: Wayne State University Press, 2006), pp. 1–14.

10 Jane Sillars and Myra MacDonald, 'Gender, spaces, changes: emerging identities in a Scotland in transition', in Neil Blain and David Hutchison (eds), *The Media in Scotland* (Edinburgh: Edinburgh University Press, 2008), pp. 183–98.

11 John Brown, 'The land beyond Brigadoon', *Sight & Sound*, 53: 1 (1983/4), pp. 40–6; p. 45.

12 In 1919 the literary critic G. Gregory Smith coined the term 'Caledonian Antisyzygy' (the idea of dueling polarities within one identity) as a recurring feature in the Scottish character. See G. Gregory Smith, *Scottish Literature: Character and Influence* (London: Macmillan, 1919).

13 Sarah Neely, 'Stalking the image: Margaret Tait and intimate film-making practices', *Screen*, 49: 2 (2008), pp. 216–21; p. 216.

14 Ian Goode, 'Scottish cinema and Scottish imaginings: *Blue Black Permanent* and *Stella Does Tricks*', *Screen*, 46: 2 (2005), pp. 235–40; p. 237.

15 Jonathan Murray, 'Blurring borders: Scottish cinema in the twenty-first century', *Journal of British Cinema and Television*, 9: 3 (2012), pp. 400–18; p. 403.

16 Mette Hjort, 'Affinitive and milieu-building transnationalism: the *Advance Party* initiative', in Dina Iordanova, David Martin-Jones and Belén Vidal (eds), *Cinema at the Periphery* (Detroit: Wayne State University Press, 2010), pp. 46–66.

8

Fantasy, fallacy and allusion: reconceptualising British landscapes through the lens of children's cinema

Suzanne Speidel

The British Landscape, more than almost any other, save perhaps that of the Netherlands, has been shaped by humans. The countryside is a fabrication, an artifice, reinvented every so many years or generations to match and mirror the latest currents in farming, industry, road building or the rush of people to and from the city. Even seemingly unchanged landscapes, like those of the Lake District, are not exactly still. Once, before Wordsworth, the Lakes would have been known to outsiders, if at all, as a place and topography too wild by half. For the past 150 years they have been a playground, at first for Romantic travellers in search of the 'sublime', and now for trekkers, climbers and holiday-makers in motor homes and bright sports and leisurewear. Nothing stays the same.[1]

This observation, by writer and architecture critic Jonathan Glancey, occurs in the introduction to a book of photographs by John Davies entitled *The British Landscape*. Davies' volume contains images of cityscapes and of rural peaks and crags, but it is dominated by what might be termed 'in-between-scapes' – that is, town edges marked by allotments, or countryside intersected by railways, motorways, farm buildings, quarries, collieries and cooling towers. Davies' photographs and Glancey's introduction reframe a familiar, received binary between the human-made urban on one hand and the natural, untouched countryside on the other. In Davies' photographs the urban, the industrial, the rural and the agricultural are knitted together, variations on built environments and 'fabrication'.

Within the British film industry and its critical reception, a rural–urban dichotomy is strongly evident, particularly since two distinct genres – social realism and historical or 'costume' drama – have traditionally been held up as synonymous with 'quality cinema'. The first of these – associated with the documentary movement, for example, or with Ken Loach, war-time dramas and New Wave, 'kitchen sink' films – brings to mind the urban through its focus on social problems and working communities. The second genre – associated with biographical films as well as with literary adaptations – brings to mind the rural through its frequent focus on pre-industrial England and/or the privileged, land-owning classes. Because of the dominance of these two genres an urban–rural binary is ingrained in our cultural perception of British cinema, which is often seen as characterised by either grey, realist 'grit' or nostalgic pastures green.

What both genres have in common is that they are defined by expectations of authenticity. That this is the case with social realism is clear, and the prevalence of the genre within British cinema has prompted Andrew Higson to define British film culture as 'profoundly mistrustful of anything other than a particular de-dramatized naturalistic form: "style" becomes something which gets in the way of the message of the film'.[2] With this in mind, it is perhaps not surprising that costume drama, also known as 'heritage' cinema, has been critiqued (most influentially by Higson) for the distorting nostalgia of its *mise-en-scène*: Higson's study of heritage films of the 1980s and 1990s begins with the assertion that 'certain English costume dramas of the period seemed to articulate a nostalgic and conservative celebration of the values and lifestyles of the privileged classes … in doing so an England that no longer existed seemed to be reinvented as something fondly remembered and desirable'.[3] Yet, even with heritage cinema, the presence of verisimilitude, at least, is assumed and valued, particularly in its emphasis on historical props, costumes and detail. The debates around heritage cinema, which grew out of the films and politics of 1980s and 1990s Britain, have been particularly polarised and polemical, with heritage cinema accused of nostalgia, conservatism and even Thatcherism on one hand and defended as populist, feminist and progressive on the other. A key issue, which separates the genre's detractors from its defenders, is the degree to which authenticity and verisimilitude are assumed to be the films' aim, since it is in effect a failure to fulfil such presumed intentions, and a failure in the related aesthetic of realism, which are at the heart of accusations that the films idealise the past through pastoral imagery celebrating the land owned by the ruling elite.

This is made clear by Andy Medhurst's assertion that 'For every British film concerned with respectful, meticulous reconstruction of the past, there are a dozen more which treat history as a great big dressing up box, where a genteel commitment to period verisimilitude is discarded for the romping joys of frocking about'.[4] Thus Medhurst cites 'the heaving cleavages and swished capes of Gainsborough and Hammer' as a direct, favourable contrast to 1980s costume drama. Ironically, advocates of heritage films also cite Gainsborough and Hammer, aligning period films with the extravagance and sexual daring of melodrama and horror. In these readings historical verisimilitude is not seen as a key preoccupation of the genre – rather historical, often pastoral settings give licence to sexual freedom and taboos because they signal a removal of contemporary institutions, prejudices and pressures.

If traditionally the two 'quality' genres within British cinema have been social realism and period drama, the films that are generally cited as the antithesis of these are associated with escapism and excess. Thus Higson laments the 'ossification' of the realist aesthetic because it 'represses the traditions of the gothic, the expressionist, the melodramatic, the "magic" realist'.[5] The prejudice against these modes has now been extensively analysed, particularly by the contributors to Charles Barr's *All Our Yesterdays* (1986).[6] In fact Barr's landmark anthology was a key work in a tide of revisionism within the study of British films that has in many ways reworked traditional, critical values of 'quality' cinema. Thus what Julian Petley has dubbed the 'lost continents' of fantasy, melodrama, horror and crime films within British cinema rapidly became its newfound land, and are now the staple ground of British film studies. At the same time the nature of critical revisionism inevitably entrenches critical binaries, since the fantasy, extravagance and excess of Powell and Pressburger, for example, or Hammer horror and Gainsborough melodrama, are thereby positioned in opposition to social realism and period drama; they are the 'unBritish' British films, either because they are not set in the UK or because lighting, colour palettes and landscapes inflect supposedly British environments with exotic 'otherness' and expressive excess.

In this confusingly well-trodden critical terrain, the overlooked, hybrid genre of the children's film offers a useful, fresh perspective. An overwhelming number of British and Anglo-American children's films since the turn of the twenty-first century fall into the genre of fantasy, and it is noticeable that children's fiction has sometimes been co-opted by revisionists seeking to promote the genres included in Petley's 'lost continent'. In *A New Heritage of Horror: The English Gothic Cinema*, David Pirie comments that children's fiction has 'at times seemed like a last refuge for fantasy in this country'[7] while also bemoaning the unremitting realist focus of the 1997 adult-selected books shortlisted for the Guardian Children's Fiction Prize and the Carnegie Medal. However, he notes with pleasure that both prizes were awarded in the same month that Bloomsbury published J. K. Rowling's *Harry Potter and the Philosopher's Stone*, thereby signalling Rowling's seven books and their eight film adaptations as the triumphant resurrection of Britain's fantasy tradition.

The films adapted from the Harry Potter novels[8] demonstrate how effectively children's cinema can blur critical boundaries. With their stories of good and evil wizards and witches, dragons, goblins, elves and so on, they belong clearly within the realm of fantasy fiction. They also evoke the Gothic: Harry's story of 'banishment' into a non-magical, or 'muggle', world of misery and neglect, from which he returns to claim his castle (Hogwarts School), his vault of gold and his place as the magical world's saviour, has strong Gothic connotations, resembling what Angela Wright dubs 'the classic Gothic plot motif' of, for example, Sir Walter Scott's *Guy Mannering* (1829) (which Wright summarises as 'a wronged laird, raised as a merchant and a soldier, returns to reclaim his ancestral home'[9]). In the film adaptations of Rowling's novels it is specifically through rural landscapes that the Harry Potter stories are rendered Gothic, through the wild, inhospitable mountains and forests that surround Hogwarts as well as the spires, the cliff-like towers, the machicolations and the lake-side setting of the castle (which strongly resembles a French Gothic château[10]).

It is often the films' urban scenes that most obviously evoke heritage cinema, particularly the two magical London streets of Diagon Alley and Knockturn Alley, which bring Charles Dickens to mind – more specifically they resemble the lively whimsicality of the etchings by long-term Dickens illustrator Hablôt Knight Browne (or 'Phiz') as well as the darker, more grotesque plates provided by George Cruikshank for *Oliver Twist* (1838).[11] These visual references are likewise detectable in many film adaptations of Dickens's novels, ranging from British film classics such as David Lean's *Oliver Twist* (1948) to more recent productions such as Douglas McGrath's *Nicholas Nickleby* (2002).

The films' combined cast also evokes period drama, since it contains a high number of prestigious British actors, many of whom are stalwarts of the heritage genre: Helena Bonham Carter, Ralph Fiennes, Michael Gambon, Richard Griffiths, Gary Oldman, Alan Rickman, Fiona Shaw, Maggie Smith, Imelda Staunton and Emma Thompson all have recurring roles across the series (Kenneth Branagh, Jim Broadbent, Robert Hardy, John Hurt and Elizabeth Spriggs have smaller roles or appear in only one film). A similar approach to casting is evident in two other children's films I shall consider in this chapter, namely *Nanny McPhee* (Kirk Browne, 2005) and *Nanny McPhee and the Big Bang* (Susannah White, 2010), inspired by Christianna Brand's Nurse Matilda books. Between them the films feature Ralph Fiennes, Colin Firth, Derek Jacobi, Maggie Smith, Imelda Staunton and Emma Thompson. The volume of prestige (often theatrically trained) performers in all these films and the ensemble (quasi-incestuous) casting practices are highly reminiscent of heritage cinema.

Children's cinema is of particular interest because it habitually breaks down other generic distinctions. Period drama spills over into fantasy and the Gothic without evoking the values and judgements of cultural capital so redolent in the notions of 'quality' cinema versus 'lost continents'. Social problems (childhood neglect, poverty, dysfunctional family life, war-time evacuation) also often merge into fantasy and escapism in ways not usually tolerated in British films aimed at adults. (As Higson observes, it is the realist aesthetic that is deemed 'responsible engaged cinema'[12] in British film culture.) Children's cinema shares with children's literature the licence – even the requisite – to be at once didactic and playful. In her study of the illustration of children's books, Susan S. Meyer observes that in the nineteenth century the stories told to children underwent a change, in that, while 'moral tales' persisted, 'something new was added: stories were written and illustrated specifically for children and were meant to be attractive and interesting, not simply to instruct or to keep them quiet, but also to entertain them'.[13]

Of course we understand that the film industry overall seeks to entertain us, but it is the pleasure to be found in *pictures* that is particularly stressed in children's fiction: while the twentieth century saw the end to the nineteenth-century illustration boom brought about by the serialisation of novels, it is significant that the practice continues unabated in children's fiction. Children's cinema, therefore, is useful in circumventing the ingrained Puritanism that characterises British film culture and criticism, and that is evident in the valorisation of naturalism, social realism and 'responsible' filmmaking as well as in hostility towards the picturesque landscapes of heritage films.

The films' genre hybridity paradoxically redraws and reproduces previous screen renditions of British, rural landscapes: the British countryside is filtered through an array of visual allusions, which include cinematic references (such as to costume drama and other children's films) as well as the illustrated novel, the illustration of children's stories, and landscape paintings. In the case of the Nanny McPhee films, landscapes take on an allusive pastoral extremity which shades into garish artificiality, while in the Harry Potter series landscapes present us with a geographical and historical bricolage in which Britishness is mixed with North American and various European *mise-en-scène*, and the present day is set alongside Victorian, Elizabethan and medieval iconography. The films' presentation of rural Britain is at once unexpected but highly mimetic, which means that it provides fresh views and insights when it comes to landscape while also serving to reframe and magnify the techniques of British cinema elsewhere.

The films I consider in this chapter are typical of many made in Britain today, in that they are classified as UK/US co-productions (unlike, for example, *The Secret Garden* (Anieska Holland, 1993) and *101 Dalmations* and its sequel (Stephen Herek, 1996; Kevi Lima, 2000), whose funding and taxation mean that they are officially US films). They were filmed and set in Britain, albeit in a country that has a closeted magical side to it (this differentiates them from the Chronicles of Narnia films, whose principal photography took place in New Zealand and whose setting is a fantasy world). The Nanny McPhee and the Harry Potter films feature British landscapes prominently and expressively, and the global box-office phenomenon of the Harry Potter franchise means that these films in particular constitute the most viewed images of the British countryside produced in twenty-first-century cinema.

Nanny McPhee was adapted by Emma Thompson from Christianna Brand's children's book *Nurse Matilda*, the first of three stories about the Brown family and their 'terribly, terribly naughty'[14] children, who require the care of the magical Nurse Matilda in order to learn to be good. The film includes much that is the book, but changes Mr Brown (Colin Firth) into a widow, who must remarry immediately on the orders of the family's wealthy Great-Aunt Adelaide (Angela Landsbury). The film's story is inherently allusive and knowing when it comes to children's fiction: the scullery maid, Evangeline (Kelly Macdonald), learns to read with the aid of a book about a horrible stepmother; the children, well-versed in such tales, are (rightly) convinced that their prospective stepmother, Mrs Quickly (Celia Imrie), will be cruel; and the film's ending is signalled by Evangeline's prediction that the farm girl is secretly an 'educated' lady, fit to marry the hero. The film also hints at fictional parallels: aerial shots and swirling winds suggest that Nanny McPhee (Emma Thompson) flies to the Browns' house in the manner of Mary Poppins, and Evangeline's careful diction, after Aunt Adelaide has been tricked into adopting her, brings to mind Eliza Doolittle (paving the way for Evangeline's marriage to Mr Brown).

Nanny McPhee and the Big Bang is not based on Christianna Brand's sequel *Nurse Matilda Goes to Town*. Instead the story is original to Emma Thompson's screenplay and features Nanny McPhee helping the Green family, whose father is away fighting during the Second World War and whose uncle is seeking to sell the family farm from under them in order to pay his gambling debts (Nanny McPhee's magical qualities are stressed by the fact that she has not aged since the Victorian era of the first film).

The story is less knowing in its references to children's fiction than is the first film, though its central premise of the farm children and their city cousins, who learn to like and help each other, draws on the British tradition of war-time evacuation stories (such as C. S. Lewis's Narnia books). In the film the British countryside and its urban antithesis become key story motifs through the contrasts between the two sets of siblings, and this is signalled by the unfeasibly muddy farm yard (which ruins Cousin Celia's elegant town clothes). Both films feature 'single' parents in financial difficulties, as opposed to the deluded, ineffectual parents of Brand's books (the children's behaviour thus emerging as responses to emotional and domestic crises), and these family structures signal further cinematic antecedents, specifically much-loved, British children's film adaptations: in *Nanny McPhee* the motherless children in need of a maternal substitute evokes *Chitty Chitty Bang Bang* (Ken Hughes, 1968) while in *Nanny McPhee and the Big Bang* the enforced absence of the father is reminiscent of *The Railway Children* (Lionel Jeffries, 1970). The narratives offer a sly, left-wing message through Nanny McPhee's explanation (not present in the books) that she is a 'government nanny', a mischievous reclaiming of the phrase 'nanny state' as well as a condoning of a welfare system that supports families in need.

For both films, extensive sets were constructed in the English countryside, which contributes to their unfeasibly picturesque qualities. For *Nanny McPhee*, the Brown family's house and surrounding village were built in the grounds of Penn House, Buckinghamshire, near Pinewood Studios.[15] For *Nanny McPhee and the Big Bang*, the Greens' farm was constructed in the fields of Tilsey Farm, near Guilford, Surrey – the farmhouse, its outbuildings, garden and duck pond all the creation of production designer Simon Elliott.[16] The film opens with an aerial shot over English wooded countryside and green fields and descends towards the half-timbered Tudor farmhouse nestled in a gentle valley beside a field of golden barley. *Nanny McPhee* begins with even more overt images of quaint artifice, its gliding aerial shot descending to a red-brick, late Victorian, Gothic-revival house with a miscellany of pointed arches, steep gables and a pitched-roof porch. This eclecticism signals the house's film-set origins, particularly since it includes decidedly un-English elements, such as the front balcony, or gallery, which is reminiscent of American vernacular adaptations of the neo-Gothic (it brings to mind film and television American Gothic set designs (Alfred Hitchcock, 1960) as well as more playful renditions, such as the mansion in *The Munsters* (television series, 1964–6)).

Brand's novels include naturalistic, black-and-white illustrations by her cousin Edward Ardizzione. However, the Nanny McPhee films resemble more stylised traditions of children's book illustrations, such as nineteenth-century pastoral prints, as exemplified by writer-illustrators Kate Greenaway and Randolph Caldecott.[17] *Nanny McPhee* seems particularly indebted to Greenaway's bucolic images of frisking animals and solemn little girls, which were both exaggerated (illustrator Edward Crane accused her of '[overdoing] the big bonnet'[18]), and characterised by simple, flat shades produced by colour-washing a wood-block print.[19] However, the garishness of the film creates a sense of Greenaway mischievously re-coloured, a notion that is made literal through Mrs Quickly's brash tastes: her thatched cottage is pink, she dresses the children in maroon and green shepherdess outfits, and she has lambs dipped in maroon and yellow dye for her wedding day. When the wedding between Mrs Quickly and Mr Brown descends instead into a food fight with purple cake, green cream pies and pink meringues, the impression of a world re-coloured using a children's paintbox increases; Nanny McPhee's magical interference makes it snow in August, thereby 'restoring' Kate-Greenaway-esque, lacy whiteness to the rustic outfits, yet the effect is to heighten the artificiality further, since the silvery-white glow of the nuptials that follow constitutes yet another layer on top of multiple coats of colour.

In *Nanny McPhee and the Big Bang* the countryside is also full of rich, incongruous colour: Nanny McPhee inspires teamwork in the warring cousins by making the escaped piglets fly and perform a synchronised swimming routine in pond water turned azure blue (the sequence is shot from above in the manner of an Esther Williams aquamusical). The suggestion of England repainted occurs most noticeably when Celia mistakes an elegant eighteenth-century mansion for her cousins' home. The house is Palladian in style, but its austere classicism is undercut because it has been painted pink (in reality the property is Marble Hill House, in Twickenham, which is white, pink having been added with CGI).[20]

The film is full of images of rolling green meadows and fields of golden barley. The narrative's contrived qualities are emphasised when Nanny McPhee and the two oldest boys visit the War Office in London a bid to discover the fate of the Green children's father. This does not bring a dose of war-time reality: Lord

Nelson on top of his column doffs his hat, and festive-looking barrage balloons float over Battersea Power Station – one, in the shape of a pig, alludes to both the flying piglets and the cover of the Pink Floyd album *Animals* (1977), also photographed at Battersea Power Station. When the war reaches the Greens' rural idyll, it does so in the shape of a ticking unexploded bomb, which fortuitously prevents Mrs Green signing away the deeds to the farm. Again the effect is comically artificial: the bomb stands nose down, cartoonishly large and incongruous amid the rippling barley, a caricature of alien ills invading England's peaceful, pleasant lands.

Both films self-consciously signal the pictorial nature of their landscapes. At the end of *Nanny McPhee and the Big Bang*, the two girls, Megs and Celia, diffuse the bomb, helped by Nanny McPhee's pet jackdaw, Mr Edelweiss. The bird, having consumed large quantities of explosive putty, gives a hurricane-inducing burp, which whips up all the barley into twinkling shapes in the sky before depositing the harvest in exquisitely arranged rows of grainstacks. The scene brings to mind a tradition of 'haymaking' landscape paintings, such as George Stubbs's *Haymakers* and *Reapers* (1783) and John Constable's *A Hayfield near East Bergholt at Sunset* (1812). Yet even these green, blue and gold, quintessentially English images are overlaid with associations from overseas: director Susannah White has stated that the scene was inspired by haystacks in Romania,[21] while the round, domed-topped stacks that punctuate the smaller piles most obviously evoke Claude Monet's *Haystacks* series (1890–1). The resemblance to landscape painting foregrounds the pleasures of pictorial landscape, and – as with the Brown family's American Gothic house – the European quality of the haystacks heightens our sense of a fabricated, exaggeratedly playful composition.

Similarly *Nanny McPhee* contains a moment when Aunt Adelaide's carriage drives off into a misty sunset, after which an iris effect and a dissolve to a stained-glass window make it appear as if the carriage is a lead decoration within the coloured glass. This emphasises the graphic properties of the sunset and the carriage's silhouette, while the iris and the window draw our attention to the framing of the landscape. In both films the landscape is at once exaggerated and distilled, the narrative coming to rest at carefully composed, idyllic moments within rural lives and rhythms (the bringing in of harvest, the setting of the sun). The films are richly allusive throughout, and in their exuberant, mimetic artificiality they place particular emphasis on the 'reproduced' element of landscape composition.

The Harry Potter series shares with the Nanny McPhee films an allusive eclecticism, freely mixing visual and literary references. While the Nanny McPhee films confine most settings and location shooting to the Home Counties (identified by Higson as the preferred setting for heritage films[22]), the Harry Potter films cover a lot more of the British Isles, with much of the series shot on location in Scotland and the north of England. This again links the films to Gothic traditions, since the wild inhospitality necessary for the expounding of Gothic themes is not so readily available in the more populated south of the country. Neither the books nor the films specify the exact location of Hogwarts School, a geographical evasion that in itself has Gothic antecedents, as Wright notes in her study of 'Scottish Gothic' – for example, Scott sets *Waverley* (1814) in 'the northern part of the island'.[23] In the films, Scottish highland and northern-English grandeur abound. In *The Philosopher's Stone*, Quidditch practice takes place against the Norman exterior of Alnwick Castle in Northumberland; in *The Prisoner of Azkaban*, a full moon glows eerily over the misty crags of Glencoe; in *The Goblet of Fire*, Harry battles a dragon at Steall Falls, Glen Nevis; and repeatedly in the series the Hogwarts Express crosses the magnificent Glenfinnan Viaduct in Lochaber to take the children to school.[24]

These rural landscapes have the effect of rendering northern, and especially Scottish, topography as the magical 'Other', especially when they are set against the 'muggle' world, often signalled by recognisable (especially London) landmarks such as the Houses of Parliament, the Millennium Bridge and Shaftesbury Avenue. At the same time, the lack of geographical specificity helps to shift our aesthetic experience of the UK as a whole dramatically northwards, subsuming Englishness (and the traditionally dominant setting of the south-east of England) into the spectacular, sublime topographies of Scotland and northern England. The filming processes enact this literally, swallowing up interior and school-ground locations shot in southern England – such as the University of Oxford's Divinity School and the cloisters of New College – inside the uncompromising walls of Hogwarts Castle.

The exterior of Hogwarts was shot by combining real-life locations with shots of an enormous model and CGI.[25] The castle and its moods are highly changeable, and Hogwarts's assortment of structures (towers, spires, cloisters, cathedral-like halls and flying buttresses) is exacerbated by repeated not-quite matches between real-life, closer location shots and the CGI and scale-model renditions. The cumulative representations of eight films also add new elements (such as a wooden, roofed bridge and a stone viaduct, which provide entry into the castle in the later films) and alter previously existing topography, such as the route down to Hagrid's hut.

These inconsistencies add to the mystical quality of the landscape, while specific changes increase the sense of the sublime as the films progress. For example, the transplantation of Hagrid's hut from its filming location in Black Park, Buckinghamshire, for the first two films to Glencoe in *The Prisoner of Azkaban* provides a sharp contrast between the elevation of the school and the steep, rocky valley into which the children venture when they leave the premises. Christine Riding and Nigel Llewellyn point out the origins of the word 'sublime' ('a conjunction of two Latin terms, the preposition *sub*, meaning below or up to and the noun *limen*, meaning limit, boundary or threshold'), arguing that the concept encompasses a 'sense of striving or pushing upwards against an overbearing force'.[26] In art that connotes the sublime, views upwards and landscapes that elevate towards the heavens are recurring motifs – for example, Claude Lorrain's Baroque *Landscape with the Nymph Egeria and Numa* (1669), in which Rome is seen to the right of the frame high above Lake Nemi and the Temple of Diana, or Thomas Seddon's Victorian *Jerusalem and the Valley of Jehoshaphat from the Hill of Evil Counsel* (1854), in which Jerusalem is perched to the left on a steep, rocky hilltop. The closing shots of *The Philosopher's Stone* and *The Order of the Phoenix* are constructed similarly to these sublime landscapes, the camera rising or tilting to encompass, in the first film, Hogsmeade station in the foreground and Hogwarts (its spires partly enveloped in mist) to the left of the screen, and, in the fifth film, the forest and lake in the foreground and Hogwarts, below billowing clouds, rising up behind to the right.

In these images the sublime constitutes a tranquil or celebratory evocation of nature, typified in art by John Martin's Romantic depiction of *The Plains of Heaven*, (1851–3) (included in his *Last Judgement Triptych: The Apocalyptic Sublime in the Age of Spectacle*), with its gentle undulations and clouds, soaring mountains and serene waters. Elsewhere in the films the sublime emerges, as Riding and Llewellyn put it, 'as expressions of awe, dread and terror',[27] whereby the magnificence of nature and landscape imbues a corollary sense of human insignificance or despair. From *The Prisoner of Azkaban* onwards, the *mise-en-scène* becomes increasingly dark, composed predominantly of blues, greens and greys, or else shrouded (even enveloped) in blackness. The third film also introduces the reaper-like dementors, who bring icy darkness with them and do in fact instil despair in their human prey. As Harry frantically defends his unconscious godfather, Sirius, from swarming dementors on the stony shorefront of the frozen lake, the mood is reminiscent of the other two paintings in Martin's triptych, namely *The Great Day of His Wrath* (1851–3) and *The Last Judgement* (1853), with their thunderous clouds and damned souls falling into the abyss.

Throughout the series Hogwarts and its environs evoke the Gothic – both the horror and the fairy-tale ends of the spectrum. The castle itself mingles the French medieval château with Scottish baronial architecture, although its most obvious antecedents are in fact Disney castles, as exemplified in *Snow White and the Seven Dwarfs* (William Cottrell et al., 1937), *Cinderella* (Clyde Geronimi et al., 1950) and *Beauty and the Beast* (Gary Trousdale and Kirk Wise, 1991) – as well as Disney's theme parks. These are at once elaborate and simplified structures, emphasising the outlines of pointed spires and unfeasibly tall, narrow towers.

The films' allusiveness again mixes Britishness with pastiches that are distinctly non-British. In *The Prisoner of Azkaban* and *The Order of the Phoenix*, the village of Hogsmeade looks exaggeratedly Germanic: its snow-covered houses with enormous, steep gables and spear-like chimneys are reminiscent of illustrations of *The Fairy Tales of the Brothers Grimm*, such as those by Arthur Rackham (1909),[28] as well as German Expressionist embellishments of this tradition, such as the house of inventor Rotwang in Fritz Lang's *Metropolis* (1927). These references are made explicit in *Harry Potter and the Deathly Hallows: Part 1* when Hermione (Emma Watson) narrates the Deathly Hallows fairy tale, 'The Tale of the Three Brothers'. This is simultaneously shown in animation, using computer-generated 'puppets' that strongly resemble Rackham's wood-block-print, black, silhouette figures such as those of 'The Golden Goose'.[29] The effect of this animated interlude is to emphasise Expressionist and fairy-tale *mise-en-scène* elsewhere in the film, such as the steeple tower where Grindelwald is imprisoned and the Lovegoods' black, lopsided house. Thus British ruralness exists within a multi-layered, transnational intertextuality, which magnifies and complicates the treatment of landscape, mixing the familiar and the alien, the actual with the exotically fictional.

Although the landscape is pictorial in its grandeur and pastiche, this is combined with non-pictorial properties, which are distinct to cinema, such as the films' high degree of camera mobility. This is more marked in the later films, in the wake of groundbreaking CGI in Jackson's *Lord of the Rings* trilogy, which brought to mainstream films a soaring, diving, circling cinematography more readily associated with computer games. In *The Order of the Phoenix* the camera races low over the lake before almost skimming tree-tops in a careering upwards crane, then ascends high over the quadrangle where children are milling about after the Christmas holidays. Such shots owe something to tourist-industry, television advertising (and may themselves be an influence on Scotland's National Tourist Organisation's current 'Visit Scotland' campaign), though their computer-enhanced speed and agility also produce non-naturalistic, sometimes vertigo-inducing effects. The films' aerial shots also invest the British Isles with an artificial sense of scale: *The Chamber of Secrets* opens with the camera at cloud level, before it descends to show a vast suburban sprawl, filling almost the entire screen with row upon row of identical houses. This heightens the distinction between the rural magnificence of the magical world and the stifling conventionality of Harry's muggle relatives. Yet, the effect is also startling, retaining the UK's familiar, modest, tightly packed housing while imbuing the country itself with a US sense of proportion.

The Harry Potter films also knit together a whole array of historically based, visual allusions, making for striking, sometimes incongruous juxtapositions. Set in contemporary times, they place today's fashions, streets, transport and technology alongside Dickensian dress, Tudor houses, fairy-tale villages, pagan monuments, collegiate quadrangles, candle-lit banquets, a medieval castle and a steam train. From *The Prisoner of Azkaban* onwards the steep route down to Hagrid's hut is lined with huge, henge-like stones, while the round hut itself has a primitive, Pictish quality. In *The Goblet of Fire* the Quidditch World Cup Stadium looks like a brand-new Olympic venue, while the tents beside it resemble a battle encampment from the Wars of the Roses – just as the flags and banners of the Hogwarts Quidditch pitch suggest a medieval jousting tournament. In the final film, after the 'Battle of Hogwarts', close-scale shots of the ruined castle bring to mind bomb-ravaged Europe in 1945.

This historical bricolage matches the stories' generic hybridity: as well as Gothic motifs such as lost inheritance and murdered parents, the novels pose mysteries and scatter clues, in the manner of detective fiction; present quests for the three young heroes, as in epic poetry; and show us Harry's maturation into adulthood, evoking the Bildungsroman. Lord Voldemort's valorising of 'pure blood' also lends political, dystopian dimensions to the fiction: as 'muggles' and 'mudbloods' face persecution, imprisonment or even murder under the auspices of the 'Muggle-Born Registration Commission',[30] it becomes clear that this is in fact a parable for children about the horrors of modern totalitarianism and ethnic cleansing.

While the earlier films employed dystopian iconography (such as the banner depicting the Minister of Magic in *The Order of the Phoenix*, reminiscent of Stalinism – and also *Citizen Kane* (Orson Welles, 1941)), *Harry Potter and the Deathly Hallows: Part 1* extends this to its depiction of the country at large. Harry, Ron and Hermione (Daniel Radcliffe, Rupert Grint and Emma Watson), in hiding and in search of Voldemort's magical 'Horcruxes', walk across fields as sinister smoke trails from enemy 'Death Eaters' shoot across the sky above them; they wander through a burnt-out caravan park (reminiscent of *Mad Max* (George Miller, 1979)), along mud flats under the Severn Bridge and between cooling towers (while on the soundtrack the voice of a resistance radio station reads a list of 'missing witches and wizards'). In this film, 'fabricated' rural landscapes, as in those found in John Davies' photographs, are very much in evidence in the form of such 'in-between' lands. This is suggestive of the work of Iain Sinclair, particularly since our three heroes walk through normally non-pedestrian spaces, in montages reminiscent of the interminable transience of Sinclair and Christopher Petit's *London Orbital* (2002).

Elsewhere in the film the teenagers travel around the country using magical 'apparition' (they walk when Ron's injury prevents this), materialising in Shaftsbury Avenue or Hogsmeade and escaping just as abruptly to precarious, rural sanctuaries, such as the Forest of Dean. Since enemies can also 'apparate', any sense of the countryside as magically safe is undermined, and at times rural landscapes look primordial or alien (as when Harry and Hermione camp on a vast 'shelf' of jigsaw-like, fragmented rocks – the 'limestone pavement' at Malham Cove, North Yorkshire). The film is characterised by generic uncertainty, partly through the inclusion of liminal fringe-lands instead of a reliance on a rural–urban binary, and partly because the act of 'apparition' repeatedly re-locates and dislocates the story, so that the narrative takes on the form of a road movie without travel. The irresolution of *Harry Potter and the Deathly Hallows: Part 1* is also exacerbated by its aerial shots (particularly those filmed directly from above, rendering topography difficult to fathom), which take on the quality of a dispassionate survey of Britain on the brink of ruin. In this film, therefore, historical eclecticism extends into a nightmare vision of a dystopian, even apocalyptic, national future.

Landscape in the Harry Potter films sometimes evokes a mood that is close to Freud's notion of the uncanny. While the films' fantasy genre seems to lessen its claim to the uncanny (because its alien properties can be accounted for within the realm of the fiction), it is rendered both familiar and strange through generic hybridity: the films' affinities to period drama are rendered startling through their modern-day setting and vice versa, and their transnational intertextuality is rendered strange through its Britishness and vice versa. Similarly, what Robert Stam terms 'concretization'[31] (whereby film adaptation makes visible what novels describe) also makes extraordinary the experience of *seeing* the (familiar) world of Rowling's fiction within film-industry, generic contexts. For example, in *Harry Potter and the Deathly Hallows: Part 2*, contemporary teenagers engage in explosive 'shoot-outs' with wooden wands against the backdrop of a medieval, Gothic castle. These scenes may be 'natural' to Rowling's diegesis, but they are also curiously incongruous within the generic conventions of cinema.

All the films I discuss in this chapter make flagrant use of pastiche. The notion of pastiche has been put forward previously in defence of heritage cinema,[32] by arguing that the genre displays, not slavish *re*construction of period authenticity, but the constructed nature of traditions, ideologies and authority. What children's period films show us is how pastiche also functions as 'illustration', with the allusive artificiality of many shots imbuing the image with extradiegetic emphasis not dissimilar to an illustrative plate or print within a book. The allusions are often transnational and pan-historical, evoking neither period detail nor Britishness but rather eclectic, recognisable, intertextual images of 'ruralness' (such as the country house, the Gothic castle, the farm yard or the harvest), which serve to augment stories through their connotative meanings and previous representations. This technique is in fact frequently employed in heritage cinema: in Joe Wright's *Pride and Prejudice* (2005), for example, lengthy tracking shots show us that the home of the Bennet sisters is surrounded by a moat, bringing a fairy-tale quality to Longbourn, which is itself transformed into a castle, or perhaps an island of maidens, on which an assortment of princes land in order to prove their worth. In Roman Polanski's *Tess* (1979), meanwhile, fields of golden corn and dappled sunshine evoke the Romanticism of J. M. W. Turner, yet, as with Turner, brush-stroke-like swirls of grey cloud and darkness quickly transform innocent warmth into brooding environments that threaten tragedy. In such moments, landscapes are co-opted into the symbolic with both childlike, literal boldness and allusive, figurative complexity. This suggests that the analogy of the book illustration – with its connotations of embellishment – may be a more useful one for our understanding of heritage films than are the realist values associated with British quality cinema.

The eclectic, stylised qualities of the landscapes I have analysed do not excite debate, largely because the films themselves are scarcely taken seriously in the critical circles that have spent decades contesting the aesthetics and ideologies of British period drama. What contemporary children's cinema suggests is how peculiarly puritanical British film culture remains; British film criticism is not yet tolerant of home-grown, visual pleasure or indeed excessive genre hybridity, and heritage cinema is still struggling with critical strictures that seem unwilling to allow it be, or do, more than one thing at once. Perhaps a change is afoot: certainly Belén Vidal's study of the figural in period film constitutes a welcome break from old, entrenched positions.[33] Children's films enjoy a status at once overlooked and privileged in British cinema, granted expressive freedom because they are 'just for children'. Of course a great many adults have watched and enjoyed the films I discuss here. It is difficult to classify them as lost continents, though they are perhaps the unacknowledged 'playgrounds', the happy sightseer's destination, in the depiction of British landscapes on film.

Notes

1 Jonathan Glancey, 'Introduction', in John Davies, *The British Landscape* (London: Chris Boot: 2006), pp. 5–7.
2 Andrew Higson, ' "Britain's outstanding contribution to the film": the documentary-realist tradition', in Charles Barr (ed.), *All Our Yesterdays: 90 Years of British Cinema* (London: British Film Institute, 1986), pp. 72–94; p. 76.
3 Andrew Higson, *English Heritage, English Cinema: Costume Drama since 1980* (Oxford: Oxford University Press, 2003), p. 12.
4 Andy Medhurst, 'Dressing the part', in Ginette Vincendeau (ed.), *Film/Literature/Heritage* (London: British Film Institute, 2001), pp. 11–14; p. 11.
5 Higson, 'Britain's outstanding contribution to the film', p. 76.
6 Charles Barr (ed.), *All Our Yesterdays: 90 Years of British Cinema* (London: British Film Institute, 1986).
7 David Pirie, *A New Heritage of Horror: The English Gothic Cinema* (London: I.B. Tauris, 2008), p. 13.
8 *Harry Potter and the Philosopher's Stone* (Chris Columbus, 2001), *Harry Potter and the Chamber of Secrets* (Chris Columbus, 2002), *Harry Potter and the Prisoner of Azkaban* (Alfonso Cuarón, 2004), *Harry Potter and the Goblet of Fire* (Mike Newell, 2005), *Harry Potter and the Order of the Phoenix* (David Yates, 2007), *Harry Potter and the Half-Blood Prince* (David Yates, 2009), *Harry Potter and the Deathly Hallows: Part 1* (David Yates, 2010), and *Harry Potter and the Deathly Hallows: Part 2* (David Yates, 2011).
9 Angela Wright, 'Scottish Gothic', in Catherine Spooner and Emma McEvoy (eds), *The Routledge Companion to the Gothic* (Abingdon: Routledge, 2007), pp. 73–82; p. 78.
10 See Banister Fletcher, *A History of Architecture* (London: Athlone Press, University of London, 18th edition, 1975), p. 613.

11 See David Bland, *The Illustration of Books* (London: Faber and Faber, 1962), p. 72; John Harthan, *The History of the Illustrated Book* (London: Thames and Hudson, 1981), p. 201.

12 Higson, ' "Britain's outstanding contribution to the film" ', p. 77.

13 Susan E. Meyer, *A Treasury of the Great Children's Book Illustrations* (New York: Harry N. Abrams, 1983), p. 13.

14 Christianna Brand, *The Collected Tales of Nurse Matilda* (London: Bloomsbury, 2007; first published 1967), p. 9.

15 See www.pennhouse.org.uk/filming/filming.htm (accessed 19 September 2013).

16 See '*Nanny MacPhee 2*: Behind the scenes,' www.wildaboutmovies.com/behind_the_ scenes/nannymcphee2-behindthescenes (accessed 19 September 2013).

17 Greenaway's work includes *Under the Window* (1879) and *Marigold Garden* (1886). Caldecott's work includes *The House that Jack Built* (1878) and *The Frog Would A-Wooing Go* (1883). See Meyer, *A Treasury of the Great Children's Book Illustrations*, pp. 109–25 and pp. 95–107.

18 Cited in Meyer, *A Treasury of the Great Children's Book Illustrations*, p. 114.

19 See Meyer, *A Treasury of the Great Children's Book Illustrations*, pp. 94–9 and pp. 109– 15. See also Brand, *The Collected Tales of Nurse Matilda*, p. 131.

20 See http://visitinghousesandgardens.wordpress.com/2013/03/10/marble-hill-house-tea-and-twittering-in-twickenham/ (accessed 19 September 2013).

21 See '*Nanny MacPhee 2*: behind the scenes'.

22 See Higson, *English Heritage, English Cinema*, p. 26.

23 Sir Walter Scott, *Waverley* (1814); cited in Wright, 'Scottish Gothic', p. 77.

24 See www.movie-locations.com/movies/h/harry_potter1.html#.UbnVXhxFF2c (accessed 19 September 2013).

25 See www.wbstudiotour.co.uk/en/tour/hogwarts-castle-model (accessed 19 September 2013).

26 Christine Riding and Nigel Llewellyn, 'British art and the sublime', www.tate.org.uk/ art/research-publications/the-sublime/christine-riding-and-nigel-llewellyn-british-art-and-the-sublime-r1109418 (accessed 19 September 2013).

27 Riding and Llewellyn, 'British art and the sublime'.

28 See, for example, 'Rumpelstiltskin', in *Grimm's Fairy Tales: Twenty Stories*, illustrated by Arthur Rackham (London: Heineman, 1973), pp. 39–43; p. 42.

29 See 'The Golden Goose,' in *Grimm's Fairy Tales: Twenty Stories*, illustrated by Arthur Rackham (London: Heineman, 1973), pp. 22–8.

30 J. K. Rowling, *Harry Potter and the Deathly Hallows* (London: Bloomsbury, 2007), p. 206.

31 Robert Stam, 'Beyond fidelity: the dialogics of adaptation', in James Naremore (ed.), *Film Adaptation* (London: Althone, 2000), pp. 54–76; p. 68.

32 See Pam Cook, *Screening the Past: Memory and Nostalgia in Cinema* (Oxford and New York: Routledge, 2005), pp. 1–21.

33 Belén Vidal, *Figuring the Past: Period Film and the Mannerist Aesthetic* (Amsterdam: Amsterdam University Press, 2012).

9

Picturesque, pastoral and dirty: uncivilised topographies in *Jane Eyre* and *Wuthering Heights*

Stella Hockenhull

An agitated young man stands dejectedly in a dark, dilapidated and unkempt room before throwing himself to the floor and banging his head repeatedly on the ground in apparent frustration and suffering. At this point a dissolve suggests a flashback and the camera, hand-held and set at a low angle, forms its own pathway through coarse upland grasses to reveal a gloomy and bleak moorland setting. Two dimly lit figures, one hooded and both with faces in shadow, appear in silhouette against a darkening sky. At this moment the camera reveals a number of birds circling menacingly above, but the only sound is from the howling wind as the figures head towards the distant, murky outline of a stone building. The structure is barely visible through the swirling mist. As they near the property their faces remain obscured and torrential rain and dejected barking dogs obstruct their passage, providing a further threat as well as an impediment to their progress.

In sum, through aspects of *mise-en-scène*, editing, cinematography and sound, the above analysis might suggest that this film forms part of the horror genre or, in terms of its grim setting, that it shares traits with British social realism. However, surprisingly this is an analysis of the early sequences of a 2011 adaptation of Emily Brontë's classic novel *Wuthering Heights*. Described by its director Andrea Arnold as 'gothic, feminist, socialist, sadomasochistic, Freudian, incestuous, violent and visceral',[1] this version of *Wuthering Heights*, along with a number of other contemporary 'heritage' films, signals significant changes in the genre,[2] particularly in terms of their representation of the landscape. Gone are the idyllic English pastoral scenes that present images suitable for National Trust frontispieces. Instead the spectator is presented with the harsh realities of rural life in the nineteenth century, with the countryside relating more to what Andrew Higson terms 'dirty realism': an expression that describes films that recount medieval England and that possess 'a fuller sense of *mise-en-scène*, lighting and cinematography … it is not simply that the landscape becomes bleaker, the dwellings more austere, and the streets, lanes and villages filthier. England/Britain generally becomes a far more dangerous place to inhabit; it is closer to nature, more primitive, less civilised'.[3] A number of the current crop of British costume dramas present wild, rugged landscapes devoid of the picturesque traits of their predecessors, instead evoking a sense of menace wrought from these settings. This chapter charts the trajectory of the various substantial debates around landscape and heritage before focusing on a number of more recent productions. Albeit adaptations from classic literature, through their use of landscape many contemporary films including *Wuthering Heights* appear more realist in style.

Andrew Higson, a determining figure on the heritage genre, has identified two specific categories associated with British cinema: heritage and realism. While suggesting that these are diametrically opposed, he links them solely insofar as heritage attempts a realistic and authentic adaptation from its literary source. However, this is the only comparison that he makes because, as he points out, 'paradoxically, the two genres most frequently cited in debates about British cinema as a national cinema seem to pull in opposite directions, and to embody different ideological perspectives'.[4] Indeed, these categories were initially distinct from one another.

The term 'heritage' was first coined by Charles Barr to describe an earlier body of Second World War films seen as patriotic inventions of a national past. Films such as *This England* (David MacDonald, 1941), later renamed *Our Heritage* for Scottish release, cover a variety of time frames in a nostalgic vein, with pastoral evocations and emphasis on the rusticity of the nation. Even earlier than the Second World War, however, Higson identifies a picturesque presentation of the landscape noticeable in British cinema and prominent in Cecil Hepworth's silent film *Comin' Thro' the Rye* (1924). In this adaptation of the Victorian novel by Helen Mathers (1875), Higson detects what he terms a pictorial interpretation of the countryside that connotes 'the dominant and enduring image of the British land'.[5] *Comin' Thro' the Rye*, at the time of its release in the inter-war years, was perceived as a tasteful film, receiving particular praise for its Englishness wrought from its 'delicacy of touch and the beauty of [its] countryside settings'.[6] Indeed, as Christine Gledhill notes, many early silent films combine the pictorial with the pastoral, and Hepworth's countryside, and other films made in the aftermath of the First World War, 'represents not only nostalgia for what is lost. As its agricultural productivity declines, it becomes a site of fantasy in which desires are reformed, for retreat but also for self-discovery and re-energising connection with different rhythms.'[7] Hepworth was keen to distinguish his work from Hollywood productions, and many films of this period and beyond offer similar bucolic representations in an attempt to introduce a sense of patriotism and the concept of nationhood.

The heritage film was to triumph much later through the Merchant Ivory productions of the mid-1980s and early 1990s. This period witnessed a surfeit commencing with *Chariots of Fire* (Hugh Hudson, 1981) and included *A Room with a View* (James Ivory, 1985) and *Howards End* (James Ivory, 1992). Later deemed what Alan Parker derogatorily termed 'the Laura Ashley school of filmmaking',[8] these films attempted to replicate and invent a national legacy on screen through their use of setting and the English country house, offering deep focus; lengthy takes of the landscape that consisted of, invariably, a comfortable part of southeast England;[9] and an approach that emphasised the 'primacy of *mise-en-scène* over narrative'.[10]

The celebration of the country house and the fetishisation of the landscape as a construct of nation was part of a culture that turned away from the present towards a conservative pastoral Englishness. This resulted in 'the past ... displayed as visually spectacular pastiche, inviting a nostalgic gaze that resists the ironies and social critiques so often suggested narratively by these films'.[11] Providing cultural kudos for an international market, the heritage films transformed the past into a museum piece identified through their slow-paced narratives, close attention to *objets d'art* and 'highly selective vision of Englishness attached to pastoral and imperial values where the past as spectacle becomes the main attraction'.[12] Higson groups such adaptations set between approximately 1800 and 1939 as heritage films of the 'modern past'.[13]

The conservative/fetishised pastoral is particularly noticeable in the 'modern past' film adaptation of E. M. Forster's *Howards End*. Director James Ivory used wildlife cinematographer Tony Pierce-Roberts to leisurely explore the minutiae of the flora and fauna surrounding the property that is the subject of the title. Part-way through the film, the Wilcox family congregate at Howards End to discuss the problematic bestowment of the house to Margaret Schlegel (Emma Thompson) by Ruth Wilcox (Vanessa Redgrave) on the latter's deathbed. The sequence commences with Margaret's visit to the hospital, where she presents Mrs Wilcox with a bunch of meadow flowers, an act that, in part, prompts the sick woman to bequeath her beloved property to her younger, sympathetic counterpart. A slow-motion dissolve from Mrs Wilcox signing a document to an extreme close-up of a bed of roses introduces the spectator to the house for the first time. Accompanied by soft music, a series of close-up images of a variety of flowers are presented to the spectator, and these remain on screen for a number of seconds. Ensuing similar displays fill the frame, until the camera pans slowly to the left at a low angle to exhibit a planting of narcissi in close-up and a red-brick house in the distance. There is little narrative motivation for these images at this point, and, rather than guide the spectator directly to the property and its inhabitants, the camera continues to range, subsequently accommodating a small orchard also replete with flowers. From this lavish floral spectacle, an angled view of the pretty cottage picturesquely adorned with wisteria is presented, followed by a further edit to a full frontal view of the house from a distance. This sequence completes what might normally be constructed as one establishing shot, albeit this succession of images has used nearly 50 seconds of screen time before an interior shot witnesses the Wilcox family gathered around a table to discuss the will.

Such lavish photography of the landscape is a repeated motif throughout *Howards End* and this pastoral presentation offers a nostalgic reconstruction of an imperial and post-colonial past,[14] enabling the spectator to witness an invented 'golden age, one that the novels depict as already tainted and unstable'.[15] Many of the films appeared during the Thatcher years in Britain, a period that arguably denied cultural difference, instead wistfully harking back to what might be perceived as better times. These films, along with a rapid development of a museum and heritage culture in Britain, provided links with the past through their association with stately homes and National Trust properties; as Amy Sargeant notes, 'in the field of Heritage Studies, cinema and broadcasting are widely recognised as effective means of presenting and marketing Britain's past'.[16]

By the mid-1990s, this idealisation of the past and, in turn, the fetishisation of the landscape were being modified with the release of films such as *Jude* (Michael Winterbottom, 1996) and *The Wings of a Dove* (Iain Softley, 1998), both deliberately disregarding heritage characteristics. In the former, Winterbottom calculatingly commences and completes the film with monochrome landscape sequences, and he refuses to permit the camera to linger on the topography for other than narrative plausibility. Thus, in place of picturesque surroundings, the settings in *Jude* are dismal, austere and overcast. When a young Jude (James Daley) and his schoolmaster, who is leaving the village of Marygreen to secure a future, survey the city of Christminster from on high, the camera frames both in silhouette set against bright sunshine as they gaze wistfully into the distance. Nonetheless, the light that initially bathes the city soon disappears, providing a sense of foreboding and, far from idyllic pastoral imagery, the setting now appears raw and unaccommodating.

The film also commences ominously with an overhead shot of Jude scattering seed in a furrowed field: these initial sequences of the boy's past were produced using black-and-white film stock. This imagery portentously forecasts his bleak future, which is also monochromatically summed up in the closing sequences of the film when Sue (Kate Winslet), dressed in black, kneels over the snow-covered graves of her children – a point noted by Pamela Church Gibson, who suggests that 'the landscape seems hostile, and the townscapes become progressively bleaker as their [Jude and Sue's] lives become more difficult'.[17]

In a similar vein, Shekhar Kapur's *Elizabeth* (1998) avoids any idyllic presentations of the landscape in favour of a raw realism. In the opening sequences, the erstwhile Bollywood director introduces brutal images of the persecution of Protestant heretics in the reign of Queen Elizabeth I before cutting to the young queen (Cate Blanchett) dancing with her ladies-in-waiting in the fields. Initially, a group of colourful figures is seen moving in the distance foregrounded by the sparkle of the sun on wet grass, albeit they are out of focus. Here the landscape is not centralised or overstated in any way; rather, Kapur is only concerned with revealing narrative information regarding the relationship between Elizabeth and her lover, Robert Dudley, Earl of Leicester (Joseph Fiennes), and the sundrenched fields adorned with spring flowers signal the last true moment of freedom for the young princess. The opening credits of *Elizabeth* have already dispelled any expectation of a nostalgic period piece, with rousing choral chant and blood-red backing to the credits interspersed with images of floating crosses. Described as a 'monarchy' film,[18] *Elizabeth* denies the spectator idyllic vistas derived from a slow editing pace; instead Kapur varies camera angles and perspectives while juxtaposing shots of short duration to create a sense of menace and evoke fear. Northumberland was chosen as the prime location for the film, in a conscious decision justified by the film's producer, Alison Owen, who has said, 'We wanted to get away from the "chocolate box" feel so many period movies have ... Northumberland is beautiful, but in a very stark way.'[19]

Claire Monk has termed *Elizabeth* and a number of other films 'post-heritage', mainly as a result of their preoccupations with sexuality and gender, and she also notes that they are marked by their distinctive if restless cinematography. For her, *Elizabeth* forms part of a sub-genre of heritage; it treats its 'audience to the visual, literary and performative pleasures associated [with heritage but] pointedly seeks to distance itself through various strategies from the supposed conservatism' of the genre.[20] Writing in 2007, Jessica Durgan too observes this aspect, particularly in the later adaptation of *Pride and Prejudice* (Joe Wright, 2005). She argues that, unlike *Howards End*, which favours the long take and deep focus to create what are ostensibly still images, Wright uses unusual camera angles and theatrically staged filming in keeping with a number of his contemporaries in order to minimise the figures in the landscape. Similarly, his constant camera movement succeeds in eliminating the pictorialism of the earlier heritage films. Described by Higson as 'more dirty realist than picturesque',[21] Wright's version of *Pride & Prejudice*, rather than glamourising the period, has more in common with a realistic portrayal of the nineteenth century. Thus, whereas Monk discusses a post-heritage strain in British cinema of the late twentieth and early twenty-first centuries, Higson notes that the rural imagery of the contemporary British 'premodern past' film is more aligned with the grittier aspects of realism, which he labels, as noted above, 'dirty realism'. For Higson, whereas the 'modern past' is sanitised and picturesque, the British medieval past is presented as dark, mysterious and dirty, and is therefore more accurate in its depiction. He uses the film *King Arthur* (Antoine Fuqua, 2004) as an example, noting these qualities particularly in relation to the film's use of landscape, which contains:

numerous spectacular wide shots of bleak, windswept hills, with grey clouds above and knights on horseback galloping in silhouette in the distance. The uncultivated grass may be a vibrant, fertile green, but the landscape is frequently swirling with mist, and the sun rarely shines. Lighting generally is gloomy, with heavy clouds preferred for daytime exteriors, occasional scenes in dark forests and other scenes shot at night; interiors are invariably gloomy.[22]

Sometimes films depicting the past mix the rustic and realist in their topographical representation. For example, in Kapur's sequel to *Elizabeth*, *Elizabeth: The Golden Age* (2007), Britain is pastoral and rolling – a Britain to be defended – when used as a backdrop for the Virgin Queen (Cate Blanchett). However, Mary Stuart, Queen of Scots (Samantha Morton), is seen predominantly in a 'medieval' landscape: in this precipitous terrain, the unforgiving and bleak hills of Scotland prevail, overpowering and diminishing her figure, although the two landscape variations ultimately converge through the spectacle of the Armada, whereby the picturesque heritage becomes realist drama.

Rugged moorlands and dark, impenetrable forestation correlate with the notion of an ancient past, and these bleak characteristics are very often as much about setting as historical specificity. More recently, these backdrops have also been emerging in films of the 'modern past': films that are 'different, dramatically heightening the rough touches, moving towards the sublime and away from the picturesque, revelling in landscapes that are much more wild, uncultivated and often bleaker than anything *Sense and Sensibility* or *Ladies in Lavender* can offer'.[23] This description might also include films such as Arnold's *Wuthering Heights*. Just as the *mise-en-scène* of the medieval past is depicted on a grand scale, and just as *King Arthur* opens with 'vast vistas across open land' with 'the battle [taking] place in a primeval landscape, flanked by a dark and mysterious forest, while mist swirls around the combatants',[24] Arnold creates a comparable situation through archaic rusticity and adverse weather conditions.

Compliant with Monk's notion of post-heritage, *Wuthering Heights* places emphasis on sexuality and gender, and particularly on its associations with nature. In the early sequences, the setting functions as a sensual and forbidden space where the young Heathcliff (Solomon Glave) and his friend Cathy (Shannon Beer) engage in adolescent sexual play. Frequent images of Heathcliff gazing through windows, both from the inside and outside, indicate his yearning for Cathy, whose manifestation is inextricably linked with the untamed landscape.

The rural in Arnold's film is tough and uncompromising, yet sensual and in tune with the natural world. Narratively it functions as a space of privacy for the young lovers, yet visually it is bleak, operating as a site for cruelty and bloodletting. When Heathcliff initially ventures out on his first day at Wuthering Heights, Cathy's brother Hindley (Lee Shaw) rides past him on his horse, roughly brushing the young boy to one side. The injured, panting Heathcliff glances up, clasping his stomach in pain before, from a low angle, Cathy first appears in view, the camera panning slowly upwards from her dirty shoes to frame her concerned face. Here, grime is indicative of a more realist aesthetic and operates as social commentary on the lives of the protagonists. Cathy asks Heathcliff to follow her as she disappears into a stone barn, and he glances up at the hills on the horizon, appearing as a Rückenfigur[25] contemplating the landscape, his back to the camera as though yearning for a preferable alternative to his miserable existence.

In Arnold's uncompromising adaptation, the introduction of animals into the story symbolises the unarticulated and repressed emotions of Heathcliff and Cathy. When the young boy eventually follows her, she is framed in extreme close-up and viewed from his perspective as she bridles her horse. Placed in near proximity to the animal's face, she gently inserts the bit in its mouth and, at this juncture, the horse's soft muzzle fills the frame, the act and shot attaining a sensuous and tactile quality. From this, the camera tilts upwards to include her hands slipping over the horse's head, and as she does so she gently places her finger into its ear, the act filmed in extreme close-up, appearing painstaking yet erotic. Throughout this process she is observed by Heathcliff until the camera creates an eyeline match with Cathy, who returns his gaze before turning back to complete the process with the horse; both animal and Cathy are backlit, creating a romantic lighting effect and, at this juncture, she succeeds in captivating the young boy and generates a foundation for their enduring obsessive relationship.

Just as Arnold uses a horse in her previous film, *Fish Tank* (2009), to symbolise the constrained life of her central character, Mia (Katie Jarvis), so the fauna in *Wuthering Heights* becomes significant for a variety of visual and narrative reasons. The animal provides the means for the two to ride together onto the moorlands, and it is also important in demonstrating Mr Earnshaw's (Paul Hilton) favouritism of Heathcliff and dislike of his own son – a situation recognised by both boys and evident when Earnshaw offers Heathcliff the first choice of a mount. Similarly, the horse operates to suggest the tension and growing desire between Heathcliff and Cathy. At one point, they ride across the empty countryside whereby Cathy's hair, seen in extreme proximity to the camera, blows gently in the wind. Heathcliff is seated behind her and, as the camera withdraws slightly, the boy closes his eyes and, enraptured, buries his smiling face in her tresses. The camera subsequently tilts downwards to display his hand placed against the animal's flank, signifying the tactility of the moment. The colour of Cathy's hair matches the mane of the horse, and the suggestion seems to be that the adventure produces a basic animal instinct in the boy. As Kate Stables, in her review of the film, notes, Arnold's 'rough, elemental reading of *Wuthering Heights*, replete with casual brutality, Ted Hughes-like scrutiny of wildlife both dead and alive … will jolt audiences weaned on the romantic tropes of previous versions just as Brontë's uncouth beast of a book did its Victorian readers'.[26]

The unforgiving landscape in Arnold's film becomes synonymous with Heathcliff and Cathy's relationship. As their bond develops, Arnold uses hand-held camera and intimate close-ups to chart their rapport on the isolated moorlands. Robbie Ryan, the cinematographer for the film, believes that, for Arnold, hand-held camerawork was a necessity: 'Andrea forbids tripods on the set. She just loves handheld. She doesn't do it any other way.'[27] Sometimes swathed in low mist, and encompassed by the fog, the landscape becomes a playground where the two chase and tussle, bodily smearing one another with mud. As the film progresses, the countryside becomes bleaker and more inhospitable, and Arnold uses pathetic fallacy to conjure up a sublime visual vocabulary. Lone windswept trees, seen from a low angle, struggle on the horizon as though mirroring the hardships experienced by the couple and, at the end of the film, branches from nearby vegetation clatter against Heathcliff's bedroom window, suggesting Cathy's persisting presence long after her death. Similarly, throughout the film, stormy weather constantly reflects and predicts emotional tumult between the two.

While the moorland backdrop functions to bring the young couple together, Arnold also brings the landscape and fauna indoors. When Cathy introduces the foreign Heathcliff to the various aspects of British nature, she does so through inanimate objects, and this visual imagery is prioritised over speech and narrative detail. In one such sequence Arnold confounds and disorientates the spectator by introducing a series of close-ups of lapwing feathers, pieces of heather and animal skulls set against a blue backdrop, these objects initially materialising as though posed for a still-life painting. An edit then reveals Cathy seated alongside the flora and fauna as she patiently explains the origins of various objects to Heathcliff. Her favourite bird, she discloses, is the lapwing, and she gently brushes a feather across the boy's cheek. From this point on he is entranced by these birds in flight, and furthermore they become a symbol of his love for Cathy. Later, and from a now adult Heathcliff's (James Howson) point of view, a flock of lapwings is witnessed hovering and swooping against a clear sky, afterwards functioning to evoke Cathy's (Kaya Scodelario) betrayal; indeed, she boasts of her collection before offering them to her new suitor and eventual husband, Edgar Linton (James Northcote), although they are a symbol of love between her and Heathcliff. Finally, following Cathy's death and after Heathcliff has become the legal owner of Wuthering Heights, the latter walks outside, and Arnold hints at the presence of Cathy. Seen from Heathcliff's point of view, a lapwing soars overhead and a feather detaches, fluttering gracefully to the ground. He does not pick it up, but walks away alone while a flashback reveals him and Cathy as children, accompanied incongruously by a contemporary piece of folk music from British band Mumford and Sons entitled 'Enemy' (written specifically for the film). Throughout this adaptation, Arnold interweaves extreme and intense images of nature with the narrative. As Ryan states, 'every lunch, I'd run away with the camera and shoot nature, whether it be a moth, a caterpillar or a dead rabbit'.[28] However, this close scrutiny of the natural world, which might not seem dissimilar to the close-ups used in *Howards End*, consists of rotten apples, insects and Heathcliff's cruel slaughter of sheep and rabbits.

Wuthering Heights only follows the conventions of the period drama insofar as it adheres to Brontë's nineteenth-century setting; beyond that it differs, operating on the more epic scale of the pre-modern past. There is little dialogue, and no score, apart from the closing contemporary soundtrack, yet the diegetic sounds evoke a primeval and visceral feel to the film. Arnold brings the rural landscape indoors both through Cathy's animal and plant collection and through the use of the ceaseless wind that surrounds and pervades the house. The director further flouts convention by introducing a black Heathcliff, who operates as an outsider to the family and also, through racial tensions, to the bigoted, incestuous community of rural Yorkshire. Another aspect that enables the post-heritage label lies in the cinematography. Throughout, Ryan, who also filmed *Fish Tank* for Arnold, adopts Heathcliff's point of view to demonstrate the outsider's segregation. As Patricia Thomson notes, 'skipping lightly over the Gothic elements and melodrama emphasized in previous adaptations of the novel, Arnold's film zeroes in on the book's darker themes: the cruelty of man, the indifference of nature, and the isolation of its needy characters'.[29]

Arnold elected to shoot the film in 1.33:1 academy ratio, a format she had previously used in *Fish Tank*, to capture the faces of the characters, in particular Heathcliff, rather than using the more traditional widescreen ratio often associated with landscape photography. As she comments, 'I like the headroom. I think it gives a lot of respect to the person.'[30] Her decision encourages a spectatorial upwards glance experienced through Heathcliff's point of view, particularly as he gazes at the lapwings, an aspect that widescreen does not permit. Rather than the 'precise and loving photography' of the country house and landscape, Arnold encourages the distortion of the image, an idea she admits is based on the work of the American photographer Todd Hido. Just as Hido 'shoots through his car window' and 'drives somewhere and takes these beautiful photographs of landscapes, but they're all distorted because there's rain or a bit of snow on the windscreen',[31] so *Wuthering Heights* follows suit by displaying images of the characters peering through distorted glass.

As noted, many films of the modern past also draw to some extent or extensively on a dirty realist aesthetic in their use of landscape. Cary Fukunaga's adaptation of Charlotte Brontë's novel *Jane Eyre* (2011) offers such visual vocabulary in his landscape milieu. The film opens with Jane (Mia Wasikowska) alone in a windswept, inhospitable topography, these initial shots suggesting isolation and seclusion. The sound of a heavy door opening is accompanied by a shot of a woman framed by a large stone entrance with intertwined branches covering the aperture. Perceived in silhouette, she stands inert contemplating the thicket that prevents her escape from Thornfield Hall. From this, a series of images document her passage from the confines of an orderly, manicured garden in the grounds of the austere, castellated stone building todarting to avoid the puddles and mud along a rough track while shrouded in mist, the rear-view shot of her figure diminished in the frame. Ultimately, the sequence ends with a cut to an overhead shot revealing her lone figure standing at a crossroads, the wind howling, the landscape filling the frame with no sky visible.

The woman, Jane Eyre, on discovering the bigamous Rochester's (Michael Fassbender) marriage to the insane Bertha Mason (Valentina Cervi), decides to leave Rochester's house with no destination in mind, on what should have been her own wedding day. When she is first viewed in the landscape, there is little horizon visible, the overhead shots reinforcing her vulnerability and confusion. Although the camera lingers on the lonely moorland tracks that cover the bleak, heather-covered hills that form part of the backdrop for much of the film, there is nothing of the pictorial and painterly heritage traits so evident in the earlier Merchant Ivory productions. Instead, driving rain obstructs the girl's passage and inhibits her progress until, on the horizon, she espies a building. In a similar vein to Kapur's cinematography in *Elizabeth*, frequent crane shots suggest Jane's suppression and entrapment, first by Mrs Reed (Sally Hawkins), her aunt and guardian, and then by the staff at Lowood, the boarding school where she is forced to remain until she reaches maturity.

Following Jane's arrival at the house of St John Rivers (Jamie Bell), she is rarely seen outside, and if she ventures into the landscape she appears diminished in the frame. Unlike the characters in *Howards End*, who wander the countryside in order to appreciate its beauty, and Cathy and Heathcliff, who rely on the freedom and naturalness provided by the land to progress their relationship, Jane is viewed largely indoors until the end of the film, when she eventually finds happiness in the gardens of Thornfield Hall. When she does appear outdoors she is at the mercy of the elements. Distinct from films of the modern past, the establishing shots in Fukunaga's film do not glorify the country house, or English culture. Instead, the spectator's first sight of Rochester's house is from a low angle, in darkness. The castellated mansion appears menacing and ominous, silhouetted against an equally threatening night sky, and such images appear piecemeal and are uninviting. Haddon Hall, the private country mansion in Derbyshire that featured as Thornfield Hall, is a visitor attraction, yet nowhere is this evident or heralded as such in its filmic presentation. Similarly, the setting for Lowood, Broughton Castle in Oxfordshire, is not visually sold to the spectator as a tourist site. Instead, Fukunaga focuses more on the small gamekeeper's cottage used for St John Rivers's house and the burnt-out Thornfield Hall to create the backdrop and emphasise the ghastly reality of Jane's existence.

When Jane moves to the school house where Rivers has found her a teaching position, the camera frames the remote building from a distance set among the desolate hills, thus evoking its inaccessibility. Jane ventures outside, yet from the camera's position she is barely visible in the frame; instead she is situated

against, and blends in with, the grey stone exterior. The snow-covered surrounding hills overpower the building, which is located low in the frame. That Jane is
frequently dominated by the landscape and subsumed by her surroundings indicates her circumstances and offers a sublime reading that is 'driven by Romantic
imperatives – the spiritual interplay between the human figure and the engulfing
landscapes'.[32]

If *Jane Eyre* offers the spectator a pessimistic rural *mise-en-scène*, the Derbyshire
landscape also appears to be a dangerous place to inhabit: its appearance is primordial and uncivilised. This becomes evident during Jane's time at Thornfield
Hall. She gains the position of governess to Rochester's ward, Adèle Varens
(Romy Settbon Moore), and the child subsequently informs her that a spectre
haunts the grounds. At this point the camera cuts to a shot of the structure from
behind a gravestone, and slowly pans from left to right. The turrets of the house
create a dramatic outline against the leaden and overcast sky, an aspect that Jane
comments upon, but not in terms of its aesthetics. Instead she aligns it to lack
of scope and limitation, a metaphor for the constraints of being a woman. The
cinematographer, Adriano Goldman, spoke of his desire to achieve this subtle
effect in the filming of the topography: 'Cloudy days were our dream; we wanted
the image to feel soft on the screen, with muted colors and dark-green grass and
foliage.'[33] Shot in the Derbyshire Peak District, this landscape is unforgiving and
harsh. The completed look of the film is commented upon by contemporary
critic Erica Abeel, who notes that 'the true stars are towering, dank Haddon Hall
as Thornfield, the go-to pile for English period films, and those undulating moors
that make romantics of us all … using natural lighting for the fog-wreathed cliffs
and dark bracken'.[34]

Throughout *Jane Eyre* the diminished figure of Jane is frequently seen amid
the gloom of the woods and in forested areas that are shrouded in mist. When
Rochester proposes to her they embrace and the camera withdraws to reveal the
tree under which they stand, its leaves rustling uneasily in the wind as thunder
rumbles overhead in pathetic fallacy. They run towards the house in the torrential rain, and kiss again once inside the building. The next day, Mrs Fairfax (Judi
Dench) and Jane walk towards the tree, and the film cuts to a shot of Adèle and
her French maid seated beneath. However, it has been struck by lightning and is
now in two halves, implying the couple's unpromising future – albeit this is the
place where the film will end happily when Jane returns to care for the blind and
debilitated Rochester.

Thus, the recent replacement of the idyllic grand country house and
Arcadian landscape with vast, cavernous castles, filthy peasant dwellings
and wild, remote rural landscapes is not only the preserve of pre-modern
past films but also inherent in films of the modern past, as noted in
Arnold's *Wuthering Heights* and Fukunaga's *Jane Eyre*. Nicole Armour has
commented that adaptations such as these form part of a group that pit the

individual against a collective and place emphasis on the landscape: in this case terrain, which is awe-inspiring and terrifying.[35] Belén Vidal believes that post-heritage may now be perceived as meta-heritage: a self-reflexive style with some postmodern cultural recycling.[36] This is partly indicated by the current crop of directors who arrive at the end product from a different cultural perspective; for example, Shekhar Kapur began his career in Bollywood, and the Taiwanese director of *Sense and Sensibility* (1995), Ang Lee, is a theatre studies graduate. Similarly, Andrea Arnold deliberately and dramatically changes the original novel, her bucolic landscapes offering a sublime and neo-Romantic sensibility consonant with the rusticity exhibited in films of the medieval past. Correspondingly, Californian-born Fukunaga brings his own cinematographer and individual filming style to *Jane Eyre*. His previous film, *Sin Nombre* (2009), was realist, hard-hitting and uncompromising, as were Arnold's *Red Road* (2006) and *Fish Tank*.[37] The rurality displayed in *Wuthering Heights* and *Jane Eyre* might be perceived as 'dirty realist', although the imagery displayed seems more in tune with the corresponding Romantic literary authors from which these films were adapted. For Monk, *Jane Eyre* (and in a similar vein *Wuthering Heights*) might be described as neo-classical realist, with a debt to 'the spirit of post-Enlightenment Romanticism'.[38]

Notes

1 Andrea Arnold cited in Amy Raphael, 'Love Will Tear Us Apart', *Sight & Sound*, 21: 12 (2012), pp. 34–6; p. 36.

2 The author loosely defines heritage film as a genre, although this is a term applied to a group of films whereby heritage is commodified. For further reading on issues of genre and heritage see Andrew Higson, *Waving the Flag: Constructing a National Cinema in Britain* (Oxford: Clarendon, 1997), and for more recent debates Claire Monk and Amy Sargeant (eds), *British Historical Cinema: The History, Heritage and Costume Film* (London, New York: Routledge, 2002) and Belén Vidal, *Heritage Film: Nation, Genre and Representation* (London, New York: Wallflower Press, 2012).

3 Andrew Higson, *Film England: Culturally English Filmmaking since the 1990s* (London: I. B. Tauris, 2011), pp. 214–15.

4 Higson, Waving the Flag, p. 27.

5 Higson, *Waving the Flag*, p. 30.

6 Higson, *Waving the Flag*, p. 30.

7 Christine Gledhill, *Reframing British Cinema 1918–1928: Between Restraint and Passion* (London: British Film Institute, 2003), p. 95.

8 A number of commentators refer to this, including Stella Bruzzi, *Understanding Cinema: Clothing and Identity in the Movies* (London: Routledge, 1997) p. 35.

9 Tana Wollen, 'Over our shoulders: nostalgic screen fictions for the eighties', in John Corner and Sylvia Harvey (eds), *Enterprise and Heritage: Crosscurrents of National Cinema* (London and New York: Routledge, 1991), pp. 178–93.

10 Sarah Street, *British National Cinema* (London and New York: Routledge, 1997), p. 103.
11 Andrew Higson, 'Re-presenting the national past: nostalgia and pastiche in the heritage film', in Lester Friedman (ed.), *British Cinema and Thatcherism* (London: University College London Press, 1993), pp. 109–29; p. 109.
12 Vidal, *Heritage Film*, p. 8.
13 Higson, *Film England*.
14 However, not all films present the landscape as a commonly felt yearning for an idyllic past; they sometimes present it specifically through the nostalgic voice of the narrator. Whereas Guy (Rupert Everett) in *Another Country* (Kanievska, 1984) reminisces about his time in England before his move to gloomy and drab Moscow, the film's ending is also a critique of the flaws of the period (1930s), particularly in terms of the attitudes towards homosexuality, albeit lingering shots of the English pastoral still pervade.
15 Higson, 'Re-presenting the national past', p. 122.
16 Amy Sargeant, 'Making and selling heritage culture: style and authenticity in historical fictions on film and television', in Justine Ashby and Andrew Higson (eds), *British Cinema, Past and Present* (London and New York: Routledge, 2000), pp. 301–15; p. 301.
17 Pamela Church Gibson, 'Fewer weddings and more funerals: changes in the heritage film', in Robert Murphy (ed.), *British Cinema in the 90s* (London: British Film Institute, 2000), pp. 115–24; p. 120.
18 Kara McKechnie, 'Taking liberties with the monarch: the royal bio-pic in the 1990s', in Claire Monk and Amy Sargeant (eds), *British Historical Cinema: The History, Heritage and Costume Film* (London and New York: Routledge, 2002), pp. 217–36.
19 Alison Owen cited in Andrew Wilson, 'All the queen's castles', *Mail on Sunday* (10 October 1998), p. 20.
20 Claire Monk, 'Sexuality and heritage', in Ginette Vincendeau (ed.), *Film/Literature/ Heritage: A Sight and Sound Reader* (London: British Film Institute, 2001), pp. 6–11; p. 7.
21 Higson, *Film England*, p. 170.
22 Higson, *Film England*, p. 210.
23 Higson, *Film England*, p. 209.
24 Higson, *Film England*, p. 204.
25 The notion of the momentary in art history is frequently represented through the lone figure in the landscape, a person facing away from the spectator known as a *Rückenfigur*. This is literally translated as a back figure, and encourages the spectator to adopt the same position. The concept suggests liminality and the mind searching for something while trying to retain what is familiar. For further reading see Joseph Leo Koerner, *Casper David Friedrich and the Subject of Landscape* (London: Reaktion, 2009).
26 Kate Stables, 'Review: *Wuthering Heights*', *Sight & Sound*, 21: 12 (2011), p. 82.
27 Robbie Ryan cited in Patricia Thomson, 'Wild passion', *American Cinematographer*, 93: 5 (2012), pp. 42–51; p. 46.
28 Thomson, 'Wild passion', p. 45.
29 Thomson, 'Wild passion', p. 42.
30 Andrea Arnold cited in Thomson, 'Wild passion', p. 43.
31 Ryan cited in Thomson, 'Wild passion', p. 44.

32 Claire Monk, 'Eyre conditioning', *Sight & Sound*, 21: 10 (2011), p. 45.
33 Adriano Goldman cited in Rachel Bosley, 'Production slate: a Jane Eyre for today', *American Cinematographer*, 92: 4 (2011), p. 18.
34 Erica Abeel, 'Jane Eyre', *Film Journal International*, 114: 4 (2011), p. 130.
35 Nicole Armour, 'Alone together: tricky negotiations between the individual and the collective as seen in a select group of offerings', *Film Comment*, 47: 6 (2011), pp. 62–3.
36 Vidal, *Heritage Film*.
37 Although it is beyond the scope of this essay to discuss more examples, similarly, Saul Dibb, director of *Bullet Boy* (2004), a gritty urban drama, moved on to direct *The Duchess* (2008), which also conforms to the notion of post-heritage.
38 Monk, 'Eyre conditioning', p. 45.

10

Folk horror and the contemporary cult of British rural landscape: the case of *Blood on Satan's Claw*

Paul Newland

It's in the trees! It's coming!
The Night of the Demon (1957); 'Hounds of Love', Kate Bush (1985)

British rural landscapes have long operated as imaginative spaces in which horrific, ghostly or uncanny narratives unfold. One need think no further than the Gothic tradition in literature – for example, representations of dark, menacing rural landscapes feature from Horace Walpole's novel *The Castle of Otranto* (1763) through Mary Shelley's *Frankenstein* (1818) and Emily Brontë's *Wuthering Heights* (1847) to Bram Stoker's *Dracula* (1897) and beyond. These narratives often incorporate mystery; a sense of danger or real or imagined threat; and themes of death, decay and madness. Sometimes they are marked by ancient curses or troubling truths lurking in long, dark shadows. Gothic stories often feature remote, run-down castles or mansions, and can take place in landscapes that seemingly have lives and secrets of their own. Picturesque ruins in remote rural locations are a key trope in Gothic literature and art. So too is the recurring sense of wild, untamed nature. Moreover, British (but also European) folklore is populated with demons that dwell in the forest.[1] Writing about landscapes in British film and television horror, Peter Hutchings employs the term 'dark heritage' in order to encapsulate such menacing landscapes.[2] He also notices an uncanny landscape 'suffused with a sense of profound and sometimes apocalyptic anxiety'.[3] Significantly, this landscape 'can signify Britishness as much as, if not more than, the critically privileged heritage dramas'.[4] But such landscapes can also be marked as 'alternative' spaces – either as spaces seemingly untouched by urban modernity, rationality or the type of progress informed by the Enlightenment, or as spaces in which these prevailing ideologies might be challenged. Often these are landscapes in which mysterious objects, cultures or indeed practices from a distant (often pagan) rural British past might be uncovered. Tanya Krzywinska notices that 'the sacred landscapes of ancient Britain have become entrenched in the popular imagination under the seductive sign of "transgression" '.[5] British cinema and television – just as much as British literature – have facilitated the development of these types of imaginative rural landscapes. As we will see, a range of such texts flourished in British culture (not just cinema) during the late 1960s and 1970s, and have been feted by a cult audience in subsequent years.

In this chapter I want to argue two separate (but related) things. Firstly, focusing primarily on the cult film *Blood on Satan's Claw* (Piers Haggard, 1971), I want to explore the generic qualities of a range of Gothic and so-called 'folk horror' films (but also films and television programmes not clearly of the horror genre but that nevertheless display familiar 'folk' tropes) and to think about how far rural landscape plays a part in their aesthetic and appeal. Secondly, I want to demonstrate that we are witnessing a contemporary 'cultification' of folk horror that is manifesting itself as a subcultural reappraisal of a range of rural 1960s and 1970s texts, but also the development of new, contemporary texts that draw on and mine (and are indeed haunted by) their textual antecedents – especially in the ways in which they often pit the rural 'anti-modern', 'natural' and/or pagan landscape against the technocracy of modernity.[6] What we see in these texts, then – and also in the cult discourse that increasingly circulates around them – is a distinct romanticisation of a dark British (but especially English) vision of a pagan, pre-modern or proto-modern rural past, and a focus on what might still be alive now 'in the present' in such spaces. These films are not simple or straightforward celebrations of (or evocations of) traditional customs, though. They might often instead be read as potentially radical in their evocation of a rural-based critique of modernity, technocracy, mass culture, mass production and consumerism, and in their engagement with the potential outcomes of ideologies of 'progress'.

In a significant article on rural horror and what he terms an 'anti-idyll', David Bell argues that 'in Britain, the rural idyll is a settled landscape mapping out a social order across a picturesque terrain – especially its construction as "village England" '.[7] Rural horror texts evidently disrupt this. Bell is also specifically interested in 'articulations' of the rural through horror films in which the 'victim' is coded as urban and the setting and the 'monster' are coded as rural.[8] This chimes with the idea that rural horror can often be read as a response to rapid modernisation and socio-cultural change – as a kind of Freudian return of the repressed. Developing his analysis, Bell notes the vast horror genre repertoire of rural locales – such as deserted mansions, cottages and indeed whole villages – and the 'endless permutations' of city folk 'transplanted' to the country – on camping trips, out hiking, touring or exploring, on school trips or as soldiers.[9] The rural, then, 'offers isolation and an alien environment'.[10] But Bell also writes that a rural 'white trash' identity trades on assorted myths – 'inbreeding, insularity, backwardness, sexual perversion (especially incest and bestiality)'.[11]

164 *British rural landscapes on film*

Peter Hutchings argues that the menacing cityscapes and landscapes that form part of a 'dark heritage' 'are in their own way just as picturesque and market-able as their more conventionally pretty counterparts'.[12] Furthermore, again, it is 'anxieties about modernity and modern social change' that arguably explain the appearance of what Hutchings terms an uncanny 'British anti-landscape'.[13] He writes of 'savage, pagan and ancient landscapes' that often involve

> moving away from the south-east to the geographical fringes of England (Cornwall, for example), or leaving England entirely for Scotland or Wales or islands off the coast. All of these provide locations for nasty stories about the countryside and what happens to outsiders – usually urbanites who provide figures of identification even when they themselves are not especially attractive – who venture there.[14]

What comes across here in Hutchings's work is how far rural horror in Britain often develops out of a distinct spatial tension between proto-modern, modern and indeed postmodern urban centres (and London and the Home Counties particularly) and distant, seemingly peripheral places – deserted, isolated, inac-cessible, strange and apparently backward locales in which things, cultures and ideas that lie buried might rise at any time.

Folk horror

A History of Horror with Mark Gatiss was a three-part television series originally aired on the digital channel BBC4 in October 2010. In the second episode, 'Home Counties Horror', Gatiss set up the horror genre productions of the key studios, Hammer, Amicus and Tigon, as a primarily southern English enterprise and concern. Gatiss noted that, while a great number of British horror films have recreated Gothic spaces in studios, a number have also made much more crea-tive use of real locations in Britain. At one point in this episode, Gatiss strolls with the film director Piers Haggard through a bucolic rural valley on a warm summer's day to the location of the ruined church of St James that features in key, memorably disturbing sequences in a film he made decades earlier: *Blood on Satan's Claw*. The cinematographer Dick Bush shot here and around Bix Bottom in Oxfordshire (interiors were shot at Pinewood Studios).[15] It is evident in the film itself – but also Gatiss's interview with Haggard – that the picturesque rural location of this ruined church (some of which dates from the Saxon and Norman periods) and its environs were hugely important. Haggard remarks in the programme that 'the nooks and crannies of woodland, the edges of fields, the ploughing, the labour, the sense of the soil, was something I tried to bring to the picture'. Intriguingly, Haggard was interested in what lies 'in the earth'. This – as we will see – is a common theme of British rural horror.

Gatiss refers to *Blood on Satan's Claw* as a prime example of a short-lived sub-genre he terms 'folk horror', along with *Witchfinder General* (Michael Reeves,

1968) and *The Wicker Man* (Robin Hardy, 1973), which 'shared a common obsession with the British landscape, its folklore, and superstitions'. According to Gatiss, 'out of the three films, *Blood on Satan's Claw* deserves wider appreciation'. But Gatiss was not the first to notice a preponderance of 'folk horror' films in Britain. Writing in an article published in 2002, Leon Hunt saw 1966 to 1976 as a period of British film history that saw a rise in representations of the pagan rural: 'magic's prime locale was now the countryside'.[16] Tanya Krzywinska also noted that films such as *The Witches* (Cyril Frankel, 1966), *Cry of the Banshee* (Gordon Hessler, 1970), *Blood on Satan's Claw* (1971) and *The Wicker Man* (1973) evoke aspects of contemporary counter-cultural lifestyles (more on this later),[17] and that *Blood on Satan's Claw* and *The Wicker Man* specifically place pagan sacrifice 'centrally as the source of horror'.[18]

While 'folk horror' was indeed a rather short-lived sub-genre initially, in later years it has become a significant cult concern. Contemporary interest in this phenomenon is evidenced in a preponderance of blogs and websites.[19] Furthermore, folk horror is increasingly becoming an object of academic study: evidence of this can be seen in the fact that, a dedicated conference, 'A Fiend in the Furrows', was held in Belfast in September 2014. *Blood on Satan's Claw* has become a key text in this sub-genre, with countless blogs given over to it alone. This contemporary folk horror cult can at least in part be put down to the rise in popularity in cult circles of folk music, 'neo-folk', visionary music and seemingly obscure film and television soundtracks – the *Blood on Satan's Claw* soundtrack was released on CD and as a limited edition vinyl LP by the cult Trunk Records label in 2007. Indeed, a popular and/or unusual soundtrack often provides a film with a ticket to cult status – this was also in part the case with the still much better known *The Wicker Man*, which has become a 'textbook "cult" movie',[20] thanks in no small part to its extraordinary soundtrack composed (and often performed) by Paul Giovanni.[21]

While folk horror and the cult discourse that surrounds it have tended to focus primarily on English folk customs and landscapes, interest does extend to Wales and Scotland. Jeffrey Richards notices that Scotland, as well as Ireland and Wales, has been characterised by wild landscapes, music, song and the supernatural.[22] Furthermore, Tim Edensor recognises the 'rural wistfulness and disempowering sense of loss' depicted in these filmic representations of Scotland.[23] Duncan Petrie remarks that rural Scotland tends to be represented as a picturesque, 'wild and often empty landscape'.[24] He notices the development of the trope of the 'island' in filmic representations of Scotland – of remote, isolated spaces, as exemplified by *I Know Where I'm Going!* (Michael Powell and Emeric Pressburger, 1945), which of course is not a horror film but nevertheless shares many of the spatial tropes of folk horror (as, to a certain extent, does another Archers film, *A Canterbury Tale*, 1944).[25] But it is rural landscapes of England (and specifically southern England) that primarily encapsulate the key, enduring spaces of folk horror.

Blood on Satan's Claw then and now

Blood on Satan's Claw (also released as *Satan's Skin*) was made by Tigon British Film Productions.[26] Written by Robert Wynne-Simmons and set in seventeenth-century England, the film tells the story of a village taken over by demonic possession. It stars Patrick Wymark as the resident judge, Linda Hayden as possessed teenager Angel Blake (a hugely ironic name that also echoes the great visionary poet and artist William) and Barry Andrews as Ralph, a kindly ploughman. Ralph works for Mistress Banham (Avice Landon), who owns the country house that sits in the centre of a typical southern English rural landscape. Mistress Banham employs Ellen Vespers (Charlotte Mitchell) as her domestic servant. Other key characters in the film – and the main figures of adulthood and authority – are the squire (James Hayter), the vicar (Anthony Ainley) and the doctor (Howard Goorney). Leon Hunt accurately describes *Blood on Satan's Claw* as 'an intoxicating, if not entirely coherent, blend of rural horror, generational conflict and *fin de siècle* bleakness'.[27] Intriguingly, it is a story 'set against the onset of the Enlightenment'.[28]

The rural landscape – shot on location – is a key aspect of *Blood on Satan's Claw*. Indeed the opening shot offers a distinctly painterly view of the rural landscape. The camera is at ground level, at a slightly canted angle, looking up a hilly field. The spectator is thus placed in the earth. In the foreground, laid out on the earth, is a simple ploughman's lunch – a jug and leather bag with some broken bread and apples. Through wisps of grass to the right of the screen we can see a ploughman following his horse, moving slowly along the brow of the hill from right to left.[29]

11 *Blood on Satan's Claw*

The next shot is a close-up of the horse's hooves on the muddy earth – again, from a very low angle. The loam-covered wheels of the plough follow heavily on. The third shot is also of the horse's hooves and plough, similarly from a low angle, but now following closely behind. Hand-held shots of the ploughman's face are subsequently intercut with further, very-low-angle shots of the horse and plough, which serve to evoke both a sense of energy and a sense of dread. Much is made throughout this sequence of the haptic materiality of the ploughed soil – its 'weight' – and our implied relationship to the earth. The distinct sense of tension is further facilitated by the soundtrack, which features cawing crows and the cries of a Cathy (Wendy Padbury) from across the field (we view her from behind some branches, like some voyeuristic woodland beast or spirit). A shot follows of a crow and pigeons gathered at ground level, with what appears to be a large piece of bone in the foreground – the camera is again in the earth. But the ploughed furrows here are also suggestive of a controlled, organised, tamed, enclosed and owned space – a proto-modern, rationalised space in otherwise wild nature.

Mark Wilkinson's playful, evocative music increases the sense of dread in this sequence – the sense that something malevolent is lying beneath the surface of the soil but also, as such, everyday life (and, as this is our point of view, by extension, *our*, modern way of life). The music works to communicate a strange, uncanny tension between modernity, the ancient and the otherworldly. Played on the ondes Martenot (a twentieth-century instrument that produces eerie, wavering notes), the music manages to evoke an evil spirit, elements of folk tradition and modern technology simultaneously. So in *Blood on Satan's Claw* the rural landscape and the soundscape work together to produce a space of thematic and temporal tension.

The final shot of the title sequence of the film is of the farmhouse, built away from the village, with cows and chickens in enclosed pens in the foreground. What is immediately apparent about this image is that this is a space defined by walls, fences and hedges. Indeed, the camera is positioned outside this 'owned' territory. In light of this shot and others in the film that depict the rural landscape, we can read *Blood on Satan's Claw* within the historical context of the enclosures – a period in England that saw much common land and crop land shared since feudal times fenced off and given over to private ownership. The Enclosure Act was passed in 1773; subsequent acts followed from the 1840s. With enclosure, farms left the centres of old villages and settlements, often to be built in the middle of the cultivated and newly controlled landscape. Pastures were ploughed up and trees and hedges were uprooted. Enclosed landscapes were exemplified by straight lines, fields and (often hawthorn) hedges. As the geography of the rural English landscape changed with the enclosures, so too did the economic and socio-cultural landscape. Rural workers were often paid very low wages by landlords; some subsequently migrated to towns to find work. Effectively, then, the enclosures facilitated the creation of a landless working class.[30] The art historian Michael Rosenthal points out: 'Until around 1760 the general reaction to uncultivated landscape was distaste. It was preferred cultivated, because farming rendered it ordered and intelligible, made it into patterns of fields and tracks intimately connected with the village and the great house for the benefit of which the ground was farmed.'[31] In other words, wild landscapes have often been imagined as uncontrolled and uncontrollable. As Rosenthal further puts it, 'the look of a landscape reveals the society which inhabits it. A cultivated one denotes civilization, but because a wild one indicates a more savage population, the onus is always to maintain the development of agriculture.'[32] Thus, *Blood on Satan's Claw* employs a cultivated, enclosed rural landscape to denote a nascent, civilised modernity that cannot fully purge the wild and untamable. Elsewhere in the film characters are often shot in the forest, behaving playfully like elves or sprites, peering out through branches and bushes, or forcing their way through dense undergrowth. The woods are thus marked as an irrational space (in opposition to the controlled fields) where the cult activities come to a sickening peak, with the ritualised rape. So *Blood on Satan's Claw* encapsulates a complex space characterised by a distinct tension between wild, untamed nature; the contemporary control and cultivation of the land for primarily economic purposes; and ruined evidence of older civilisations and communities.

In some ways *Blood on Satan's Claw* resembles another Tigon film, *Witchfinder General*, which presents the lush green beauty of the East Anglian landscape as a seventeenth-century space in which unspeakable horrors are being perpetrated, this time by Vincent Price's character, Matthew Hopkins, and his acolytes. But, like *The Wicker Man*, as we have seen, *Blood on Satan's Claw* has often been read as a period, seventeenth-century-set articulation of contemporary counter-cultural concerns, and, especially, as documenting the slow and painful death of the initial optimism of this youth-led movement. As such, these films can be read as texts that see potential horror in the contemporary battle between modernity and tradition – especially in terms of rapid shifts in socio-cultural values.[33] Certainly Angel Blake and the other adolescents in the film are reminiscent of late 1960s 'flower children', and, as Tanya Krzywinska has pointed out, 'the anarchic outbreak of barbarous behavior in the film has a transgressive appeal that would not be lost on the well-developed counter-culture'.[34] Rudolph Arnheim once argued, 'The monster has become a portrait of ourselves and of the kind of life we have chosen to lead.'[35] There might of course be a number of reasons why a film such as *Blood on Satan's Claw* should speak to presentist concerns. As David Sanjek points out, 'To remain worthy of attention, the British horror film would have to embrace the monstrous in audience and viewer alike.'[36] This suggests that, while these horror films of the 1970s might have had a narrative interest in ancient cultures, they also spoke to the concerns of contemporary audiences – perhaps, above all, to ensure an audience.[37]

In his book *The Making of a Counter Culture* (1969), Theodor Roszak argued that the counter-culture could be understood as a reaction against the 'technocracy': 'that form in which an industrial society reaches the peak of its organizational integration'.[38] For Roszak the counter-culture was a transnational phenomenon. This counter-culture was not organised, as such, but was instead 'something in the nature of a medieval crusade'.[39] Furthermore, Noël Carroll has argued that 'horror cycles emerge in times of social stress' and that 'the genre is a means through which the anxieties of the era can be exposed'.[40] So we might read the explosion of folk horror films in Britain in the late 1960s and 1970s as a manifestation of anxieties about rapid change. As Vic Pratt points out of *The Wicker Man*, 'the present is piled on top of the past, evoking a distinctly plausible world of folk tradition'.[41] Indeed, Pratt notices that 'the political fervor of the counter-culture might have been damped down, but the yearning to replace the old order with something more authentic and spiritually fulfilling still smouldered beneath the surface'.[42] Again, here – as in *Blood on Satan's Claw* – we have the sense of something dark lurking beneath everyday modern life, something that might be more visible in rural surroundings. But, significantly, as I want to argue in more detail later on, we might also read the contemporary, recent development of a cult around these texts as a response to changes in millennial Britain.

It is important to point out that *Blood on Satan's Claw* can also be read within the contexts of coeval developments in cinema outside Britain. For example, Bernice Murphy argues that the post-1970 period saw the growth of what she refers to as 'backwoods horror' in US cinema.[43] Clearly *Blood on Satan's Claw* has some common ground with these American films, even if for Murphy they are often more obviously engaged with the relationship between chaos and order within a distinctly 'new world' or 'new frontier' context. But *Blood on Satan's Claw* should certainly of course be considered within the context of a long and rich history of representations of rural landscapes in British films.

One of the most important early British films to feature significant location shooting (like *Blood on Satan's Claw*) was *Night of the Demon* (Jacques Tourneur, 1957), which begins with a sequence filmed at Stonehenge in which the voice of the narrator imparts: 'It has been written, since the beginning of time, even unto these ancient stones, that evil supernatural creatures exist in a world of darkness.'[44] *Night of the Demon* forms part of a 1950s cycle of British films identified by Christine Geraghty that mark rural villages as sites of resistance to modernity, or at least as distinctly dangerous places for urban characters to go.[45] While the films Geraghty discusses are not horror films, they do chime with similar concerns. For example, *Quatermass II* (Val Guest, 1956) features a sinister modern refinery, and *Village of the Damned* (Wolf Rilla, 1960) – adapted from John Wyndham's novel *The Midwich Cuckoos* – features a rural village overwhelmed by an invasion of extraterrestrial children.

The Hound of the Baskervilles (Terence Fisher, 1959), *The Mummy* (Terence Fisher, 1959), *The Plague of the Zombies* (John Gilling, 1966) and *The Reptile* (John Gilling, 1966) were the key period-set English 'rural horrors' made by Hammer. *The Hound of the Baskervilles* is primarily set on Dartmoor (in Devon) and *The Mummy* is set in an unspecified part of the English countryside. Both *The Plague of the Zombies* – 'the English capitalist aristocracy as voodoo-practising slave-masters, zombifying their workforce to increase the production rate in a Cornish tin mine'[46] – and *The Reptile* are set in rural south-west England. But it is significant that Hammer rarely left the studio when shooting its Gothic horrors. Indeed, while these films feature a modest amount of location shooting, most of their exteriors are studio setups. As such, these films do not tend to feature many wide landscape shots – in other words, rural landscape very rarely operates at the level of the pictorial (or indeed as spectacle) in these films. However, unlike *The Plague of the Zombies* and *The Reptile*, the Cornish-set non-Hammer film *Doctor Blood's Coffin* (Sidney J. Furie, 1961) does feature sequences shot on location (on a Cornish beach).[47] It should be pointed out that some locations do appear (and indeed reappear fairly often) in Hammer films, such as the impressive Oakleigh Court in Windsor. Interviewed in *A History of Horror with Mark Gatiss*, the producer Anthony Hinds remarks that such locations employed in Hammer films tended to be 'within walking distance of the studio'. Amicus operated out of Shepperton Studios and also tended, wherever possible, to use local sites for the necessary location shooting for its portmanteau films. But, with films such as *Blood on Satan's Claw* and *Witchfinder General*, Tigon actively embraced location shooting.

Just as the ruined old church of St James forms an important picturesque site for the grim action in *Blood on Satan's Claw*, old ruins and pagan standing stones are a common feature of British folk horror (and other) films, usually providing a distinctly pre-modern element within a rural landscape against which the conflicted modernity embodied by the protagonists can be worked through. One memorable example of ruins employed in a film (and indeed shot on location) can be found in Roger Corman's Poe adaptation *The Tomb of Ligeia* (1964), which saw the director break with the usual British horror tradition of studio shooting to move out into the countryside on location. The Hammer cinematographer Arthur Grant shot memorable sequences in the ruined Castle Acre Priory in Norfolk for the film. But ruins and pagan sites are not the sole preserve of British horror films. A pagan stone circle also features in the cross-genre, cult, 'undead biker' film *Psychomania* (Don Sharp, 1971), for example. This 'Seven Witches' stone circle was a fabricated set, but the shooting of the sequence was still done on location in rural southern England (but not far from Shepperton).

The potentially subterranean nature of rural landscape is also a key thematic feature of Hammer films. For example, the eponymous hound in *The Hound of* the Baskervilles is concealed in a disused mine, as are the zombies in *The Plague of the Zombies*. In *The Reptile* the monstrous creature is lodged in sulphur pit beneath the isolated country house. And *The Mummy* concludes with an image of the swamp into which the mummy has vanished. These films seem to suggest, then, that dark malevolence and evil might at any time rise again, out of the British rural landscape.[48] In other British horror and fantasy films, the uncovering of a long-buried object often changes or disrupts the lives of those in the present in some way. A key example here can be found in the cult television play *Penda's Fen* (1974), written by David Rudkin and directed by Alan Clarke for the BBC's *Play for Today* series. Set in the Malvern Hills, *Penda's Fen* also evokes a tension between the past and present in one rural location. It sees a teenager, Stephen (Spenser Banks), unleash the spirit of the buried seventh-century warrior king Penda of Mercia when he plays Elgar's 'visionary chord' from *The Dream of Gerontius*.[49]

1970s rural horror(s)

Other films arguably fall within the category of 1970s 'folk horror' (or at least exist on its thematic periphery) and were shot on location. As such, they are able to focus on the apparently isolated, unchanging, pre-modern nature of certain rural locales (often, again, in south-west England), but within the context of the contemporary, 'modern' moment. One well-known example is the US director Sam Peckinpah's *Straw Dogs* (1971), which stars Dustin Hoffman as David Sumner, an American mathematician, and Susan George as his wife, Amy. Set in a Cornish village (the fictional Wakeley), *Straw Dogs* 'assembles familiar horror-in-rural England motifs (arrival of stranger in remote village, mistrustful locals, dark hints about the past)'.[50] The critic Tom Milne wrote that 'the pale horse of the Apocalypse hovers grimly over a quiet Cornish farmhouse'.[51] In *Crucible of Terror* (Ted Hooker, 1971), Jack Davies (James Bolam), an art dealer in London, and Michael Clare (Ronald Lacey), the son of a gifted sculptor, Victor Clare (Mike Raven), drive down to Cornwall to see if they can purloin any items from the old man. Victor lives as a recluse in a cottage built above an abandoned, haunted tin mine. *Doomwatch* (Peter Sasdy, 1972; an adaptation of a television series: BBC, 1970–2), made by Tigon, follows the activities of a government scientific agency. Dr Del Shaw (Ian Bannen) travels to a fictional island, Balfe (off the Cornish coast), to uncover the possible cause of the strange bodily mutations and random violence being displayed by members of a remote community. As Shaw travels across to the island, the boatman tells him, 'You'll find them a strange, close lot on Balfe.' Shaw initially puts their physical abnormalities – protruding eyebrows and thick lips – down to 'centuries of inbreeding'. *Neither the Sea nor the Sand* (aka *The Exorcism of Hugh*) (Fred Burnley, 1972) was also shot on location and primarily takes place on a peripheral island. This Tigon film stars Susan Hampshire as Anna Robinson, who travels to Jersey from mainland England. Here she develops a relationship with a young man (Michael Petrovich), who subsequently dies and returns as the undead. Lastly, *The Shout* (Jerzy Skolimowski, 1978) is also set in the south-west, and features urbane characters in an isolated rural property being terrorised – this time by an individual (Alan Bates) who claims he has the ancient aboriginal power to kill with his shout.

Some of the thematic concerns of these rural, contemporary, 1970s-set films (objects and ideas that lie buried; violence; mutation; mysticism; ritual; sexual violence or rape) can be seen in the period-set *Blood on Satan's Claw*, but also in other British films of the 1970s that are in no way horror films but might more accurately be termed art films or essay films. One example is *Akenfield* (Peter Hall, 1974), which was shot on location near Wickham Market in rural Suffolk. This film presents the everyday life of a village over three generations, but it disrupts linear time in order to do this. The life of the village is thus documented through folk rituals governed by the cyclical rhythm of the seasons, with the modernist, fragmentary formal strategies evoking the uncanny sense that the past very much exists in the present.[52] *Requiem for a Village* (David Gladwell, 1975) was also shot in rural Suffolk. This film again resists generic categorisation but certainly contains a number of common rural folk horror tropes, such as a focus on the seemingly unchanging rhythms of countryside life within the contexts of modernity, and a potentially violent and/or immoral sexuality. A notable example of a folk-horror-type event occurs in an extraordinary sequence in the film in which long-dead villagers are seen by an old man (Vic Smith) to rise up out of their graves (in slow motion) and enter the church in their Sunday best.[53] David Fanshawe's music is also key to the critical and cult success of the film, perhaps because it is 'evocative of a one immovable faith'.[54] This theme of events repeating themselves in a specific rural place can also be seen the HTV children's fantasy television series *Children of the Stones* (Peter Graham Scott, 1977), set in the fictional English village of Milbury. Another 1970s children's series, *The Changes* (John Prowse, 1975), sees people reverting to a pre-modern way of life and 'posits a mass reversion to Luddism, as the entire populace destroy their technological goods and machinery and instigate an agrarian, superstitious and intolerant society in which any mention of machines or modernity is condemned as heresy'.[55] This series was shot on location in the West Country, around Bristol, the Forest of Dean and Sharpness.

The contemporary cult of the rural

The writer Rob Young has been a key figure in the critical engagement with (and indeed articulation of) a distinctive cult of British 'folk horror'. This is a growing cult, one that incorporates 'active celebration', 'communion and community' and 'commitment' (to employ the definitions of cult offered by Ernest Mathijs and

Jamie Sexton).[56] It is also imbued with some of the mystical vision of William Blake and John Clare's simple love of the rural (combined with his madness), and with the dark mystery of writers such as M. R. James, Arthur Machen, Algernon Blackwood, Lord Dunsany, L. T. C. Rolt and Robert Aikman – and especially the films and television plays and series that adapt their ghostly works. The folk horror cult has developed out of an increased interest in obscure rural British television (often of the late 1960s and 1970s – some of which has been released on DVD) such as Nigel Kneale's *The Stone Tape* (Peter Sasdy, 1972), *Against the Crowd: Murrain* (John Cooper, 1975), the *Beasts* series of television plays (1976) and the television series *The Owl Service* (1969–70), adapted by Alan Garner from his own book (produced and directed by Peter Plummer). Other texts that have become aligned with this rural 'folk horror' cult include the television plays *Whistle and I'll Come to You* (Jonathan Miller, 1968), *Robin Redbreast* (James MacTaggart, 1970) and two episodes of the series *Shadows*: *Dark Encounter* (1976) and *The Inheritance* (1976), as well as the *Ghost Stories for Christmas* episode *Stigma* (1977) and *The Mind Beyond* episode *Stones* (1976).

Rob Young writes in his 2010 *Sight & Sound* article 'The Pattern under the Plough' of the late 1960s and 1970s in terms of a historical moment 'when Britain's creative industries unconsciously examined the "matter of Britain"'.[57] As he points out, this was not just in television and film. Musical artists such as Fairport Convention, Pentangle and Nick Drake often delved into folk archives and celebrated the pastoral. But I would also argue that others married folk tendencies to a less traditional, more progressive sensibility and often surreal or even horrific imagery that effectively blurred folk tradition and modernity, such as Genesis – especially on their albums *Nursery Chryme* (1971) and *Foxtrot* (1972) – Steeleye Span, Jethro Tull, the Trees, Comus and Lindisfarne. Young argues that such 'visionary' folk culture requires our renewed scrutiny: 'Perhaps it's time to admit that certain indigenous traits have been ignored by mainstream film critics for too long.'[58] Seeking to delineate a tradition or genre out of these texts, he writes: 'British culture frequently exhibits and even celebrates a desire to focus on the historical essence of place, and screen out modernist intrusions; or to envision buried spirits of a place bursting into the present. Alongside this runs the pervasive mystique of the pastoral, the push and pull between nostalgia and progress, the socio-political tension between country and city.'[59] Evidence of a long and enduring tradition of engagement with the past in rural place can be found in Edwardian folk song collecting, in the work of writers such as Arthur Machen, John Cowper Powys and Alan Garner; the poetry of Rupert Brooke, Richard Aldington and Edward Thomas; and the paintings of Paul Nash, Eric Ravilious and Stanley Spencer.[60] Young terms this tendency the 'antiquarian eye'.[61] Perhaps this 'antiquarian eye' can also be seen in some ways in the work of independent filmmakers such as Tacita Dean, Ben Rivers, Adam Chodzko, Stephen Sutcliffe and Matt Hulse, who have all presented folk or rural culture in their work.[62]

William Fowler writes significantly that 'in the 1980s folk offered an alternative to Thatcherite society'.[63] The sense now in Young's work is that the antiquarian eye can and should continue to gaze at rural England. In *Electric Eden* (2010), Young dedicates a chapter to apparent links between folk music and visionary and supernatural culture in Britain in a vast range of texts (including *Blood on Satan's Claw*, *The Wicker Man* and *Penda's Fen*[64]) that deal with 'the lingering pagan presence in the British landscape, and by extension, the soul of the nation'.[65] These texts, along with folk and contemporary visionary music, signal a way of seeing contemporary Britain (and its landscapes) that might potentially be radical: 'The pattern under the plough, the occult history of Albion – the British Dreamtime – lies waiting to be discovered by anyone with the right mental equipment.'[66]

Young also recognises elsewhere the rise of 'hauntology' in contemporary music criticism – a focus on the visionary work of more contemporary artists such as Broadcast, the Focus Group and Moon Wiring Club. And he notes links between these cultural spheres and the contemporary (often rural) psychogeography of artists, writers and filmmakers such as Patrick Keiller, Andrew Kötting, Iain Sinclair and Andrew Cross.[67] Further evidence of the contemporary reification of a strange, pagan vision of a contemporary Britain (fuelled by an imagined past) can be evidenced in the development and growth of the annual Green Man festival (held in rural Wales near Abergavenny) and the gonzo archaeological project to chart British pagan sites that has been undertaken by the eccentric former Teardrop Explodes singer Julian Cope. Moreover, a range of other texts evidently engage with rural landscape within the contexts of a critique of or responses to ideologies of progress and modernity, such as the work of the writer Robert Macfarlane – especially *The Wild Places* (2007) and *The Old Ways: Journeys on Foot* (2012). It is important to reiterate here then that the British (but especially English) rural landscape is continuing to play an important role in a wide-ranging subculture.

Post-millennial rural horror

British cinema has seen a number of films since around the turn of the twenty-first century that locate horror in rural landscapes. Examples include *Dog Soldiers* (Neil Marshall, 2001), which sees soldiers in isolated rural Scotland, where they come across rabid werewolves. *Eden Lake* (James Watkins, 2008), shot at Pinewood Studios and around Iver Heath, Buckinghamshire (Frensham Ponds, Black Park and Burnham Beeches), is a brutal film that again, like *Blood on Satan's Claw*, locates horror in rural youth. We might also consider *Wake Wood* (David Keating, 2010), *In the Dark Half* (Alistair Siddon, 2012) and *The Borderlands* (Elliot Goldner, 2013) as key examples of contemporary rural horror.

British rural landscapes have appeared in other ways in film. Ben Walters has noticed what he calls a 'British bathetic bucolic' strain of film and television: a 'semi-absurdist mode' in which rural landscapes provide the locale for 'urban odd couples getting holidays wrong'.[68] Walters mentions the seminal *Nuts in May* (Mike Leigh, *Play for Today*, 1976) here, but also *Withnail & I* (Bruce Robinson, 1986) and *The Trip* (Michael Winterbottom, 2010). But Ben Wheatley's film *Sightseers* (2012) seems to pull together a range of tropes – this is 'a unique and provocative confluence of genres, infusing the bathetic bucolic mode with a grand-guignol vision of murder as social critique, all mapped onto the quint-essentially American frame of a runaway couple's homicidal roadtrip'.[69] Walters notes that the couple in the film, Chris and Tina (Steve Oram and Alice Lowe), are initially motivated to escape 'the disappointing strictures of everyday life'.[70] Ben Wheatley is the primary contemporary director of films that dwell on a sense of rural horror, as Walters points out: 'Both *Down Terrace* and *Kill List* also juxtapose the English countryside with human brutality in stories focused on couples for whom murder is a shared pursuit.'[71] Walters argues that, 'as *Sightseers* progresses, a sense of unaccountability and wildness grows'.[72] Interestingly, Ben Wheatley himself admits that 'I see that weird schism of modern and ancient at the same time'.[73] Here we can see clear links to the thematic preoccupations of *Blood on Satan's Claw*. It is no surprise that Wheatley's 2013 film *A Field in England* – an exemplar of the British folk horror tradition – is gaining an increas-ingly widespread cult following.

Conclusion

Yi-Fu Tuan's books *Topophilia* (1974) and *Space and Place* (1977) have been highly influential in the field of cultural geography since the 1970s. In these publications Tuan argues that, through human perception and experience, we get to know the world through 'places'. Tuan's concept of topophilia thus effectively evokes the powerful bond that he argues exists between people and place.[74] Interestingly, Tuan argues that an awareness of the past is an important element in 'the love of place'.[75] It is this awareness of the past that arguably became diminished in the rapid industrialisation of Britain and the develop-ment of modern city life. In *The Condition of Postmodernity* (1989), David Harvey argues that the ruthless break of modernity from the past effectively involved a movement away from what he terms 'the irrationalities of myth, religion, superstition'.[76] As spatial barriers diminish within the contexts of postmodernity, so we become much more sensitised to what the world's spaces contain. British rural folk horror films such as *Blood on Satan's Claw* can be read within this context. They uncover the idiosyncratic nature of specific rural places in Britain, often, at the same time, acknowledging that there are ways of life and systems of behaviour and ideas that effectively stand opposed to (or at least might inform, in a dialectical sense) modernity (nascent or oth-erwise), technology, rationality, and industrial and post-industrial life. Indeed,

in his examination of marginal places that function as products of modernity, Rob Shields advocates that 'the social "other", of the marginal and low
cultures is despised and reviled in official discourse of dominant culture and
central power while at the same time being constitutive of the imaginary and
emotional repertoires of that dominant culture'.[77] The dark rural landscape of
Blood on Satan's Claw and the peripheral island of *The Wicker Man* might thus
be read as spatialised articulations of contemporary fears concerning rapid
socio-cultural and spatial change.

The British rural folk horror film *Blood on Satan's Claw* has become a complex
text that can be read in a variety of ways. Firstly, it articulates how far rural landscapes remain key to understanding important aspects of how modern Britain
developed (the enclosures being just one example), and what culture the prevailing ideologies of rationality and progress that fuelled the agricultural and then
industrial revolutions have effectively buried (or at least attempted to bury). The
film effectively uses a vision of rural folk culture to challenge or at least problematise the prevailing narratives of modernity, technological progress and the
Enlightenment. Secondly – and linked to this – *Blood on Satan's Claw* demonstrates that folk narratives might keep pagan memories alive (no matter how dark
and disturbing these might be), and that identities might continue to be forged
in the earth and in the elements as well as within the contexts of capitalism. If the
film is horrific – above and beyond its depiction of sexual violence and manifestations of evil – this is primarily because it demonstrates that the magical, mystical
and superstitious aspects of life that cannot rationally be accounted for always
potentially remain, and might appear at any time in the present world, to perhaps
fuel contemporary subcultural practices or otherwise.

But, in addition to this, contemporary cult interest in *Blood on Satan's Claw*
and other 1960s and 1970s folk horror texts can be read as evidence of an ongoing urge to re-engage with aspects of British culture that are not governed and
controlled by an increasingly global, glossy, homogeneous, superficial culture
industry. These texts are apparently seen to be celebrating an alternative culture
of the folk or people, and thus to play on how terrified modern urban individuals might need to be not only of old, undying aspects of the world but also of
the false truths (or indeed truthlessness) of their own modern or postmodern
existence.

Notes

1 John Rennie Short, *Imagined Country* (London and New York: Routledge, 1991), p. 8.
2 For more on the Gothic in English horror films, see David Pirie, *A Heritage of Horror:
   The English Gothic Cinema 1946–1972* (London: Gordon Fraser, 1973); Jonathan
   Rigby, Jonathan, *English Gothic: a Century of Horror Cinema* (London: Reynolds &
   Hearn, 2002).

3 Peter Hutchings, 'Uncanny landscapes in British film and television', *Visual Culture in Britain*, 5: 2 (2004), pp. 27–40; p. 29.

4 Hutchings, 'Uncanny landscapes in British film and television', p. 28.

5 Tanya Krzywinska, 'Lurking beneath the skin: British pagan landscapes in popular cinema', in Robert Fish (ed.), *Cinematic Countrysides* (Manchester: Manchester University Press, 2007), pp. 75–90; p. 84.

6 Several writers have engaged with the idea of a quest for 'folk' as an essentially anti-modern exercise – see, for example, Ian McKay, *Quest of the Folk: Antimodernism and Cultural Selection in Twentieth-Century Nova Scotia* (Quebec: McGill-Queen's University Press, 1994).

7 David Bell, 'Anti-idyll: rural horror' in Paul Cloke and Jo Little (eds), *Contested Countryside Cultures: Otherness, Marginalisation and Rurality* (London and New York: Routledge, 1997), pp. 94–108; p. 94.

8 Bell, 'Anti-idyll', p. 95.

9 Bell, 'Anti-idyll', p. 96.

10 Bell, 'Anti-idyll', p. 96.

11 Bell, 'Anti-idyll', p. 96.

12 Hutchings, 'Uncanny landscapes in British film and television', p. 28.

13 Hutchings, 'Uncanny landscapes in British film and television', p. 29.

14 Hutchings, 'Uncanny landscapes in British film and television', p. 34.

15 Derek Pykett, *British Horror Film Locations* (Jefferson: McFarland, 2008), p. 23.

16 Leon Hunt, 'Necromancy in the UK: witchcraft and the occult in British horror', in Steve Chibnall and Julian Petley (eds), *British Horror Cinema* (London: Routledge, 2002), pp. 82–98; p. 84; see also Hutchings, 'Uncanny landscapes in British film and television', p. 35.

17 Tanya Krzywinska, *A Skin for Dancing In: Possession, Witchcraft and Voodoo in Film* (Trowbridge: Flicks Books, 2000). See also Hutchings, 'Uncanny landscapes in British film and television', p. 36.

18 Krzywinska, 'Lurking beneath the skin', p. 78.

19 See, for example, evidence of the online cultification of folk horror at https://ghostingimages.wordpress.com, www.fangoria.com (a history of British folk horror), http://celluloidwickerman.com, www.folkhorror.com, http://ayearinthecountry.co.uk (which provides a folk horror review), http://sparksinelectricaljelly.blogspot.co.uk and http://breakfastintheruins.blogspot.co.uk (all accessed 4 March 2015).

20 Vic Pratt, 'Long arm of the lore', *Sight & Sound*, 23: 10 (2013), pp. 24–31; p. 26.

21 See Paul Newland, 'Folksploitation: charting the horrors of the British folk music tradition in The Wicker Man (Robin Hardy, 1973)', in Robert Shail (ed.), *British Cinema in the 1970s* (London: British Film Institute, 2008), pp. 119–28.

22 Jeffrey Richards, *Films and British National Identity: From Dickens to Dad's Army* (Manchester and New York: Manchester University Press, 1997), p. 178.

23 Tim Edensor, *National Identity, Popular Culture and Everyday Life* (Oxford: Berg, 2002), p. 148.

24 Duncan Petrie, *Screening Scotland* (London: British Film Institute, 2000), p. 32.

25 Petrie, *Screening Scotland*, p. 35.

26 For more on Tony Tenser and Tigon, see John Hamilton, *Beasts in the Cellar: The Exploitation Film Career of Tony Tenser* (Ann Arbor: Fab Press, 2005) pp. 181–5.

27 Hunt, 'Necromancy in the UK', p. 93.

28 Hunt, 'Necromancy in the UK', p. 94; see also David Taylor, 'Don't overact with your fingers! The making of *Blood on Satan's Claw*', in Stefan Jarworzyn (ed.), *Shock: The Essential Guide to Exploitation Cinema* (London: Titan, 1996), pp. 85–95; p. 88.

29 Jez Winship also notices the painterly qualities of this shot in his blog: '*Blood on Satan's Claw* (1971)', *Sparks in Electric Jelly* (5 February 2014), http://sparksinelectricjelly. blogspot.co.uk/2014/02/blood-on-satans-claw-1971.html (accessed 4 March 2015).

30 For more on the enclosures see E. P. Thompson, *Customs in Common* (London: Merlin Press, 1991); Paul Langford, *Public Life and the Propertied Englishman 1689–1798* (Oxford: Oxford University Press, 1991); M. E. Turner, *Enclosures in Britain, 1750–1830* (London, 1984); G. E. Mingay, *Parliamentary Enclosures in England* (London: Longman, 1997).

31 Michael Rosenthal, *British Landscape Painting* (London: Phaidon, 1982), p. 9.

32 Rosenthal, *British Landscape Painting*, p. 16.

33 See Krzywinska, 'Lurking beneath the skin', p. 80; Hunt, 'Necromancy in the UK', p. 93.

34 Krzywinska, 'Lurking beneath the skin', p. 81.

35 Rudolph Arnheim, 'A note on monsters', in Rudolph Arnheim (ed.), *Toward a Psychology of Art* (Berkeley: University of California Press, 1972), p. 257.

36 David Sanjek, 'Twilight of the monsters: the English horror film 1968–1975', in Wheeler Winston Dixon (ed.), *Re-viewing British Cinema 1900–1992: Essays and Interviews* (Albany: State University of New York Press, 1994), pp. 195–209; p. 197.

37 For more on the cultural contexts of horror cinema, see J. L. Crane, *Terror and Everyday Life: Singular Moments in the History of the Horror Film* (London: Sage, 1994); Andrew Tudor, *Monsters and Mad Scientists: A Cultural History of the Horror Movie*, (Oxford: Blackwell, 1989).

38 Theodor Rozsak, *The Making of a Counter Culture: Reflections on the Technocratic Society and Its Youthful Opposition* (Garden City, NY: Doubleday, 1969), p. 5.

39 Rozsak, *The Making of a Counter Culture*, pp. 1–4, 48.

40 Noël Carroll, *The Philosophy of Horror; or, Paradoxes of the Heart* (New York: Routledge, 1990), p. 207.

41 Pratt, 'Long arm of the lore', p. 27.

42 Pratt, 'Long arm of the lore', p. 30.

43 Bernice M. Murphy, *The Rural Gothic in American Popular Culture: Backwoods Horror and Terror in the Wilderness* (Basingstoke and New York: Palgrave Macmillan, 2013), p. 135.

44 Krzywinska, 'Lurking beneath the skin', p. 78.

45 Christine Geraghty, *British Cinema in the Fifties: Gender, Genre and the 'New Look'* (London: Routledge, 2000), pp. 38–54.

46 Rob Young, *Electric Eden: Unearthing Britain's Visionary Music* (London: Faber & Faber, 2011), p. 418.

47 I would like to thank Peter Hutchings for pointing this out to me.

48 I would like to thank Peter Hutchings for pointing these connections out to me.

49 Rob Young, 'The pattern under the plough', *Sight & Sound*, 20: 8 (2010), pp. 16–22; p. 22.

50 Nigel Andrews, '*Straw Dogs*', *Monthly Film Bulletin*, 38: 455 (1971), pp. 249–50; p. 250.

51 Tom Milne, '*Straw Dogs*', *Sight & Sound*, 41: 1 (1971), pp. 71–2.

52 Paul Newland, *British Films of the 1970s* (Manchester: Manchester University Press, 2013), pp. 155–7.
53 Newland, *British Films of the 1970s*, pp. 163–4.
54 Elisabeth Sussex, 'Requiem for a village', *Sight & Sound*, 45: 1 (1975/76), p. 60.
55 Young, 'The pattern under the plough', p. 19.
56 Ernest Mathijs and Jamie Sexton, *Cult Cinema* (Malden and Oxford: Wiley-Blackwell, 2011), pp. 2–3.
57 Young, 'The pattern under the plough', p. 17.
58 Young, 'The pattern under the plough', p. 17.
59 Young, 'The pattern under the plough', pp. 17–18.
60 Young, 'The pattern under the plough', p. 18.
61 Young, 'The pattern under the plough', p. 18.
62 William Fowler, 'Absent authors: folk in artist film', *Sight & Sound*, 20: 8 (2010), p. 21.
63 Fowler, 'Absent authors', p. 21.
64 Young, Electric Eden, pp. 415–46.
65 Young, *Electric Eden*, p. 415.
66 Young, *Electric Eden*, pp. 416–17.
67 Young, *Electric Eden*, p. 20.
68 Ben Walters, 'Psycho geography', *Sight & Sound*, 22: 11 (2012), pp. 30–3l; p. 31.
69 Walters, 'Psycho geography', p. 31.
70 Walters, 'Psycho geography', p. 32.
71 Walters, 'Psycho geography', p. 32.
72 Walters, 'Psycho geography', p. 33.
73 Ben Wheatley quoted in Walters, 'Psycho geography', p. 33.
74 Yi-Fu Tuan, *Topophilia: A Study of Environmental Perception, Attitudes and Values* (Englewood Cliffs: Prentice Hall, 1974), p. 4.
75 Tuan, *Topophilia*, p. 99.
76 David Harvey, *The Condition of Postmodernity* (Oxford: Blackwell, 1990), p. 12.
77 Rob Shields, *Places on the Margin: Alternative Geographies of Modernity* (London: Routledge, 1991), p. 5.

sleep furiously: interview with Gideon Koppel

Paul Newland

Paul Newland

In his excellent review in *The Guardian*, Peter Bradshaw called *sleep furiously* a 'documentary love-letter to Trefeurig'.[1] I understand you spent some of your younger years in this part of rural west Wales. How far does the film feel like an engagement with or representation of 'home' for you, and how far does the landscape – as you captured it – feel homely or not to you?

Gideon Koppel

Yes – I spent two formative teenage years living in the community of Trefeurig, although my family had been going there for weekends and holidays since I was about eight years old. Peter Bradshaw is insightful in his use of the phrase 'love-letter' – there was and still is an equation in my mind between *sleep furiously* and a collection of associated but disjointed memories that lay dormant – like the image of bundles of letters covered in dust, found in an attic. And there is also a quality of 'love' in my relationship with Trefeurig: both my parents are or were (my mother is still alive and my father died over 30 years ago) German Jewish refugees. This part of mid-Wales has a reputation for being a closed society – one that is inhospitable, if not overtly antagonistic towards outsiders. My parents were very much outsiders – yet against all odds they found a sense of belonging in this place and community.

As a child, I had little or no conscious knowledge of my parents' histories, nor of the Holocaust. This was something rarely if ever spoken about at home; silence seemed to be one of my parents' ways of dealing with their suffering and loss – perhaps an attempt to protect their children from absorbing some-thing of this 'forgotten' history. But of course it wasn't forgotten and in some

12 *sleep furiously*

ways they did not survive their experiences. So the idea of being Jewish was a mystery to me; I did not know what it was, what it meant ... it carried in some ways a quality of Freud's idea of the 'unthought known', though at school I often got teased and bullied for being a Jew. I suspect this apparent anti-Semitism I experienced then was more of a naïve and generalised intolerance of difference; I doubt whether any of my contemporaries had any idea about Jews and Jewish culture. Nevertheless it was out and out racism. My father's outrage at this situation was palpable – I was sent to boxing and judo lessons once a week with the clear purpose to learn how to inflict physical damage on my tormentors. I have no doubt that on an unconscious level this was more than a clue – even for a small child – of the hidden turbulence from where I indirectly came ... in blunt terms: my heritage of persecution and nomadism.

Why do I digress to describe this aspect of myself? Because there must have been something in me that recognised the poignancy of that sense of belonging that grew in my parents as they established a small-holding in the hills of mid-Wales. To have and work a piece of land in a community that tolerated them must have created a powerful sense of achievement, which filtered down to me in the form of a kind of love for this community and landscape that they were allowed to become a part of.

That part of mid-Wales is an absorbing landscape – one that continues to stim-ulate me. While living there as a child ... particularly being involved in 'living off the land' – growing vegetables and rearing animals – I became more sensitive to the quality of time, the rhythms, rituals and cyclical nature of life there. The valleys in the Trefeurig area are narrow. Despite the sparse population and the sense of isolation there can be qualities of intimacy in the environment. On most days – if the clouds have not drifted down – you can see and hear the daily activities of neighbours. If the weather is calm and windless, it is possible to hear a conversation taking place on the other side of the valley – perhaps a mile away – with the same clarity as if you were next to those people. At the same time, the narrow valleys and height of the hills can create an alienating quality – a darkness and foreboding. At those times the landscape feels hermetic, though this feeling might be broken for a moment by the glimpse of the sea ... an infinite horizon. This not only created or perhaps appealed to an already present sense of melancholia; it also provoked the strong desire to escape.

This is all to say – my engagement with landscape in *sleep furiously* is less about quantifying or polemicising stuff around the environment. There were no considerations about 'representing' or 'capturing' the landscape. It is not the manifest landscape I explore in my work – what is important is the latent and imaginary world evoked by what I experience around me. In that sense the landscape becomes an embodiment of histories and traces of life I find, which are discovered by using the camera and microphone as microscopes. The making of images involves processes of translation and evocation. So, for example: space is translated to place; nature into culture and people in community. And it is the consequent movement through landscape that becomes an approach to creating narrative – one that works associatively, in effect a lattice of meandering paths. In Paul Celan's Büchner Prize acceptance speech 'Der Meridian', he spoke about encountering the self in the explorations undertaken through poetry: 'These are also paths among so many other paths, on which language becomes audible; these are encounters, paths of a voice to a perceiving other, creaturely paths, perhaps a conceived existence, a sending forth of the self to the self, searching for one's self... a kind of homecoming.'

'A kind of homecoming' is perhaps as close as I get – in my thinking and in my work – to acknowledging an existence of 'home'. Perhaps coloured by my inherited nomadic disposition, the idea of 'home' for me is a mirage. It is an image that – in moments of vulnerability – I conjure up with a hope of comfort and security. Celan's 'a kind of homecoming' is like the mathematical concept of 'tending towards' zero ... that is to say, zero itself cannot – by definition – exist.

Paul Newland

I wonder if you might offer a further insight into the poetic nature of your work on *sleep furiously*. You mention Paul Celan here, and clearly you draw on literary and other cultural traditions in your work.

I would suggest that the film evokes some of the concerns of the pastoral tradition of poetry as exemplified by Edmund Spenser's *The Shepheardes Calender* (1579). Paul Alpers, in his book *What Is Pastoral?* (1996), argues that the recurring theme of the pastoral is the focus on the rustic lives of shepherds. This can be traced back to Hesiod, Virgil and, later, Theocritus. *sleep furiously* would seem to evidence elements of this key pastoral theme – and perhaps even the library van driver is a kind of shepherd of the community. The pastoral also appears to be concerned with the relationship between urban centres and the bucolic countryside. Is the poetic power of *sleep furiously* linked in any way to the relationship between the rural remoteness of Trefeurig and the contemporary urban centres in which the film was screened, reviewed and talked about in such glowing terms?

But might the film also be termed Romantic or neo-Romantic? (I am thinking especially here of potential links to the work of Wordsworth and Coleridge's *Lyrical Ballads*, for example.) Can you say something about how you think the film might perhaps be evocative of or draw on some of the concerns of pastoral or Romantic poetry?

Gideon Koppel

The first answer to your question is that the 'poetic nature' of my work on *sleep furiously* – if there is a 'poetic nature' – is an idiom within the film and is not a result of any consciously formed construct. That is to say 'poetry' is not something I would or even could strive for … it is elusive. I imagine that a writer can set out to create a poem … but they cannot determine whether their words will be poetic …

Again quoting Celan – because I am in the middle of developing a feature-length film exploring his life and work – writing an early commentary on his poems:

'What matters for this language … is precision. It does not transfigure, does not "poetize", it names and composes, it tries to measure out the sphere of the given and the possible.' In a strange way, this could be a description of how I worked with the camera and microphone. That is to use the imaginary frame of the camera to construct a stage, a landscape in which gestures of humanity are played out. Philippe Lacoue-Labarthe writes in *Poetry as Experience*:

There is no 'poetic experience' in the sense of a 'lived moment' or a poetic 'state.' If such a thing exists or thinks it does – for after all it is the power, or impotence of literature to believe and make others believe this – it cannot give rise to a poem. To a story, yes, or to a discourse whether in verse or prose. To 'literature', perhaps at least in the sense that we understand it today. But not to a poem. A poem has nothing to recount, nothing to say; what it recounts and says is that from which it wrenches away as a poem.

As I understand it – Lacoue-Labarthe is suggesting a similar paradox: that to experience a poetic moment as 'poetic' takes you out of that moment.

I do not know of Edmund Spenser's *The Shepheardes Calender* ... nor Paul Alpers's *What Is Pastoral?* – so I really can't comment on your suggestion. This notion of 'the pastoral' seems to be infused with a sentimentality and nostalgia that I hope aren't evidenced in *sleep furiously*; as I see it, they are qualities connected to a Christian spirituality that is simply not part of my culture or value systems, which are firmly grounded in the material. I think that there is nothing achieved in that kind of retrospective longing ... like Raymond Williams said, 'to be truly radical is to make hope possible rather than despair convincing'. If I make claim to any intention on behalf of *sleep furiously*, it was to offer – albeit in my inimitable, melancholic way – a quality of hope. The shot of the tree at the very end – the one that most people miss because it is after the credits – that is the very clearly intended image of hope.

But I do agree with your comment that 'the pastoral also appears to be concerned with the relationship between urban centres and the bucolic countryside'. This seems to be one of Williams's ideas – as I understand it – that the juxtaposition between the rural and urban can become a significant form through which society recognises itself and its problems. It is a contrast that suggests a quality of narrative. I immediately think of my fascination with bus, car and train journeys where, with concentration and excitement, I follow the movement from the built-up urban into a rural landscape ... or the other way round. Sometimes that transition is sudden and clear ... sometimes gradual and indecisive. ... Recently I flew into Mexico City and was astonished by the abruptness with which the density of human habitation started and then how it seemed to go on for ever ... suddenly the desert became urban conurbations, which we flew over for at least 40 minutes. Then there are those juxtapositions that are bound into a singular image ... and maybe a juxtaposition of sound and image. The most poignant of those for me in *sleep furiously*, and one that was carefully formed from actuality in the post-production process, occurs towards the end of the film. We see a scene being played out between a farmer, his sheepdog Meg and a sheep who has just given birth. Midway through the drama, a low-flying military jet crosses the valley with a menacing roar. We don't see the jet, nor does anything about the landscape or mood of the drama played out suggest the potential presence of such a high-tech aircraft. Rather than take out this almost anachronistic element, we gave it a more defined presence. It becomes another moment in the film in which the ecologies and dramatic struggles between nature and human are played out like the many scenes where machines and mechanical action are juxtaposed with nature and the natural. Here my terms of reference are clear: two pictures which I always refer to because they are so powerful in their evocation of an advancing modernity – *The Fighting Temeraire* (1839) and *Rain, Steam and Speed* (1844) – both by Turner and both in the National Gallery.

An aside. Some of your questions seem keen to elicit answers that make scholarly deductions. I am not a scholar and, although I have read some Wordsworth,
I read like a magpie … or like Hanta, a character from Hrabal's novel *Too Loud a
Solitude*: 'When I read, I don't really read: I pop a beautiful sentence in my mouth
and suck it like a fruit drop or I sip it like a liqueur until the thought dissolves in
me like alcohol, infusing my brain and heart and coursing on through the veins
to the root of each blood vessel.' In the past few years, aspects of making art have
been increasingly absorbed into the institution and language of academia – in
particular the 'PhD by practice' has become a common and [poignantly ambigu-
ous] 'terminal' qualification for artists. There seems to be a growing tendency in
British universities to award doctorates to artists, or people assuming the mantle
of artist, without sufficient scrutiny of whether the work makes an original contribution to knowledge or understanding – the basic tenet of doctoral research.
This new fashion – perhaps encouraged more for economic reasons than for any
real pedagogical reasons – is growing new expectations of the rhetoric expected
from artists. While this might be an interesting phenomenon, there is the danger
that art work made as 'research' often misses the point – because fundamentally
art does not carry any signs or messages. As Deleuze's confident statement makes
clear: 'The work of art is not an instrument of communication. The work of art
has nothing to do with communication. The work of art does not contain any
information at all.' This is not to say that I am opposed to serious and rigorous
analysis of art. Quite the contrary: I think that it is necessary – on the most basic
level, borrowing Duchamp's notion that without an audience there is no art. But
I do worry that this new trend is sanitising and making synthetic the important
discourse between art and academia.

At the time of making *sleep furiously* I was reading W. G. Sebald's novel
Austerlitz, a work with many resonances of what might be 'my story': the history
of my parents as Jewish refugees fleeing Nazi Germany; a journey that meanders,
with a constant sense of 'not knowing', through specific places and landscapes
along a spatial trajectory from north Wales to the East End of London – coinci-
dentally, some of the places of my own story.

The writings of Sebald led me to read Peter Handke's play *Kaspar*. The world
of Kaspar had a particular resonance with my own feelings of isolation from
living in Trefeurig – feelings compounded by the inevitable sense of regression
having returned to live in the place of my childhood and youth. I found a strong
identification with Kaspar's struggle for language, for words – his cry 'I want to
be someone like somebody else once was.' Handke describes *Kaspar* as a play
'which does not show how it really is or how it really was with Kaspar Hauser, it
shows what is possible with someone'.

For me, Handke's words suggested a landscape – an internal landscape – that
provoked important questions without any room for nostalgia or sentimentality.
So, I wrote to Handke, describing the film I was making, and asked whether

I could come to Paris to talk with him about it. One month later, over lunch eaten in the heat of an early autumn afternoon, we talked. Peter listened to the descriptions of what I had been filming and looked bemused whenever I expressed a doubt in what I was doing – 'trust your instinct', he said firmly. We talked about the nature of stories and he pointed me towards his collection *Once Again for Thucydides*. Each story is an evocation of a moment, place in time and gesture, and each as if, just then, time had stopped and that experience had been looked at under a microscope. Peter's words were and remain very important for me ... and the conversations continue.

I am aware there is a quality of contradiction to my answers ... which I would like to address because it concerns how my work is perceived and the broad strokes of classification imposed on it, in this case notions of 'documentary'. I have often spoken about my concern with the term 'documentary' and how it is used in film and media studies. In that context 'documentary' is often conflated with 'factual television programme making' and illustrated journalism. My view of documentary film is more affiliated with strands of so-called experimental filmmaking. This idiom of filmmaking is driven by curiosity – the filmmaker explores their chosen world with the camera and microphone as a means of consciously translating experience and not simply recording it. An important reference here is Dziga Vertov's *Man With a Movie Camera* (1929), and significantly, in his manifesto *The Council of Three* (1923), Vertov writes that 'the main and essential thing (of cinema) is the sensory exploration of the world through film'. I perhaps sometimes overemphasise the idea that *sleep furiously* is an internal landscape and a fiction.

There is of course, on some level, a specific form of engagement with actuality and a 'realism' that I need also to acknowledge. It is a quality of realism that I was really interested to find described in an essay on Van Gogh by Meyer Shapiro (1946). He writes: 'I do not mean realism in the narrow, repugnant sense that is acquired today ... but rather the sentiment that external reality is an object of strong desire or need, as a possession and potential means of fulfilment of the striving human being, and is therefore the necessary ground of art.'

Paul Newland

I am fascinated by the apparent tensions thrown up by your admission that you feel you perhaps overemphasise the idea of the film as 'internal landscape' and 'fiction' and that at the same time you have to acknowledge some level of realism. When I saw *sleep furiously* for the first time, in the Aberystwyth Arts Centre Cinema (fairly close to Trefeurig), I was struck by how some local people were evidently engaging with the film – in short, nodding to each other and pointing out people and places they knew. Clearly they wanted – or expected – the film to be some kind of 'home movie'! It goes without saying that my experience of the film as a then-outsider in Ceredigion was very different. I was struck by its melancholy, bucolic reverie, and intrigued by its poetry.

I absolutely agree with you that, if the film does encapsulate 'realism', as such, it is not documentary realism. But the film was shot in a specific rural landscape and at a specific historical moment. And it does focus on real people engaging in quotidian activities, and frames their 'gestures of humanity', as Celan put it.

Earlier you said, 'what is important is the latent and imaginary world evoked by what I experience around me'. Can you say a bit more about this in terms of your thoughts on the potential 'realism' of the film (perhaps building on your point above about Van Gogh)? And, linked to this, how precisely was the internal landscape (or imaginary world) of the film inspired by the real rural Welsh landscape (and 'rural people') that the film depicts?

Gideon Koppel

Those tensions are very important for me in the process of making a film. I think that they are the tensions between a more analytic and strategic self and the freedoms of 'making' or 'playing'. There are times when I am so immersed in 'making' that intellectual reason is lost and I don't care about the parameters of different terminologies and implications of different classifications. It is perhaps close to Keats's notion of 'negative capability'. The psychoanalyst Christopher Bollas, who has written very interestingly about 'free association', describes this form of thinking in 'The Evocative Object World':

> You are riding in a train, absorbed by the sights flying by. It passes an airport, crosses a canal, traverses a meadow, climbs a long, low hill graced by rows of vineyards, descends into a valley choked with industrial parks. ... Each location evokes sets of associations. The airport reminds you of the coming summer and your holiday abroad. It recalls the plane that brought you to this part of the world in the first place; the never-ending expansions of airports. ... Crossing the canal you think of a longed-for trip on a canal boat, yet to be accomplished, signifying the potential remainders of a life. ... You think of your mother and father-in-law's former house which was alongside a small canal. You might also think of the dentist and a root canal. And so it goes.

Bollas's description of free associative thinking also links back to the ideas I spoke about earlier – the way movement through a landscape forms narrative pathways.

Your comment on the different relationships audiences have with *sleep furiously* is important. Of course some local people were very involved with elements of the film, almost as an extension of their day-to-day life. ... I guess that is because they had pre-existing relationships with many of the places and characters in the film. ... They could incorporate parts of the film into their complex and continuous self-narratives. Perhaps the film also enabled local people to see aspects of their world and the everyday from a new perspective – which in a sense can create new values in their lives. But finding the familiar in *sleep furiously* was not the monopoly of people who lived locally. I became aware that many people from Jewish emigrant backgrounds who saw the film also engaged with dynamics that were already familiar to them. But in that case those dynamics are not as easy to identify in the film as a recognisable character, or place. Again I make the distinction between the manifest landscape and the latent landscape.

I don't really understand your questioning about the 'realness' of *sleep furiously*. It isn't real: it is a film. It is a shadow of the world. Perhaps like T. S. Eliot's shadow in 'The Hollow Men':

> Between the idea
> And the reality
> Between the motion
> And the act
> Falls the Shadow

Since the film was released, I have spoken and written about the ways in which *sleep furiously* is a fictional construct. It is also as Vertov described a 'sensory exploration of the world'. Yes, you are right, the film is made from a foundation of observed actuality, but these observations undergo such complex processes of interpretation and translation before emerging on the screen as sequences of picture and sound, it is impossible to equate one with the other. That is to say: to ask what the precise nature of the relationship is between *sleep furiously* and as you put it 'the real rural Welsh landscape (and "rural people")' seems to be missing the point. What is key is the idea of Paul Klee's, that 'art does not reproduce the visible … rather it makes it visible'.

There are people who have reviewed, commented on, analysed… *sleep furiously* in ways that have been illuminating and energising for me. John Banville's essay in *Sight & Sound* and Mark Ford's review in *The Guardian* are published examples. I would like to share an unpublished personal letter I received from David Fraser Jenkins (art historian and formerly curator at Tate Britain):

> I write to you about what seems to me an extraordinary contradiction, that your film is so close to your father's paintings, sculpture and aesthetics, and yet no one mentions this, and perhaps does not even suspect it.
>
> I wonder how many people are there who are aware of this connection, and also, following on from that, how many other films or writings there may be that had a vastly important other half to what they are about, which no one has ever realized (and I am reminded also of one of my favourite films, Paolo Sorrentino's *Consequences of Love*, which only makes sense as an allegory of the process of dying, as is made clear in the film, yet, again, this is never mentioned in reviews, nor again in this *Time Out* guide).
>
> It seemed to me the first time I saw your film, which was at Tate Modern, that spots of blank colour that occur a few times make clear this connection with a certain kind of painting, and that the colours have a relation to those used by Heinz.[2] The patterns of light in the film are like the patches of light and shade in

his drawings and paintings. The relation of all of these to the farm is like the way that he suspended his later paintings from a wigwam of sticks.

The whole attitude of individual persistence alongside the uncaring seasons of nature is like his unique and self-centred notes on the loneliness of perception. The family closeness is like so many of his pictures. And the occasional oddity of things is like such strange events he showed from time to time, as the 'crashed airplane' in one picture.

I don't see the film as just a portrait of the village (as if some later *Under Milkwood*), or even just as being about your family. It has overall, and I suppose other people must feel this, a cumulative force of visual symbols, to do with the operation of the visual arts within the making of a life, which individuals can only brush against but can feel this eruption from within, as in the particular means of making the film. This is something I have felt so often from certain works of art, because I look at pictures, and I see your film as a visual commentary on Heinz's work.

Of course I also think of the whole film as a requiem, which makes up the other half of the arch which begins with the story of Heinz's life in Berlin and then as an exile. The film then returns your father to his burial in Wales, and seems to me to express that whole dreadful saga of European history – which of course I have also felt in recent visits to Germany. Heinz's art was devoted to re-configuring a visual language, which ended up abstracted but nevertheless gathered together in his studio and in his constructions. But your film at last gives a conclusion to this whole archway, embedding the activities of colours and movements that he had seen and preserved into the eccentric life of the village, and under the eyes of your mother. Just in the same way the formal language of film makes a space out of slight movements, which has to be convincing to be any good. By taking up your father's vision you have been able to re-enact this within something actually seen in Wales.

Notes

1 Peter Bradshaw, review of *sleep furiously*, *The Guardian* (29 May 2009), http://www.theguardian.com/film/2009/may/29/sleep-furiously-film-review (accessed 23 March 2016).
2 Heinz Koppel (1919–80), painter born in Berlin and father of Gideon Koppel.

12

Film and the repossession of rural space: interview with Patrick Keiller

Paul Newland

Paul Newland

Robinson in Ruins features a lot of shots of rural areas around the Cherwell Valley. Many people who have seen your other work, and are familiar with your background in architecture, will perhaps be more aware of your representations of urban areas (London in particular, of course). Shooting in rural Oxfordshire, did you find that setting up shots of these landscapes required you to adopt different approaches (to the framing of the shots, for example)?

Patrick Keiller

I think it was the other way round. At the outset, the film didn't have a title, didn't necessarily involve anyone called Robinson, and I wasn't sure where I would go. I had auditioned some distant locations, but making the film moved much more slowly than I had expected, and was diverted by things I found along the way until I arrived, very fortuitously, at what became the film's final destination. I had visited this before starting, but did not learn of its historical significance until the day I went there with the camera.

However, I had taken some decisions before starting out. After making enquiries about HDCAM, of which I had some experience, and the Red camera, then nearly available, I decided to originate the footage as 35mm negative, using the Caméflex camera with which I had photographed *London* and *Robinson in Space*. I wasn't sure whether to make any prints. My objective was to produce the highest resolution digital version for retail, a disc (the current offering is DVD and Blu-ray in one box) or perhaps something better in future. At the Tate last year, we showed both the footage in the exhibition and the film in the lecture theatre as ProRes (HQ) files, which worked very well. By the time the film was finished, making prints seemed an unnecessary expense, but the finished digital cinema version confirmed the decision to originate on film stock. The cinematography began rather suddenly, when I noticed a first camera subject (the plywood-encased house) that I thought might not be there for much longer. This also offered a good opportunity to compare two film stocks (using the grain of the plywood, as in an early sequence in *London*) and was very near where I live.

I had not worked with the camera since 1995, having made two other projects in the interval, both originated with electronic cameras in 16 × 9 ratio. Whether or not the new film was to be printed, I knew the retail versions would be 16 × 9 (1.78:1). The earlier Robinson films were academy ratio, 1.37:1, and their retail versions are 4 × 3. There is a slot in the Caméflex's viewfinder that looked as if it was intended to accept something, so I cut a 16 × 9 rectangle in a piece of transparent acetate and put it in the slot, as a guide. If there had been any prints, they would have been either 1.85:1 or 1.66:1, though the latter is not common in the UK. 4 × 3 is the ratio of many of Turner's best-known larger works (often ~36″ × ~48″). I've not so far found any paintings that are 1.78:1, though Claude's *The Enchanted Castle* (1664) is 87.1 × 151.3, which is 1.74:1. This is quite close to √3:1 (1.732:1).

The 16 × 9 ratio was initially a bit difficult (even though I had worked in it before), as many architectural and landscape subjects are tall. I noticed the problem early on, attempting to make images of a post box outside the Bodleian Library, a subject I'd had my eye on for years. To begin with, I used my widest lens (18.5mm) more often than in the earlier films. But I soon became accustomed to the ratio, and the lens was used less often. Both the ratio and the film stock may have had some influence on the choice of camera subjects, as they usually do, but other considerations were, I think, more important: some years before, I had decided that in future I should try to develop the film's spatiality by exploring fewer locations in greater detail, and as a result I moved slowly. I soon encountered several nearby sites that were central to the film's enquiry, so there seemed to be nothing lost by not travelling very far.

I was also anxious not to repeat myself. Travelling about the country in 2007, I thought it might be difficult to avoid making images resembling those of *Robinson in Space*. The landscape didn't seem to have changed enough in twelve years to justify another film. As it turned out, however, the three films progress from the largely urban spaces of *London* to the peripheral landscapes of *Robinson in Space* to the southern, arable landscape of English enclosure and the rise of the 'new gentry', events that resonate with our predicament today.

Paul Newland

I am very interested that you mention the work of the painters Turner and Claude here. It is clear to me that the notion of landscape is still highly contested. Critics argue that landscapes can be used in multiple ways – for example, observed and enjoyed or inhabited and worked. In the work of British landscape painters in the tradition of Claude, landscapes tend to appear as classical, balanced compositions, often with a perspective that, through recessive depth, emphasises a sense of detachment – these landscapes are seemingly there to be gazed upon, so to speak. But later painters such as Gainsborough often uncovered the politically charged nature of landscape as it is lived. In *Robinson in Ruins* you are clearly engaged with the politics of landscape in rural England, and appear to be thinking about the tensions at the heart of the landscape I mention here. Can you perhaps say a bit more about the decisions you made to shoot specific rural landscapes – camera position, perspective and so on? How far did you want the film to 'show' landscapes to the viewer, or how far do you feel the film on the whole, as a political text, effectively attempts to reimagine or even 'reclaim' landscapes otherwise owned or indeed 'enclosed'.

Patrick Keiller

There aren't very many images in the film that I'd call landscapes, in the sense of views. I tended to avoid them, so they only appear occasionally. The camera subjects are more often relatively small scale: the plywood-encased house, the post box, a road sign with lichen growth, the Boyle-Hooke plaque, a false megalith, a transformer substation, a mobile phone mast, pipeline markers, a milepost, flowers, trees and so on. The first that I'd call a rural landscape is a view of Harrowdown Hill, about fifteen minutes after the start. It's a view north from the edge of the nearest village, Longworth, in the direction of RAF Brize Norton, not far away on the other side of the Thames. The flights in and out of Brize Norton are not very frequent, but I imagine that the weapons expert David Kelly would have been aware of its proximity. I made three takes, two with a 28mm lens and one with a 50mm lens. One of the 28mm takes is in the film.

The next such view is of the Harwell site from the Ridgeway, at 20:52, with Didcot power station beyond, photographed in April. It was difficult in that it involved walking a long way with the equipment, and waiting quite a long time for light, this after an unsuccessful attempt the previous afternoon. The synchrotron (the 'Diamond Light Source') is visible on the right of the frame. I made three takes during the morning with 35mm, 50mm and 150mm lenses, all centred on a small wind turbine near the edge of the site. Only the 50mm take is in the film.

Towards the end of the film, between 1:20:32 and 1:22:21, there is a sequence of three views north-west centred on a derelict cement works chimney, photographed on 16 October with 28mm, 50mm and 150mm lenses from a high viewpoint near a farm called Folly Farm, in Common Road, Beckley. The chimney, which has already been seen at 1:12:37 and been mentioned as a destination, is only easily seen here in the 50mm and 150mm frames, and in the 28mm and 50mm frames the subject is primarily the harvesting of a crop of maize in the field in front of the camera. The set-up wasn't planned – I just happened to drive past on my way to thank the people at the farm for something. The 28mm and 50mm takes both begin before the maize harvester and its attendant tractor and trailer enter the frame and cross it from right to left. The machinery is very noisy and one is aware of its presence before it enters the frame and after it has left. Before the machinery first appears in the 28mm frame a man enters from the left unexpectedly and runs across and out on the right. In the 150mm frame, neither the maize nor the machinery is visible, but the machinery can still be heard as it moves away.

I recently found an article 'Place-Names' by O. G. S. Crawford, which begins:

I. FOREST TERMS.
Many puzzling place-names explain themselves after a study of medieval forest documents, and of books like Turner's *Select Pleas of the Forest* or Baillie-Grohman's *Master of the Game*. Amongst these is 'Folly' which occurs all over the country, often on sites where Roman remains have been found. Baillie-Grohman says (folio edition, p. 198):

> The position taken up by the shooter to await the game was called his *standing* or *tryste*, and a bower of branches was made, to shelter the occupant from sun and rain as well as to hide him from the game. Such arbours were called *berceau* or *berceil* in old French, from the word *berser* (to shoot with a bow and arrow). They were also called *ramiers* and *folies* from rames or branches, and *folia*, leaves, with which they were made or disguised. It would be interesting to know if any of the so-called *follies* that exist in different parts of England cannot trace back their name from being originally a shooting-hut built on the place of some ancient *folie*.[1]

> There can be little doubt that Mr. Baillie-Grohman is correct in his opinion. When the position of the different Folly woods, Folly farms and follies is investigated, it is found that a great many of them do occur within the limits of the royal forests. It is not possible, of course, to give an exhaustive list, but two good examples are Folly Farm near Marlborough and Foliejon Park in Windsor Forest. Those who knew the Vimy Ridge will recall the ruins of the Ferme de la Folie (nicknamed the Glass house), whose position on the edge of the escarpment was exactly like that of Folly Farm above the Kennet valley.[2]

Folly Farm in Beckley, opposite what was once Beckley Common, is at the edge of Stowood, of which Victoria County History offers:

> Until disafforestation by Charles II Stowood was the northernmost portion of Shotover and Stowood forest; with its centre in the manor of the Derehyde in Shotover, it was administered by the bailiff of Shotover aided by other forest officials; its history during this period therefore cannot be disentangled from that of Shotover and the rest of the royal forest.[3]

My camera position seems to have been close to what might have once been that of a huntsman in a royal forest.[4]

The film was made as part of a project of which I have written that it was prompted by what appeared to be a discrepancy between, on one hand, the cultural and critical attention devoted to experience of mobility and displacement and, on the other, a tacit but seemingly widespread tendency to hold on to formulations of dwelling that derive from a more settled, agricultural past. While making the film, I began to notice that many of its images were of signs, markers, paths and, occasionally, views from more or less elevated viewpoints. Writing about rock art, Richard Bradley refers to a distinction between the tenure exercised by settled farmers, 'a stable pattern of settlements, boundaries and fields, not unlike the world we inhabit today', and that of hunter-gatherers and other mobile peoples, based on 'paths, places and viewpoints', to which one might add markers, like those made by tramps and other itinerants, and rock art. I began to hope the cinematography might involve an implicit critique of Heideggerian 'agricultural' dwelling, or enclosure, or that its wandering might amount to a kind of 'possessioning', like that at Otmoor in 1830, but perhaps I was forgetting that there are other kinds of hunting than those undertaken by hunter-gatherers – 'prospect-hunting', for instance. On the other hand, there aren't many such 'prospects' in the film, and there are a lot of markers and signs, so maybe it's OK.

Paul Newland

Your points here remind me of an important book, *The Image of the City* (1960), by the American urban planner Kevin Lynch. In this book, Lynch discusses the ways in which we form mental maps of urban areas, through what he calls their 'imageability'. He argues that our mental maps of cities are built out of paths (streets, pavements, other channels in which people travel); edges (perceived boundaries); districts (relatively large sections of the city that have a 'character'); nodes (focal points, intersections or loci); and landmarks.

It seems to me that, through your focus on signs, markers, paths and so on, *Robinson in Ruins* perhaps develops a mental map of this part of rural England (through its imageability, if you will) – a map that might facilitate its 're-possessioning'. Can you perhaps say a bit more about how far you see *Robinson in Ruins* functioning as a new 'mental map' of a landscape, as opposed to a representation of a landscape that is there to be 'looked at' as spectacle (as is quite often the case in cinema)?

Patrick Keiller

One difference between a city and a film, considered as assemblies of images, is that in a city one is likely to have some awareness of the spatial relationships between the individual 'imageable' sites, hence the concept of a mental map, but in a film the succession of images doesn't itself convey that, and I don't think one can assume prior topographical knowledge on the part of the viewer. As I mentioned earlier, after *Robinson in Space* I had thought that if I was to make another film it should address fewer locations and devote more attention to each. This is more or less how *Robinson in Ruins* turned out, especially towards the end, where some of the locations are intervisible and the ambient sound continues over picture edits so as to create, I hope, a sense of a locality rather than merely a succession of individual perspectives.

I've addressed mapping more directly in three exhibitions[5] that assembled moving pictures in space, rather than in succession in time, the most recent being *The Robinson Institute* (Tate Britain, 27 March 2012 to October 2012), developed from the film and laid out to represent its elliptical journey. The introductory panel included a geological map of Oxfordshire and Berkshire on which the journey and the film's camera subjects were marked.[6] Four re-edited sequences of footage from the film were displayed with the other exhibits at appropriate points along the journey, and a longer re-edit was displayed on a larger screen above the centre of the exhibition with ambient sound but no narration, the exhibition's text panels and captions taking over the narrative function.

If the film does enable a 're-possessioning' of some kind – as I hope it might – I think this would be achieved though the particular character of the images (hence my resorting to phrases such as 'the transformative potential of images of landscape'), the choice of camera subjects and the idea of a walk undertaken with a declared purpose. The latter is introduced by the narrator soon after the beginning of the film: 'From a nearby car park, he surveyed the centre of the island on which he was shipwrecked: "The location", he wrote, "of a *Great Malady*, that I shall dispel, in the manner of Turner, by making *picturesque views*, on journeys to sites of scientific and historic interest." '

I'm not exactly sure why my protagonist thinks that Turner intended to dispel a malady, or how his 'picturesque views' (that is, the books of engravings based on his watercolours) might have done so, and I didn't explain in any detail what the malady is, but I imagine it has something to do with Baudelaire's 'Great Malady, Horror of Home' and, more specifically, with some characteristics of that 'home' – Anglo-American attitudes to the economy, military adventures, education (the line accompanies a view over Oxford, 'a centre masquerading as a margin'), property and so on – all of which one might wish to dispel in order to re-possess the landscape, its having fallen – in the protagonist's view – into the wrong hands. In 2009, pressed for a tag-line for the film, I had offered: 'In early 2008, a marginalised individual sets out to avert global catastrophe, hoping to trigger the end of neoliberalism by going for a walk.' By the time the film was finished, this didn't feel quite right, but the performative aspect of the film was established early on: when I began the cinematography in 2008, I wasn't aware of the 'possessioning' of Otmoor in 1830, but I did recall other examples of circumambulation and so on – the attempt to exorcise the Pentagon in 1967, *London Orbital* and so on.

Paul Newland

I agree with you that the ambient sound in the film facilitates the sense of a rural locale. In her written work on the film, Doreen Massey notices that many of the 'natural' sounds are suggestive of 'the contemporaneous existence of other things'.[8] She also writes of the 'openness' of this landscape. What importance did you place on sound as you were making the film? And how far do you think the 'repossession' of the landscape you speak of in the film is facilitated by the sounds we hear?

Patrick Keiller

The location sound is all post-synchronised, as it is in the earlier Robinson films. The Caméflex camera is quite noisy, and, as the cinematography is nearly always undertaken under time pressure, I've almost never recorded sound when making pictures with it. We did try once or twice when photographing *Robinson in Space*, but the results were not very satisfactory and were not used. For projects originated with electronic cameras, on the other hand, I've always recorded direct sound. For the first two Robinson films, Larry Sider made some recordings himself (the sound of Concorde landing, for example, in *London*) and found others ready-made (there is some effects-library wind in *London* that turned out to have been recorded for Antonioni's *Blow-Up*), but for *Robinson in Ruins* I recorded the ambient sound myself, mostly at or near the location in each picture about a year after the visit with the camera, so that the sounds were of the same season. None of the picture locations were very distant, so it was easy to revisit them, and the sound recording was a welcome change from editing and writing narration. I accumulated a lot of ambient sound, which was very expertly selected and fitted to the edited picture by Chu-Li Shewring.

When post-synchronising sound, one can be (and, in any case, necessarily is) selective. For example, Hampton Gay and the several nearby locations towards the end of the film are quite near Oxford airport, so that the sound of a light aircraft landing or taking off, or some other loud engine noise, is very frequent, much more so than the sight of a plane. When photographing the pictures, I hadn't noticed how noisy the airport is, and I took some trouble to avoid recording a lot of aircraft noise, so that the sound in the film is to some extent a fiction.

Similarly, some of the locations were subject to much more traffic noise than is heard in the film. I imagine the film's sound might enable 'repossession' both in this way and, more generally, in heightening awareness of what is present at the location, some of which isn't visible. I was particularly keen to include birdsong.

The finished film gives the spoken narration precedence over the ambient sound, but the DVD and Blu-ray versions offer the option of a soundtrack without narration, as I thought some viewers might like to experience the location sound more fully. This was one of several decisions – like the inclusion of the map and the duration of the film's longest takes – that hint at other modes of exhibiting the material, as in the subsequent exhibition.

Notes

1 O. G. S. Crawford, 'Place-names', *Archaeological Journal*, 78 (1921), pp. 31–46. In this quotation Crawford referes to Baillie-Grohman, *The Master of Game*, p. 98. In fact *The Master of Game* was written by Edward of Norwich and edited by William A. and F. N. Baillie-Grohman.

2 Crawford, 'Place-names'.

3 British History Online, 'Stowood', in *A History of the County of Oxford, Vol. V: Bullingdon Hundred* (London: Victoria County History, 1957), www.british-history.ac.uk/report. aspx?compid=101900 (accessed 23 February 2016).

4 British History Online, 'Beckley', in *A History of the County of Oxford, Vol. V: Bullingdon Hundred* (London: Victoria County History, 1957), www.british-history.ac.uk/image. aspx?compid=101881&filename=fig6.gif&pubid=1126(accessed 23 February 2016).

5 Keiller: 'The first and largest of these was a moving-image reconstruction of the interior (mostly) of Chhatrapati Shivaji Terminus in Mumbai on thirty screens in a large interior, resembling that of a railway station, at Le Fresnoy, Tourcoing (*Londres, Bombay* 12 October 2006–24 December 2006). Thirty sequences of HDCAM varying in length between about ninety seconds and about twenty-seven minutes were arranged in a configuration like that of their camera viewpoints in the station in Mumbai, creating an interlacing of actual and virtual space. The second exhibition, at the British Film Institute (23 November 2007–3 February 2008), comprised sixty-eight topographical films of the UK in about 1900, one to three minutes long, from the British Film Institute archive, arranged on forty-six interconnected maps. It was displayed as five "regional" sequences on five screens configured in the approximate relationship of their regions. Visitors to the exhibition could intervene in the displays, moving about the "landscape" of films and maps using the control functions of a DVD player. If no one intervened, each screen played its regional sequence, with each film introduced with a map, but the underlying navigable landscape of each display comprised the same material. The navigable DVD, developed over several years, had already been exhibited in other ways.'

6 Keiller: 'I had already used the same map when making the chapter menu for the film's preview DVDs, with the chapter buttons marked as months located in the appropriate

places on the map. It survives in the British Film Institute's DVD release, although in this the chapters are listed more conventionally. The map also appears in the book *The Possibility of Life's Survival on the Planet* [London: Tate Publishing, 2012], which accompanied the Tate Britain exhibition.'

7 Iain Sinclair and Chris Petit, *London Orbital* (London: Granta, 2002).
8 Doreen Massey, 'Landscape, space, politics: an essay' (n.d.), https://thefutureofland-scape.wordpress.com/landscapespacepolitics-an-essay (accessed 14 April 2015).

Index